Major Issues in Cognitive Aging

Oxford Psychology Series

Editors

Mark D'Esposito   Daniel Schacter
Jon Driver   Anne Treisman
Trevor Robbins   Lawrence Weiskrantz

Major Issues in Cognitive Aging

Timothy A. Salthouse

OXFORD
UNIVERSITY PRESS

2010

OXFORD
UNIVERSITY PRESS

Oxford University Press, Inc., publishes works that further
Oxford University's objective of excellence
in research, scholarship, and education.

Oxford   New York
Auckland   Cape Town   Dar es Salaam   Hong Kong   Karachi
Kuala Lumpur   Madrid   Melbourne   Mexico City   Nairobi
New Delhi   Shanghai   Taipei   Toronto

With offices in
Argentina   Austria   Brazil   Chile   Czech Republic   France   Greece
Guatemala   Hungary   Italy   Japan   Poland   Portugal   Singapore
South Korea   Switzerland   Thailand   Turkey   Ukraine   Vietnam

Published by Oxford University Press, Inc.
198 Madison Avenue, New York, New York 10016

www.oup.com

Oxford is a registered trademark of Oxford University Press

Library of Congress Cataloging-in-Publication Data
Salthouse, Timothy A.
Major issues in cognitive aging / Timothy A. Salthouse.
p.   cm.—(Oxford Psychology series ; 49)
ISBN 978-0-19-537215-1
1. Cognition—Age factors.   2. Memory—Age factors.   3. Cognition in old age.   I. Title.
BF724.55.C63S217 2010
155.67′131—dc22
2009016487

9   8   7   6   5   4   3   2

Printed in the United States of America
on acid-free paper.

Preface

I recognize that it is somewhat presumptuous to use the phrase "major issues" in the title of this book because there is likely little agreement with respect to which issues are truly "major." Nevertheless, the phrase was chosen deliberately because the topics to be discussed were intended to represent some of the most important in the field, and thus the phrase serves to characterize the focus of the monograph. Unlike an undergraduate textbook, in which selected findings are reported in a manner to convey currently accepted interpretations, there is no attempt in this monograph to survey the entire field of cognitive aging. Instead, the book is designed more like a graduate seminar in that ideas are presented at least in part in the hope that they might stimulate further thought and research.

Of course, there are several different types of graduate seminars. Some are very narrow and focus on the methodology and results of a limited number of specific studies. Others take a broader perspective, and rather than concentrating on individual studies, the replicated results across multiple studies are the primary information of interest. This monograph is designed to be like the latter type of seminar in that it is an attempt to identify and discuss some of the most important issues in the field of cognitive aging in an attempt to extract broad and generalizable principles.

A key consideration in an endeavor such as this is how major issues are determined. There would probably be little disagreement with the assertion that not all topics and research questions are equally important, in the sense that they each have the same potential to contribute to substantial increases in knowledge. However, the challenge is in identifying the questions likely to be most informative in advancing understanding of the phenomenon.

Since one of the roles of scientific theories is to determine which questions are important, one approach might be to rely on theories to help designate major issues. However, there is sometimes a tendency for the focus of theories to become progressively narrower as the theories are subject to investigation and refinement, with the consequence that the questions often shift from general to specific. In order to minimize the impact of this tendency, major questions could be defined as those that are meaningful regardless of the particular theory because they transcend topics restricted to a few theories.

Another approach that might be used to identify major issues is to determine whether they are considered important in different disciplines, such as psychology, neurology, and epidemiology. The rationale is similar to that based on whether issues are applicable to many theories in that questions that transcend the focus of a specific discipline could be considered among the most important. Still another approach that might be used to identify major issues is to rely on a historical perspective by assuming that questions that have persisted through time without resolution may be among the most important in the field.

Finally, major questions might be identified from the set of questions used as guides for reporters when they are writing a story. That is, one way of characterizing understanding is when one has answers to what, when, where, why, and how, and in that sense these can be considered major issues.

Input from each of these approaches was used in the current monograph to guide in the identification of major issues. The issues discussed here are certainly not all of the important questions, but I believe they are among the most fundamental questions in the field, and they often get neglected when researchers get immersed in the details of specific research questions.

What I consider to be among the major issues in the field are each the focus of a separate chapter. Chapter 1 is concerned with the relations between age and cognitive functioning, and Chapter 2 addresses the question of whether the age–cognition relations differ for between-person (cross-sectional) and within-person (longitudinal) comparisons and, if so, why. The focus in Chapter 3 is the advantages and disadvantages of a narrow or broad focus on cognitive aging phenomena, and Chapter 4 deals with how potential causes of cognitive aging can be investigated. The issue in Chapter 5 is how normal cognitive aging is distinct from pathological aging, and Chapter 6 addresses the questions of why there are not greater consequences of age-related cognitive declines and what can be done to prevent or minimize them. At the beginning of each chapter a number of important related questions are listed. My view is that these questions are somewhat secondary to the major issues, but they are nevertheless important in the field.

The chapter format was chosen to emphasize major issues, with minimal distractions associated with discussions of specific details and inclusion of citations. However, much of that information is clearly necessary, and hence it is presented in a Notes chapter at the end of the book.

An important disclaimer should be mentioned at the outset. I believe that it is no longer possible to be exhaustive in the coverage of all of the literature relevant to cognitive aging because of the growth of the field in so many different directions. As recently as a decade ago an author could attempt to survey the field from the perspective of a cognitive psychologist or a neuropsychologist and hope to be reasonably comprehensive by focusing primarily on articles published in three or four major journals. However, now such an effort would represent only a small fraction of the relevant literature because research on aging and cognitive functioning is published in journals based in the disciplines of psychology, neuroscience, neurology, radiology, health psychology, psychopharmacology, epidemiology, public health, endocrinology, and more. Fortunately, exhaustive coverage is not as critical in this type of book because the goal is to summarize major themes in the research rather than provide a comprehensive catalog of all relevant findings.

Contents

Major Issues in Cognitive Aging

1

Relations between Age and Cognitive Functioning

Major issue: What are the relations between age and cognitive functioning? Related questions: Are there different age trends for different types of cognitive variables? Do the individual differences in cognitive functioning become greater with increased age? When does age-related cognitive decline begin? How large are the age-related effects? Is age kinder to the initially more able?

The well-recognized demographic changes related to population aging have led to increased interest in all aspects of aging, cognitive as well as physical. In this book the focus is on mental, or cognitive, aspects. It is noteworthy that negative views about the cognitive abilities of elderly adults have been expressed for thousands of years. For example, in the *Republic*, Plato (ca. 360 BC) said that " . . . a man when he grows old . . . can no more learn much than he can run much." And William James, revered as the father of American psychology, wrote in his classic 1890 book, *Principles of Psychology*, "Outside of their own business, the ideas gained by men before they are twenty-five are practically the only ideas they shall have in their lives. They cannot get anything new. Disinterested curiosity is past, the cognitive grooves and channels set, the power of assimilation gone. . . . Whatever individual exceptions might be cited to these are of the sort that 'prove the rule.' "[1]

However, more optimistic views about cognitive aging have also been frequently expressed. To illustrate, Solon in about 600 BC was quoted as saying that "I grow old ever learning new things." Responding to early findings reporting age-related cognitive declines, a researcher in 1927 wrote that "Even if these tentative results point to the actual limitations of the establishment of new associations in age, they do not yet prove that learning capacity ever completely ceases in the average case."[2] Another early researcher on aging wrote that " . . . no one is ever too old to learn . . . There is no veto-power to learning exercised by age at any period in the normal life span. Relative decrement occurs, it is true, but in amount this is less than the difference in rate between moderately fast and moderately slow learners of equal age."[3]

Although there is no shortage of opinions about cognitive aging, it sometimes seems that relatively few of the claims are based on well-established empirical evidence. Perhaps more than in many other areas of scientific research, assertions about cognitive aging may be influenced as much by the authors' preconceptions and attitudes as by systematic evaluation of empirical research. The pronouncements are sometimes based on personal impressions, or when evidence is cited it is often weak, such as the results of a single study with a small sample of research participants of uncertain representativeness, and measurements with unknown reliability.

The primary goal of this book is to summarize some of the robust and replicated research findings concerned with the effects of aging on cognitive abilities and to discuss potential causes and consequences of these effects. Many of the findings will be illustrated with results from research projects conducted in my laboratory over the past 30 years.[4] Details about the samples of participants and specific outcomes of the studies can be found in published reports of the research, but some information can be mentioned here. Nearly all of the individuals participating in the research reported themselves to be in good to excellent health, and most had completed at least some college. They ranged from 18 to 98 years of age, and when the data are combined across studies, results for some variables are available from over 8,000 individuals.

Comparison with Physical Functioning

It is useful to begin by comparing cognitive aging with physical aging. Assessments of physical ability could be based on unsystematic observations, such as inferring that someone is strong if he or she can lift heavy boxes or move large pieces of furniture. However, comparisons involving these types of judgments are unlikely to be very precise because the boxes could vary in weight and ease of handling, and movement of furniture could involve obstacles such as stairways and tight corners, which might require agility as well as strength. Assessments of physical ability could be improved by basing the comparisons on standardized procedures, such as grip strength measured with a sensitive dynamometer, the heaviest weight that can be lifted over one's head, the speed of running a specified distance, and so forth. Moreover, in order to maximize the role of basic capacities as opposed to acquired skills, assessments of physical ability could be designed to avoid capabilities that might be specific to particular sports, such as hitting a baseball.

Comparisons of this type frequently reveal patterns of nearly linear declines in various measures of physical ability starting from when people are in their early to mid 20s. To illustrate, Figure 1.1 portrays the world records for the speed of running several distances as a function of age. The results in this figure clearly indicate that increased age is associated with progressively lower levels of physical performance because these data indicate that the fastest 65-year-old was able to run at only about 75% the speed as the fastest 20-year-old.[5] Few people would probably be surprised at these results, and it is unlikely that many individuals would view them with alarm or dismay. Because people are seldom expected to run 1,500 meters, or even 100 meters, at their maximum speed, age-related declines such as these are probably not perceived as imposing major limitations on one's daily activities.

Now consider how cognitive functioning is assessed. One could rely on unsystematic observations, such as inferring that someone has a good memory if he or she can remember the names of people met last year or details of events from his or her childhood. However, because these types of observations are inherently subjective and are based on activities and situations that have multiple determinants that could vary across people, they are not very useful for the purpose of making comparisons of different people, or

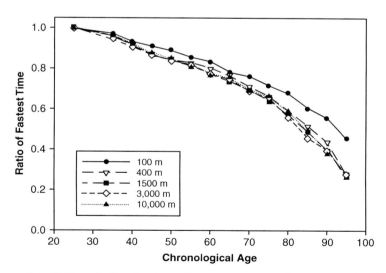

Figure 1.1. Ratio of the best performance at each age to the best performance across all ages. Because performance is measured in units of time, the plotted values are the reciprocals of the actual ratios to express values as proportions of the best performance.

of the same people at different ages. Instead, just as with the assessment of physical ability, more objective information might be obtained by using standardized assessments to measure various dimensions of cognitive functioning, such as memory, reasoning, and so forth.

Cognitive tests can be viewed as standardized situations designed to evaluate specific capabilities. They are not intended to represent everything that is interesting or important about cognition, but rather are designed to provide an objective indication of an individual's level of performance on some limited aspect of functioning. Although a very large number of cognitive tests have been developed, it is important to note that there are not yet any well-accepted tests of attributes such as judgment, common sense, wisdom, or quality of real-life decision making. Because some aspects of cognitive functioning have not been investigated, no scientific evidence is currently available about their possible relations to age, and thus they do not receive much discussion in this book.

Examples of the types of tests frequently used in cognitive aging research are illustrated in the next two figures. Each test is standardized in terms of the instructions, administration procedures, and the items that are presented, which allows people to be compared in terms of their ability to perform as instructed. The items in memory tests are frequently presented successively with the examinee asked to reproduce them either immediately following the last item, or after a delay ranging from seconds to decades. The materials in the other tests can be presented simultaneously or successively, and either with or without time limits. Because perceptual speed tasks are typically very simple, performance is usually assessed by the number of items that can be completed in a specified period of time. As with tests of physical ability, cognitive tasks are usually designed to evaluate the capabilities of individuals in a manner that is influenced as little as possible from acquired knowledge or skills.

Different Approaches

Assessment of cognitive ability with tests such as those illustrated in Figures 1.2 and 1.3 has been investigated from at least five somewhat different perspectives. The perspectives have often been pursued independently, with little communication or interaction among one another, and sometimes even with no awareness of the results from the other perspectives. The boundaries between them are becoming blurred in recent years, but it is probably still the case that few researchers are familiar with the results from more than one or two of the perspectives.

The *psychometric* perspective relies on standardized tests to evaluate differences across people. This research approach is characterized by moderately large (e.g., in the hundreds of individuals) samples of people who are each administered several different types of cognitive tests. Researchers within

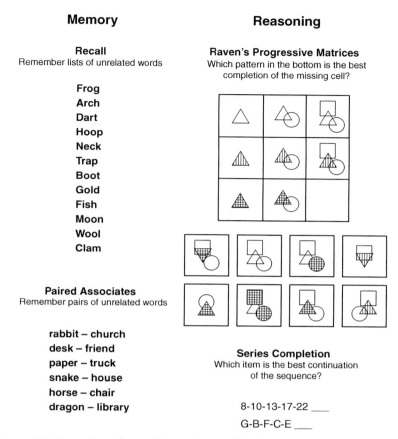

Figure 1.2. Examples of cognitive tasks used in the assessment of cognitive functioning of adults.

this tradition frequently examine relations among the scores from different tests and interpret the results in terms of levels of cognitive abilities such as memory, reasoning, or speed. Psychometric researchers are seldom interested in the details of how a particular level of performance is achieved, or in the neural substrates that are active while the task is being performed, but instead are primarily concerned with how different cognitive variables are interrelated and the implications of those relations for how people differ from one another.

The *experimental cognitive* perspective tends to rely on tests or tasks designed to investigate specific theoretical processes. The studies are often based on relatively small (e.g., less than 50 individuals) samples of research participants, and in the context of research on aging the individuals are frequently recruited from two groups, with one group

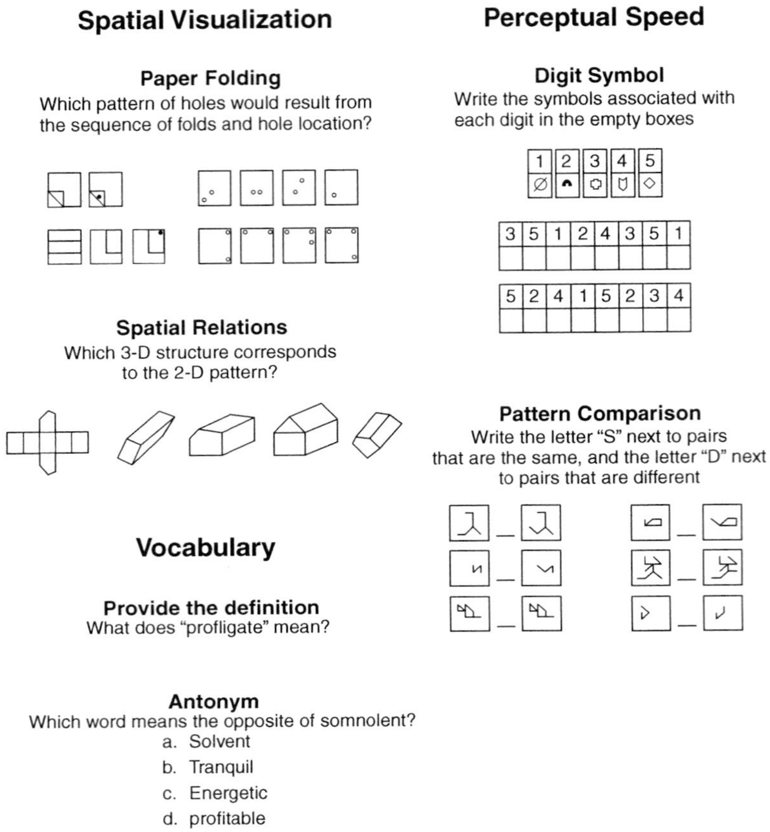

Spatial Visualization

Paper Folding
Which pattern of holes would result from
the sequence of folds and hole location?

Perceptual Speed

Digit Symbol
Write the symbols associated with
each digit in the empty boxes

Spatial Relations
Which 3-D structure corresponds
to the 2-D pattern?

Vocabulary

Provide the definition
What does "profligate" mean?

Pattern Comparison
Write the letter "S" next to pairs
that are the same, and the letter "D" next
to pairs that are different

Antonym
Which word means the opposite of somnolent?
    a. Solvent
    b. Tranquil
    c. Energetic
    d. profitable

Figure 1.3. Additional examples of cognitive tasks used in the assessment of cognitive functioning of adults.

consisting of college students and the other consisting of adults over the age of 65. Several different versions or conditions of the same task are often administered to allow the results to be interpreted in terms of the efficiency of particular processes or strategies hypothesized to be responsible for performance in the task. However, the analyses typically focus on a single variable and tend to ignore any relations that might exist among variables from different tasks. Until recently, researchers working within the experimental cognitive perspective had little interest in neurobiological substrates.

In the *neuropsychological* perspective the tests are often selected to reflect the functioning of particular brain regions, frequently determined from results of studies with individuals who have localized brain damage. The samples can range from a few individuals to 50 or more, and the results are often interpreted in terms of the efficiency of various brain structures.

Neuropsychological researchers are typically not interested in the relations that exist among variables, or in the influence of factors other than the functioning of particular brain regions as determinants of level of performance.

The *cognitive neuroscience* perspective includes aspects of the experimental cognitive and neuropsychological perspectives, but it differs by obtaining measures of brain activation while participants are performing cognitive tasks. Because most neuroimaging procedures are expensive, the sample sizes in cognitive neuroscience research are usually quite small, often only involving 12 or fewer young adults and 12 or fewer older adults.

The *epidemiological* perspective relies on brief tests of general cognitive ability because they are used to screen large numbers of people, and only a few minutes can be devoted to each individual. This research tradition often limits the assessment to very general aspects of cognitive functioning, but the samples in epidemiological studies can be very large, frequently in the thousands.

The preceding taxonomy is only one way of organizing approaches to research in cognitive aging, and other classification schemes could certainly be proposed. For example, the research could be categorized according to the type of cognitive ability that is primarily studied, according to the age range of the individuals included in the studies, and according to whether the research involves cross-sectional or longitudinal comparisons. In fact, an argument could be made that three subfields of cognitive aging might be distinguished based on differences in the backgrounds of the research teams, the dominant journals where the research is published and the lack of cross-citations. One subfield focuses on characterizing and explaining cross-sectional age differences between adults in their late teens or early 20s and adults in their 60s and 70s. A second subfield is primarily concerned with factors affecting longitudinal change in presumably healthy adults over the age of 65, and a third subfield is interested in the detection and characterization of the early stages of dementia in older adults. One major issue in the field is the extent to which the same causal factors and mechanisms are operative in these different subdisciplines within cognitive aging.

The preceding taxonomy is also not exhaustive because animal models of cognition could be mentioned as another perspective. Researchers working with nonhuman animals often use tasks resembling those used with humans, and as will be discussed in Chapter 2, there are many parallels in the two sets of results. However, the animal cognition perspective is less integrated into the cognitive aging research literature than the five perspectives mentioned above, and thus it will only be briefly mentioned in this book.

All five of these perspectives have been used to study the phenomenon of cognitive aging, but with different types of samples, procedures, and analytical methods, and with the reports often published in different journals. One of the goals of the current book is to attempt to integrate some of the major research findings concerned with cognitive aging from all five of these approaches.

Early Themes

Two broad themes about cognitive aging have been apparent from the beginning of research on this topic. The first theme is that different cognitive variables have different patterns of relations with age, and the second is that there is large variation in cognitive performance across people at any given age, such that the differences associated with age correspond to only a small proportion of the total variation that exists across people.

Different Variables Age Differently

One of the earliest findings in research on cognitive aging was that there was a pattern of stability, or even an increase with age, in measures of vocabulary and general information, and a decrease with age in measures of memory, reasoning, forming new associations, and the ability to solve novel problems.[6]

The early results indicating that different cognitive variables exhibited different age trends led to distinctions between two types of cognitive ability, one broadly referring to accumulated knowledge, and the other to the ability to generate, transform, or manipulate information. The distinction is loosely analogous to the information you already know versus your ability to acquire new information and to manipulate or transform old information. Many labels have been proposed for the different types of cognitive functioning, but the terms "fluid" and "crystallized" are probably the most frequently used in the psychological literature. Fluid abilities are conceptualized as diffuse in that they can flow into many different tasks or activities, whereas crystallized abilities refer to the somewhat stable residue of prior interactions of one's fluid ability with his or her environment. However, this terminology can be somewhat confusing in the context of cognitive aging because research within the psychometric perspective has revealed that several abilities besides fluid ability decline with increased age, such as perceptual speed and episodic memory. Another set of labels for the two types of cognitive abilities are the terms "process" and "product." Process refers to efficiency of processing at the time of assessment, and product refers to cumulative products of processing that was carried out earlier in one's life. However, it is important to recognize that all of the terms are merely labels of the different types of cognitive ability, and they are not explanations. Some theorists have linked the first type to biology and the second type to experience and culture, but these linkages should probably be viewed as tentative because both types of cognitive abilities have been found to be influenced by genetics and by historical or cultural changes.

Accurate description of the age relations on any variable requires moderately large samples of people across a wide, and continuous, range of ages. As noted earlier, much of the published research from the experimental cognitive, neuropsychological, and cognitive neuroscience perspectives on cognitive aging is based on samples from only two or three relatively narrow age ranges. If the sample sizes are large enough to have sufficient statistical power, this type of extreme-group research design can be efficient for the detection of group differences[7], but it is of limited value for characterizing the complete age relation on a variable. The omission of adults in the middle age range is understandable because many of these individuals are working and may not be as available to participate in research as college students or retired adults. Nevertheless, studies with only two groups from the extremes of the age distribution necessarily provide incomplete information about the nature of age relations across the entire period of adulthood.

Meaningful comparisons of age effects on different variables also require that the variables are sensitive across a wide measurement range and have adequate reliability. Some cognitive tests are designed to screen large numbers of people for dementia in epidemiological studies and are too easy for most people, whereas many tasks developed by cognitive psychologists and neuropsychologists have not had their reliability established. For the reasons just mentioned, results from the psychometric perspective tend to be the most informative for characterizing age trends in cognitive functioning.

Most of the measures of performance obtained from cognitive tests are in different scales, and therefore they need to be transformed to the same units to allow age trends to be compared across different tests. One possibility is to use the proportion of correct answers or the proportion of the maximum score as the common scale, but proportion scores are not necessarily meaningful for all tasks, such as those based on reaction time measures. The most widely used convention is to express all scores in units of across-person variability (i.e., standard deviations) in the variable. That is, the scores are converted to standard deviations by subtracting each score from the mean of a reference distribution, and then dividing that difference by the standard deviation of the reference group. This transformation into what are known as z-scores has the advantage that the scale has the same meaning with all variables, and if the distribution is normal, the values can be expressed in terms of percentiles of the reference distribution. Specifically, -1 corresponds to the 16th percentile of the distribution, 0 to the 50th percentile, $+1$ to the 84th percentile, etc.

The use of standard deviations is based on the assumption that the distributions of scores are symmetric and bell shaped. Fortunately, this

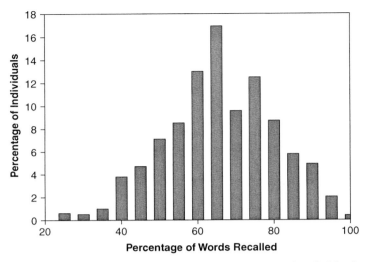

Figure 1.4. Frequency distribution of the percentages of individuals who recalled different percentages from a list of words.

assumption frequently appears justified because with moderate to large sample sizes the scores in many cognitive tasks closely approximate a normal distribution. For example, Figure 1.4 illustrates the proportion of individuals with different percentages of words recalled from a list of unrelated words. It can be seen that the distribution is nearly symmetric and shaped approximately like a bell, which are two distinguishing characteristics of a normal distribution.

A number of different reference distributions could be used when making age comparisons. For example, the scores at each age could be expressed relative to standard deviations computed across adults of all ages, or they could be expressed relative to standard deviations derived from scores of only young adults. A reference distribution based on people across a wide range of ages is informative about the placement of a group or an individual in the entire population, but it may lead to underestimation of the actual magnitude of the age trends because some of the variation in the total sample, and hence in the standard deviation used to calibrate the scores, is associated with age-related effects. This is not a problem when young adults are used as the reference distribution, and because young adulthood is the period of peak performance for many cognitive variables, the use of this reference group also has the advantage of allowing comparisons to be made against the best-performing individuals.

It is interesting that some of the most popular standardized cognitive test batteries, the Wechsler tests (e.g., Wechsler-Bellevue, WAIS, WAIS-R, WAIS III; WMS, WMS-R, WMS III) use different reference distributions for different age ranges, which has the effect of artificially eliminating the age relations on the transformed scores. The rationale for this procedure was that David Wechsler, the original developer of the tests, considered age-related decline in certain aspects of cognitive functioning to be normal, and hence that the most meaningful information for a test interpreter was the extent to which an examinee deviated from normal, as reflected by his or her performance relative to other people of the same age. However, it is important to recognize that it is no longer meaningful to examine relations of age to the age-adjusted scores when the scores are calibrated separately for different age groups.

Figure 1.5 portrays age trends in the tests illustrated earlier in total sample standard deviation units. These data are from participants in different studies conducted in my laboratory, with the number of individuals contributing to each function ranging from 2,780 to 8,085. It can be seen that there is a similar pattern of nearly linear age-related decline for memory, reasoning, spatial visualization, and speed variables, and for an increase until about age 60 followed by decline for the vocabulary variables.

Measurement of the variables in these studies was reliable, and the sample sizes were moderately large. However, the individuals were recruited on the basis of convenience (e.g., with newspaper advertisements, flyers, and referrals from other participants), and consequently they are not necessarily representative of the general population. That is, all of the participants in these studies were volunteers, and the fact that they

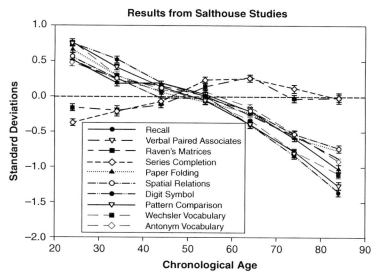

Figure 1.5. Means and standard errors of performance in different cognitive tests in the Salthouse data as a function of age, expressed in total sample standard deviation units.

volunteered to participate in a research study may distinguish them from other people. Some of the people may have participated because of possible concerns about their level of cognitive functioning, whereas others may have been motivated to participate to confirm their beliefs that they were still functioning at very high levels. Regardless of the reasons for participation, a sample may not be representative of the population when all of the members of the sample explicitly volunteered to participate. The problem of differential selection as a potential contributor to age relations in cross-sectional comparisons was recognized by some of the earliest researchers in the field[8], and it clearly needs to be considered when interpreting the results from convenience samples.

Some of the best available data on age trends in cognitive functioning are those obtained from samples used to establish the norms in standardized tests. These data are valuable because in addition to ensuring that all of the variables are reliable, most test publishers rely on stratification procedures to obtain nationally representative samples in which the numbers of individuals are matched to proportions in the population in terms of characteristics such as age, gender, race, ethnicity, years of education, occupation, and region of the country.

The next three figures portray age trends on a variety of cognitive variables from three comprehensive test batteries. Because of the manner in which the normative values are reported in the test manuals, the reference distributions in these figures are young adults. In each case the age patterns are similar, with slow growth for product measures (such as vocabulary and general information) until about age 60, followed by gradual decline, and a continuous decline from the early 20s for process measures. The right axes of the figures represent percentiles of the reference distribution, where it can be seen that by age 70 the average adult is performing at a level lower than the 20th percentile of the distribution of young adults on most of the process variables.

Because the age trends are not necessarily linear, it is informative to examine the slopes of the relations between cognitive performance and age at different periods in adulthood. Estimates of these slopes for adults under and over age 50 computed for the variables from the previous figures are plotted in Figure 1.9 (for the Salthouse data) and Figure 1.10 (for the data from standardized tests). Inspection of the figures reveals that for the product variables there is an increase with age prior to about 50 followed by decline at older ages. Declines are evident at both age ranges for the process variables, although with somewhat greater rates of decline after age 50.

Perhaps because only young and old adults have been compared in many studies, it is often claimed that there is a continuous increase in knowledge throughout adulthood. However, the results in Figures 1.5 through 1.8, as well as findings from other large-scale studies[9], suggest that performance on many standardized tests of vocabulary stops increasing at about age 60 and declines at older ages.

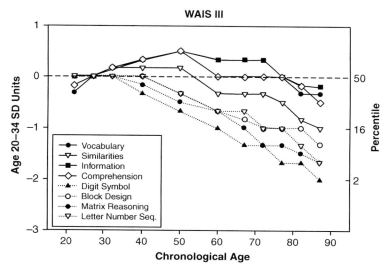

WAIS III

Figure 1.6. Means of performance in cognitive tests from the Wechsler Adult Intelligence Scale III test battery, expressed in standard deviation units from the sample of adults age 20 to 34. The vertical axis on the right represents the percentile of the reference distribution.

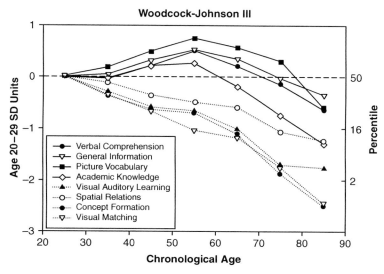

Woodcock-Johnson III

Figure 1.7. Means of performance in cognitive tests from the Woodcock-Johnson III test battery, expressed in standard deviation units from the sample of adults age 20 to 29. The vertical axis on the right represents the percentile of the reference distribution.

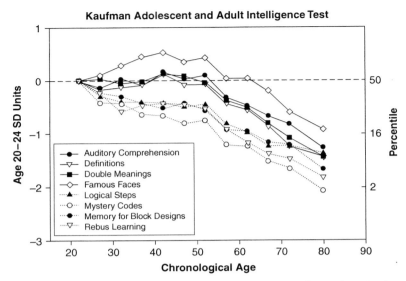

Figure 1.8. Means of performance in cognitive tests from the Kaufman Adolescent and Adult test battery, expressed in standard deviation units from the sample of adults age 20 to 24. The vertical axis on the right represents the percentile of the reference distribution.

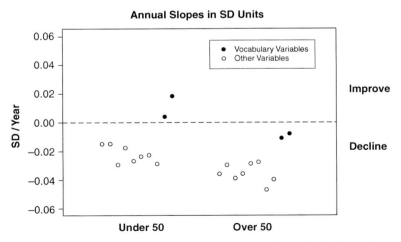

Figure 1.9. Estimated slopes, in total sample standard deviation units per year, for vocabulary and other variables for adults under and over age 50 in the Salthouse data.

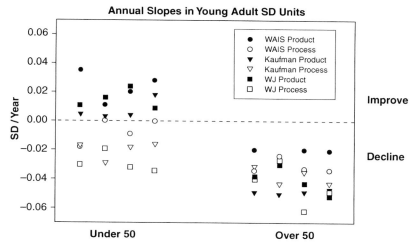

Figure 1.10. Estimated slopes, in young adult standard deviation units per year, for product and process variables for adults under and over age 50 from normative data in standardized cognitive test batteries.

Despite the lack of evidence indicating continuous increases in knowledge, it is still possible that knowledge continues to accumulate, but that it simply has not yet been documented because of the nature of the available tests. Indeed, it seems likely that current tests underestimate the true level of knowledge for most people. In order to be applicable to a large number of people, the tests have been designed to assess general, culturally shared, knowledge, but the majority of one's knowledge is probably idiosyncratic and difficult to assess in a manner that allows comparisons across different individuals[10]. It is therefore conceivable that trends reflecting greater knowledge with increased age might be obtained if tests could be devised to assess the specialized types of knowledge that are unique to each individual. Comprehensive evaluation of an individual's true level of knowledge is one of many areas where the assessment of cognitive ability is currently inadequate. This omission is unfortunate because it means that most studies of cognitive aging have focused on process variables that exhibit age-related declines, and thus the research may portray a somewhat distorted picture of the overall cognitive functioning of adults.

The results in the preceding figures indicate that variables representing reasoning, spatial visualization, memory, and speed abilities have very similar age trends. In each case there is a decrease of about 1.5 to 2 total sample standard deviation units from the 20s to the 70s. Moreover, although the negative age relations are stronger at older ages, there is no evidence in the figures of abrupt transitions or dramatic drops corresponding to the onset of menopause for women, or to the typical retirement age for men or women.

Some researchers have suggested that the patterns of age-related change in individuals may be more step-like rather than continuous. Although this is certainly possible, there is little data in support of this speculation at the current time, at least in part because it would require precise and reliable estimates of an individual's performance across a wide range of ages that are not yet available.

When the samples are large enough, somewhat different age trends can be detected with different tests of the same type of ability. For example, age trends have been reported to be more positive for measures of synonym vocabulary than for measures of antonym vocabulary, for difficult compared to easy vocabulary items, and for measures of expressive (i.e., What is the name of the object in this picture?) than for measures of receptive (i.e., Which picture represents this word?) vocabulary[11]. Moreover, it is conceivable that different age trends might be found for passive (recognition) versus active (actual use) vocabulary, although no large-scale studies have apparently been published with this type of comparison.

The point of this digression is that one needs to be cautious in drawing conclusions about age trends from a single variable, even if the assessment of that variable is reliable, and the data are based on a large and representative sample of adults. Variable-specific characteristics can affect the age relations on any particular variable, but these characteristics should not be inferred to be the major determinant of the age differences on that variable until the age relations are examined in the context of age relations on other variables.

Large Individual Variation

The second major theme apparent from the earliest cognitive aging research is that there is considerable variation among the scores for different people of the same age[12]. One way of illustrating this variability is with a figure in which the vertical axis represents scores on the variable, the horizontal axis represents age, and data points correspond to scores of individual participants. Figure 1.11 contains this type of data from a task in which participants attempted to remember as many words as possible across four presentations of the same list of 12 unrelated words. Performance in the task is represented in the figure in terms of the proportion of words correctly recalled across the four presentations. The diagonal line in Figure 1.11 represents the average age trend, which corresponds to a decrease of about 0.3% per year from the maximum. However, it is obvious that there is a great deal of variability at each age because the scores of some adults in their 20s are below the average of adults in their 60s, and the scores of some adults in their 60s are above the average of adults in their 20s. Figure 1.11 therefore makes it clear that age-related variation in cognitive test performance is only a fraction of the total between-person variation, a fact that has been recognized since the first systematic studies on cognitive aging.

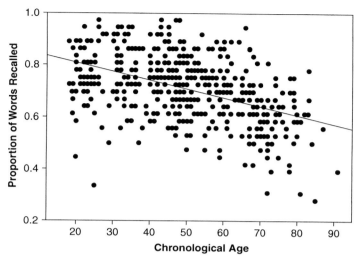

Figure 1.11. Scatter plot of the proportion of words recalled as a function of age. The solid line corresponds to the regression equation for these data.

One of the most common methods of expressing the association between two variables is with a correlation coefficient, and in the range from about 18 to 80 years of age the correlations between age and many measures of cognitive ability are typically between about–0.2 to–0.6.[13] Because the square of a correlation indicates the proportion of variance shared between two variables, correlations of this magnitude indicate that only between 4% and 36% of the total across-person variation in the scores is associated with age. The correlation between age and the recall proportion scores in Figure 1.11 was–0.46, which indicates that although the scores are clearly related to age, only about 21% (i.e., .46^2) of the total variation among the people in this measure of memory functioning was associated with age.

Results such as these indicate that between 64% and 96% of the differences among people in many cognitive test scores are associated with factors other than age. Some of the variability is due to imprecise assessment, random fluctuation, or what is broadly termed measurement error. Much of the systematic variation is probably due to stable individual difference characteristics other than age. Nevertheless, the relations between age and measures of cognitive functioning are intriguing because years from birth is a very crude variable, and yet it is associated with more of the between-person variation in cognitive performance than most other individual difference characteristics, including gender, ethnicity, or personality type.

Age and Between-Person Variability

It is sometimes assumed that people become less similar to one another as they grow older because of the diversity of occupations, leisure activities, health conditions, and experiences as they age. To the extent that people age differently, it might be expected that people would become less alike with respect to their levels of cognitive abilities as they grow older, such that the magnitude of between-person variability would increase with age. Surprisingly, quite a few empirical results are inconsistent with this expectation.

One index of variability is the standard deviation, and thus the relation between age and variability of cognitive performance can be investigated by examining standard deviations at different ages. What may be the earliest report comparing standard deviations at different ages, published in 1933, found them to be nearly constant in the range from 20 to 60 years of age[14]. Subsequent empirical findings on age differences in between-person variability have been mixed, with some reviews concluding that between-person variability of cognitive performance increases with age, and others reporting an inconsistent pattern.

Figure 1.12 illustrates standard deviations as a function of age for 10 variables from our research project. The sample sizes for different variables ranged from 2,780 to 8,058, with between 140 and 1,359 individuals contributing to the values for each data point. Examination of the figure reveals that there is little indication in these data of a systematic relation between age and amount of between-person variability, and if anything, with some variables between-person variability appears to be smaller at older ages.[15]

However, results from convenience samples are not ideal for investigating age differences in variability because the degree to which the individuals are representative of the general population could vary across age groups. Differential representativeness is less of a problem in the samples used to establish norms for standardized tests because, as mentioned earlier, the normative samples are typically selected in a manner to match the proportions in the population with respect to characteristics such as education, sex, ethnicity, region of country, urban versus rural residence, etc. Even these normative samples are likely to exclude individuals in poor health, and to the extent that level of health decreases with age and is related to scores on cognitive tests, results from normative samples may underestimate age-related increase in variability. Nevertheless, the samples used to provide the norms for standardized tests probably provide the best available data for examining age differences in between-person variability.

Figures 1.13, 1.14, and 1.15 portray standard deviations at different ages for the same standardized tests used to illustrate age trends in three comprehensive test batteries. Inspection of the figures indicates that any age trends in between-person variability are relatively small, particularly in comparison

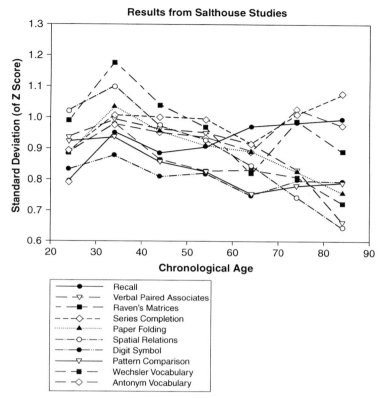

Figure 1.12. Standard deviations as a function of age for the same data (Salthouse data) portrayed in Figure 1.5.

with the age trends in the means in the same variables (i.e., Figs. 1.6, 1.7, and 1.8).

It is likely that variability would increase with age if the samples included individuals in poor health and very old adults. However, it is important to note that these results clearly indicate that age-related declines in average level of performance can occur in the absence of sizable increases in between-person variability. Relations between age and cognitive functioning therefore do not seem to be a consequence of only some people declining with many others remaining stable, because that would result in an increase in variability that is typically not found.[16]

Another interesting point to consider is that to the extent that there was an age-related increase in between-person variability, then other things being equal, the magnitude of the correlations between age and scores on the various tests would be expected to decrease with increasing age. That is, an increase in the individual difference variance not related to age would mean

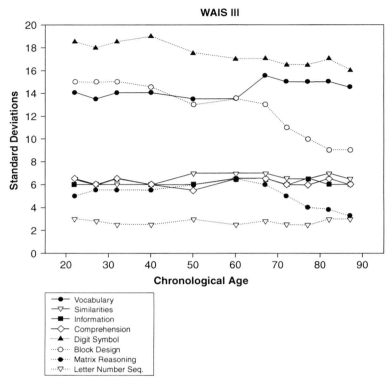

Figure 1.13. Standard deviations as a function of age for the same data (Wechsler Adult Intelligence Scale III test battery) portrayed in Figure 1.6.

that the variance that is related to age corresponds to a smaller proportion of the total variance, which implies that the correlation of the variable with age should be weaker at older ages. However, as indicated in Figures 1.9 and 1.10, for many variables the age relations are actually stronger, rather than weaker, at older ages. At least for healthy adults, therefore, age appears to be a more precise predictor of an individual's cognitive status at older ages than at younger ages.

Correlations among Variables

It is sometimes claimed that correlations among different cognitive variables increase across the adult years, which might suggest that variables and abilities become less distinct, or differentiated, as people grow older. This possibility can be examined in the same data reported earlier. Median correlations for the 10 variables from our project are reported in Figure 1.16. Notice that the

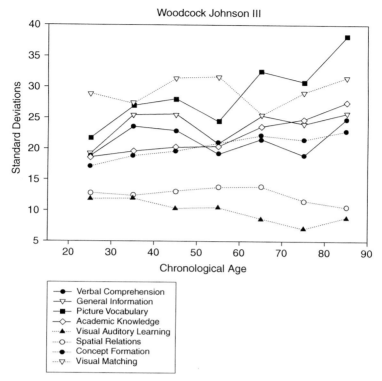

Figure 1.14. Standard deviations as a function of age for the same data (Woodcock-Johnson III test battery) portrayed in Figure 1.7.

values appear remarkably consistent from the 20s through the 70s. The figure also contains correlations between a prototypical process variable (Raven's Progressive Matrices) and a prototypical product variable (Wechsler Vocabulary). Once again there is no indication of a systematic pattern of increasing correlation with increasing age.[17] The third set of correlations in Figure 1.16 are between two measures of perceptual speed. These correlations do appear to increase somewhat with increasing age, which suggests that task-specific influences in assessments of perceptual speed may become less salient with increased age, thereby resulting in stronger correlations among the speed measures.

Correlations can also be examined among the scores of standardized tests from the nationally representative samples used to establish the norms for commercial test batteries. Figure 1.17 illustrates median correlations among variables as a function of age from several of the standardized cognitive tests reported earlier. Notice that the correlations are moderate in magnitude and nearly constant across all of the adult years. In none of

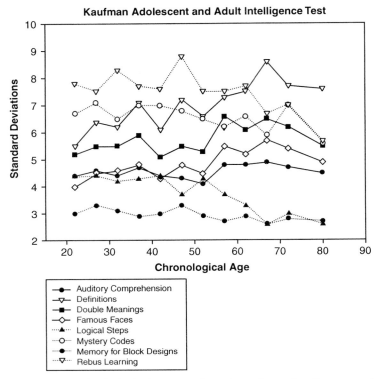

Figure 1.15. Standard deviations as a function of age for the same data (Kaufman Adolescent and Adult test battery) portrayed in Figure 1.8.

these sets of data, therefore, is there any evidence of systematic differences as a function of age in the magnitude of the correlations among variables.[18] There may be an increase in the strengths of the relations among variables in certain samples, but it is apparently not a universal characteristic of normal aging up to at least age 80.

When Does Cognitive Decline Begin?

One of the major questions concerning cognitive aging is when it begins. This question is important because the answer could have both theoretical and practical significance.[19] Not only would the search for causes likely be most successful when the focus is on the period when the phenomenon originates, but interventions intended to prevent or delay the phenomenon are likely to be most effective if they are implemented at the earliest stages of change.

It is often claimed that cognitive decline only occurs late in life, or that when it occurs it is associated with a pathological condition. Assertions such

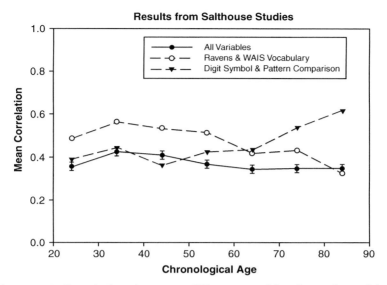

Figure 1.16. Correlations between different combinations of cognitive variables as a function of age in the Salthouse data.

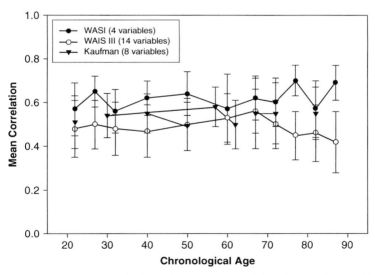

Figure 1.17. Mean correlations between combinations of cognitive variables in standardized cognitive test batteries as a function of age.

as these might seem surprising in view of the results described earlier that appear to indicate nearly continuous decline in many measures of cognitive performance from the early 20s. Some of the inconsistency is probably attributable to differential emphasis on findings from crude assessments of overall cognitive ability rather than sensitive measures of specific abilities. Different findings from longitudinal versus cross-sectional comparisons, which will be discussed in the next chapter, are likely also contributing to the discrepancy between well-documented cross-sectional age trends and certain claims about the time course of cognitive aging.

Many criteria could be used to determine when aging begins, or as the basis for assigning labels to specific ages. For example, old age could be defined as occurring when 50% of the birth cohort has died (which is approximately how life expectancy is measured). According to a definition of this type, in 1900 an old person would be someone who was 47 or older, in 2000 the beginning of old age might have been around 77 years of age, and in the not-too-distant future old age might not begin until age 85. Alternatively, cognitive aging might be considered to begin when it is first noticed by the individual or by others, or when there is a statistically significant drop from his or her level some number of years earlier. Based on their changing descriptions of the participants in their studies over time, some researchers seem to define old age as 10 years older than their own current age.

All of these criteria are somewhat arbitrary, however, and a more productive approach to determining when cognitive aging begins is to examine levels of cognitive performance across a wide age range. Lifespan age relations on process and product cognitive variables can be illustrated with data from three recent test batteries that were administered to people ranging from under 6 to over 90 years of age.[20] Each battery has one or more tests of process and product cognitive ability, and to allow across-variable comparisons, the scores have been expressed as the percentage of the maximum across all ages. Age trends for process measures are portrayed in the left panel of Figure 1.18, and those for product measures are portrayed in the right panel.

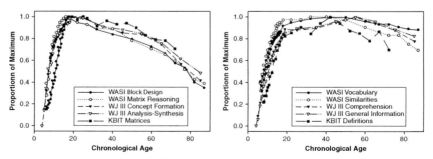

Figure 1.18. Proportion of the maximum score on 10 different cognitive tests as a function of age across the entire life span.

Inspection of these results reveals that there is a remarkably similar pattern across the variables in each sample. Specifically, for each variable there is an increase until about the late teens or early 20s, followed either by a decrease for process variables, or by a period of stability and then a decline at around age 50 or 60 for product variables. The cross-sectional age trends in process measures of cognitive ability are therefore similar to those found in measures of physical ability in that declines appear to begin in the 20s and to continue throughout all of adulthood.

How Large Are the Effects?

Another important question concerning cognitive aging is the magnitude of the age-related effects. This is a particularly relevant question because the phenomenon of cognitive aging may not be very important or interesting if the effects are small. Several methods can be used to evaluate the size of cognitive aging effects.

First, the magnitude of the differences found across the period of adulthood can be compared with the magnitude of differences found across the period of childhood. This method was originally proposed by researchers in 1933[21], who reported that for several cognitive variables the decrease from 20 to 55 years of age was about the same magnitude as the increase from 14 to 20 years of age. Similar comparisons can be derived from the lifespan data in Figure 1.18, where it appears that for the process variables, the difference between about age 18 and 80 is nearly the same magnitude as the difference between about age 8 and 18.

A second method of specifying the size of the cognitive aging phenomenon relies on information about the location of the average individual of a given age within a reference distribution. This type of percentile information is available in the earlier figures which portray the age relations both in standard deviation units and in percentiles of the reference distribution. Inspection of Figures 1.6, 1.7, and 1.8 indicates that the average individual at age 75 is at about the 10th percentile of the young adult reference distribution.

A third basis for evaluating the magnitude of cognitive aging effects consists of contrasting them with the age-related effects on various biological systems. An article published in 2001[22] reported estimates of annual decline for various body organs in units of the percentage of the maximum across all ages. To illustrate, the estimated percentage decline of the efficiency of the musculoskeletal system was 0.36%/year, for the gastrointestinal system it was 0.60%, for the respiratory system it was about 0.84%, and for the immune system it was about 1.10%. Estimates of annual decline in standardized tests of cognitive ability derived from data in the test manuals are often close to 1%/year. For example, for the WAIS III Block Design variable it is 0.72%, for the WAIS III Matrix Reasoning it is 0.97%, for the WASI Block Design variable it is 0.90%, for the WASI Matrix Reasoning variable it is 0.90%, for the KAIT Mystery Codes variable it is 0.94%, and for the KAIT Rebus Figures variable it is 0.98%.

Finally, the size of cognitive aging effects can be compared with the sizes of effects representing other types of relations. Another article published in 2001[23] summarized the strengths of a variety of associations expressed in correlation coefficient units. Some of their results are reproduced in Table 1.1, where it can be seen that the relations between age and the level of performance on certain cognitive tests are stronger than many of the relations among biomedical variables that form the basis for contemporary medical practice.

Each of these different ways of expressing the magnitude of age relations indicates that the effects of aging on certain measures of cognitive functioning are fairly large. However, it is important to recognize that because there is considerable variability, the relation between age and any measure of cognitive performance is only probabilistic, and it cannot necessarily be used to predict the performance of a given individual. Terms such as "universal" and "inevitable" are sometimes used to refer to age-related cognitive changes, but it is probably more appropriate to use terms such as "normative" (happens to most) and "progressive" (effects are larger, and more likely, with increased age).

Table 1.1. Estimated Effect Sizes (Correlations) for Different Types of Relationships

Effect	Size
Aspirin and reduced risk of heart attack	.02
Chemotherapy and surviving breast cancer	.03
Calcium intake and bone mass in post–menopausal women	.08
Ever smoking and subsequent incidence of lung cancer within 25 years	.08
Alcohol use during pregnancy and subsequent premature birth	.09
Effect of nonsteroidal anti–inflammatory drugs (e.g., ibuprofen) on pain reduction	.14
Gender and weight for U.S. adults	.26
ECT for depression and subsequent improvement	.29
Sleeping pills and short–term improvement in chronic insomnia	.30
Age and episodic memory	**.33**
Elevation above sea level and lower daily temperatures in the U.S.	.34
Viagra and improved male sexual functioning	.38
Age and reasoning	**.40**
Weight and height for U.S. adults	.44
Age and speed	**.52**
Gender and arm strength	.55
Nearness to equator and daily temperature in the U.S.	.60
Gender and height for U.S. adults	.67

Adapted from Meyer et al. (2001).

Moderators of Age Trends

Although the trends summarized in the previous figures may appear convincing, it is natural to wonder whether the cross-sectional age relations vary according to particular characteristics of individuals. This issue will be explored in more detail in Chapter 4, but results with two individual difference variables, gender and initial level of ability, will be discussed here.

Gender

There are occasional reports of more rapid cognitive aging in either males or females, but most of the claims are based on relatively small samples of unknown representativeness. Systematic analyses with larger samples tend to reveal that although there are some gender differences, with males performing higher in some tests and females performing higher in other tests, the rates of age-related decline are very similar in men and women.[24]

The two panels in Figure 1.19 portray results from two tasks in our project; a spatial relations task, and a free recall memory task. The patterns in these figures are fairly typical as males frequently perform somewhat higher than females on spatial ability tasks, and females frequently perform somewhat higher than males in verbal memory tasks. However, the important point to note in the current context is that the age trends are nearly parallel for males and females. These findings are also consistent with reports from recent longitudinal studies in which gender differences are sometimes found in the intercept parameter representing the overall level of performance, but seldom in the slope parameter representing the rate of age-related decline. It therefore appears that although males and females may have different average levels of performance on some cognitive tests, they do not differ much, if at all, in the rate at which cognitive performance decreases with increasing age.

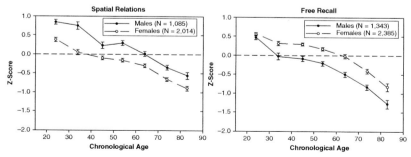

Figure 1.19. Means and standard errors for males and females on two cognitive tests as a function of age in the Salthouse data.

Effect of Initial Ability

Are people who perform at higher levels somewhat immune from age-related cognitive declines? One of the earliest reports of cognitive aging, published in 1928, investigated the effect of initial ability level on cognitive aging trends. These researchers concluded that it is " . . . probable that the influence is very slight, that the ablest man and the ordinary man show very nearly the same curve, that the decline of ability to learn begins little, if any, later in the highest one percent of intellects than in the average man." Results consistent with this conclusion have been reported in many subsequent studies, including several articles with variants of the phrase "Is age kinder to the initially more able" in the title.[25]

One way to investigate the relation between initial ability and rate of cognitive aging involves examining cross-sectional age relations for people whose performance places them at different regions of the distribution of scores at each age. That is, people at the 75th, 50th, and 25th percentiles of the distributions at age 18–30 can be compared to people at the same percentiles from the distributions at age 31–40, age 41–50, and so on. Figure 1.20 illustrates the age trends for four variables from our project in this format. Notice that the functions are nearly parallel for individuals at the 75th, 50th, and 25th percentiles in the distribution of scores at each age.

Nearly parallel age trends are also evident in the data from standardized tests. For example, Figure 1.21 portrays the age relations for individuals at the

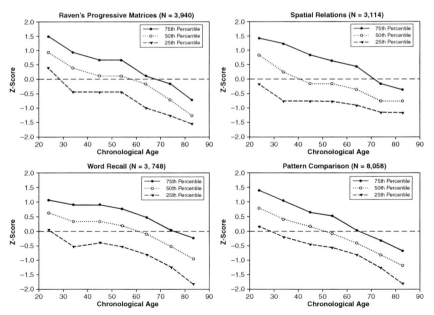

Figure 1.20. Mean levels of performance at the 25th, 50th, and 75th percentile at each age on four cognitive tests in the Salthouse data.

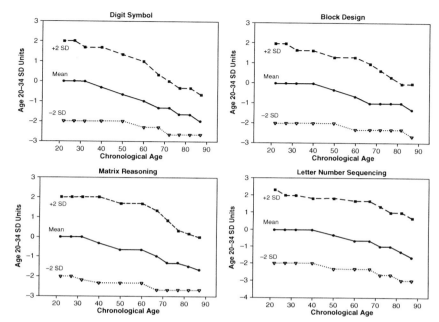

Figure 1.21. Levels of performance at the mean and one standard deviation above and below the mean at each age for four cognitive tests from the Wechsler Adult Intelligence Scale III.

mean and at two standard deviations above and below the mean for four variables from the WAIS III. It can be seen that the functions have very similar slopes, and any deviations from parallelism likely occur because the scores cannot go much lower for the lowest-performing individuals.

Different age trends for people of different ability levels could occur when the tests do not discriminate among people at high or low levels of ability because the tests are either too easy or too difficult. However, considerable evidence suggests that the age trends at different ability levels are usually parallel when sensitive tests are administered to relatively large samples.

What Is Responsible for Cognitive Aging?

Beginning with the earliest reports of age differences in cognition, researchers have considered alternative interpretations of the cognitive aging phenomenon that would minimize the negative implications of the finding that some aspects of cognitive functioning appear to decrease with age.[26] For example, the primary author of the report on psychological testing in World War I dismissed results of negative age relations observed in the sample as due to differential representativeness.[27] His argument was that higher-functioning older men were under-represented in the military because they were in critical occupations that were exempt from the draft, or because they were wealthy enough to pay for a surrogate to take their place. The observed age relations were therefore postulated to be an artifact of differential selectivity. Other early researchers speculated that age differences in cognitive performance were artifacts of differences in level of health, amount of education, level of motivation or anxiety, sensory abilities, disuse, and so forth.

It has also been asserted that many cognitive assessments are not valid because they are based on tasks that are child oriented, trivial, unrepresentative of, or unrelated to, real-world functioning. Cicero in *de Senectude* (ca. 44 BC) could be considered an early proponent of this position as he wrote: "The old remember everything that concerns them, the appointments at court, who owes them money, to whom they owe money." Age-related differences in cognitive functioning are sometimes claimed to be restricted to the period of very late adulthood, and thus may only affect a small, albeit growing, segment of the population. Another position has been that any effects that might exist are limited in scope, only happen to certain people (e.g., those with dementia or other pathologies), or only affect certain (unimportant) abilities. Still another view is that the effects may be real, but they are not permanent because the level of critical abilities can be re-acquired with appropriate intervention (e.g., diet, physical exercise, cognitive stimulation, etc.). A related perspective is that the results may reflect qualitative differences rather than quantitative deficits, and are reflections of styles, goals, or priorities, rather than actual ability. A few researchers have even suggested that some of the differences in cognitive aging could be adaptive because it may be functional to think slower as one slows down physically. Furthermore, in some cases memory failure might be considered beneficial because we would be overwhelmed if our memories kept accumulating and were not updated with current information, such as where you parked your car today as opposed to yesterday.

One of the most popular interpretations of cognitive aging is that cross-sectional age relations are artifactual because they primarily reflect characteristics of people other than age. In fact, some researchers have suggested that only longitudinal data are directly relevant to the study of aging. This position will be examined in detail in the next chapter, but it is important to note that the phenomenon of age-related differences in cognitive functioning from 18 to over 80 years of age is well documented, and it warrants explanation even if it is eventually discovered that there are different determinants of the age trends in between-person (cross-sectional) and within-person (longitudinal) comparisons. The phenomenon of cognitive aging refers to relations between cognitive performance and age, and thus large proportions of the research literature, whether from cross-sectional or longitudinal designs, should not be dismissed without careful consideration, particularly because cross-sectional age relations may have more immediate practical importance than longitudinal age relations.

Many of the preceding opinions were incorporated into the summary statement in the American Psychological Association Task Force for the 1971 White House Conference on Aging[28]: "For the most part, the observed decline in intellectual functioning among the aged is attributable to poor health, social isolation, economic plight, limited education, lowered motivation, or variables not intrinsically related to the aging process."

Although the views expressed in this statement may have reflected a consensus at that time, it is important to evaluate the validity of these assertions because if they are true then the phenomenon may be of limited interest. Chapters 2, 3, and 4 will therefore be devoted to examining these and other speculations about the causes of cognitive aging.

Personal Observations

Age-related cognitive declines are discouraging, and they seem inconsistent with the impressive level of functioning and accomplishments of many older adults. However, anecdotes and personal observations about remarkable older adults are not always scientifically valuable because they are unsystematic, the activity domains of exceptional individuals are usually narrow and self-selected, and considerable attrition may have occurred such that only the highest functioning older adults survived to be recognized.

It is nevertheless interesting that prominent psychologists have acknowledged the existence of cognitive decline in their own functioning as they grew older. For example, Donald Hebb noted " . . . the real change, I conclude, is a lowered ability to think; the loss of interest in psychological problems is secondary to that. . . . . But—between you and me, privately—the picture is one of a slow, inevitable loss of cognitive capacity."[29]

B.F. Skinner presented a talk at a professional convention, when he was 78 years old, titled "Intellectual Self-Management in Old Age." His remarks were expanded to a book titled *Enjoy Old Age*, which was originally published in 1983, and reprinted in 1997. The book contained very few citations, and Skinner acknowledged that it was not a scientific treatise, but more like friendly advice based on personal observations. However, it is interesting that Skinner accepted the existence of age-related limitations of memory and other cognitive abilities and offered several suggestions on how to minimize the consequences of cognitive declines. Among these were the following:

- Do not speak in complex sentences; try to avoid digressions or you will lose your train of thought.
- Thinking at a slower pace helps. The slowness is not a great handicap, since old people usually have plenty of time.
- Give up complicated puzzles, chess, and intellectual games that tire you. Relax your standards and read detective stories or watch some of the programs on television that you once condemned as trash.

Although the opinions of Hebb and Skinner are not necessarily more valid than the anecdotes about remarkable older adults, it is nevertheless noteworthy that they are from individuals who might be expected to be especially sensitive to cognitive changes.

Why Study Cognitive Aging?

It is clear that performance on certain tests used to assess cognitive functioning is negatively related to age, and that, at least in cross-sectional comparisons, the relations appear to begin when adults are in their 20s. The effects accumulate such that the average level of performance of adults in their 60s and 70s is substantially lower than that of adults in their 20s, and this is true not just for memory ability, but for many different types of cognitive abilities.

Several authors have noted that results such as these are often unpopular, and they have wondered why anyone would want to study cognitive aging.[30] Researchers investigating cognitive aging have sometimes been accused of implicitly accepting a "decrement perspective" because they have focused on aspects of functioning that appear to decline with increased age. It is clearly true that there have been many more studies investigating process variables that decline with age than studies investigating product variables that may increase over much of adulthood. However, one important reason is that, as mentioned earlier, the available measures of an individual's knowledge are severely limited. The critics have apparently also ignored the possibility that at least some researchers have emphasized the declining aspects because they are the aspects most in need of remediation or intervention. That is, it seems likely that a goal of many researchers is to understand the causes of the differences in order to ultimately intervene. If aspects of cognitive ability decline with age, then it is valuable to determine why that is the case and to use that information either to try to reverse the process or to prevent it from occurring in the future.

In this respect it is worth noting another parallel between cognitive aging and physical aging. The differences first need to be documented, and possible determinants of the differences identified, before the efficacy of possible interventions can be evaluated. As with physical ability, it is valuable to determine whether patterns early in life are associated with the presence, the age of onset, or the severity of limitations or pathologies that occur late in life. In physical aging, interventions with at least some documented success have been identified, such as diet and exercise, both of which are under the individual's control. A key question in the field of cognitive aging is whether there are analogous interventions that might alter the course of cognitive aging. This question will be examined in Chapter 6.

2

Within-Person and Across-Time Comparisons

Major issue: Are the age–cognition relations different in between-person (cross-sectional) and within-person (longitudinal) comparisons, and if so, why?

Related questions: What are the relative contributions of various factors, such as short-term fluctuation, selective attrition, retest and period effects on the pattern, and precision, of cross-sectional and longitudinal age trends in cognitive functioning? Do time-lag effects in cognitive performance affect the interpretation of cross-sectional age trends, as suggested by obsolescence interpretations, or the interpretation of longitudinal age trends, as suggested by inflation interpretations? Are there age differences in cognition in non-human animals raised in constant environments, and therefore presumably not subject to cohort influences? How large, and reliable, are longitudinal changes in cognitive functioning? Do changes in different cognitive variables occur together? Does cognitive change have the same meaning at different periods in adulthood?

All of the results described in the previous chapter were based on cross-sectional comparisons, and thus they reflect differences between people who not only vary in age, but undoubtedly in many other characteristics as well. It is widely recognized that comparisons of people of different ages at a particular period in time do not necessarily reflect changes that will occur within a given individual as he or she ages. This point is sometimes illustrated with a now rather dated anecdote about a visitor to Miami who observes that most of the older adults are of European descent and speak English with a New York accent, whereas many of the young adults are Hispanic and speak English with a Spanish accent. The visitor therefore infers that aging results in changes in ethnicity and in characteristics of speech. Note that the issue is not that cross-sectional differences are not genuine, or potentially important, but rather that they do not necessarily reflect processes intrinsic to aging in the sense that the differences apparent between people of different ages at a particular point in time will ultimately be manifested as changes in people as they age.

Indeed, several studies have found negative relations between age and performance on cognitive tests in cross-sectional comparisons, but either no age relation, or a positive relation, in longitudinal comparisons.[1] Figure 2.1 portrays estimates of age trends in cross-sectional and long-itudinal comparisons with results on seven composite cognitive ability scores from a popular cognitive test battery.[2] The vertical axis represents

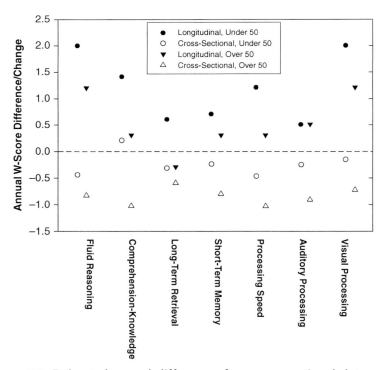

Figure 2.1. Estimated annual differences from cross-sectional data, and 1-year changes from longitudinal data, for adults under and over age 50 on seven cognitive abilities from the Woodcock-Johnson test battery.

the difference expected over 1 year based on the slopes of the age relations in cross-sectional comparisons, or on the estimated rates of change derived from longitudinal comparisons. Separate estimates are portrayed for adults under and over the age of 50 to examine the possibility of nonlinear age trends. It can be seen that all but one of the longitudinal (filled symbols) values are positive, reflecting better performance with increasing age, and all but one of the cross-sectional (unfilled symbols) are negative, indicating poorer performance with increasing age. Furthermore, both types of comparisons indicate more negative (or less positive) differences or changes for adults above the age of 50 than for those at younger ages. Results such as these clearly indicate that marked discrepancies can occur between the age trends observed in cross-sectional and longitudinal comparisons of cognitive functioning.

This point is illustrated in a slightly different way in Figure 2.2, which portrays cross-sectional and longitudinal results on variables from four separate longitudinal studies.[3] Higher scores correspond to better performance in the top two panels, but because performance in the bottom two panels is expressed in units of errors (left) or time (right), better performance in these panels is represented by lower scores. In each case, scores from the

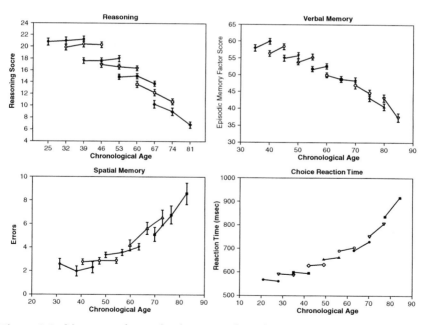

Figure 2.2. Means and standard errors of performance on different cognitive tests at different measurement occasions for adults of different ages. The connected lines represent longitudinal data from the same individuals, and different sets of lines correspond to different individuals.

same individuals are represented by points on connected lines, and those from different individuals are represented by points on different lines. It is apparent from these figures that poorer performance with increased age is evident in the between-person (cross-sectional) age relations, but that at least before about age 60, the within-person (longitudinal) age relations portray either stability, or an increase, with increasing age.[4]

One of the important questions in the field of cognitive aging is what is responsible for the different age relations found in cross-sectional and longitudinal comparisons of cognitive functioning. The major factors that have been postulated to contribute to different age trends in cross-sectional and longitudinal comparisons are briefly discussed in the following sections.[5]

Maturation

In the context of research on aging, the term *maturation* refers to processes originating from within the individual as he or she grows older. They are presumably biologically based, although not much is currently known about the specific causes. Maturation is the factor of primary interest in most developmental research, and it is what many researchers assume they are investigating in their research. However, maturation always occurs in the context of other factors whose influences must be considered and distinguished from maturation.

Statistical Artifacts

Some of the apparent discrepancies between age trends in cross-sectional and longitudinal comparisons could be attributable to a variety of statistical issues. For example, the statistical power to detect changes as significantly different from zero could be low when the intervals between test occasions are short, or when the reliability of the change scores is low. Most cross-sectional comparisons involve an age range of 40 or more years, whereas only a few longitudinal studies have followed the same individuals for more than 5 or 10 years. It is informative to consider the likely outcome of cross-sectional comparisons with an age range comparable to that of typical longitudinal retest intervals. The cross-sectional comparisons summarized in the previous chapter indicate that the age-related differences in many cognitive variables range from about–0.01 to–0.04 standard deviations per year, which correspond to differences of between–0.05 to–0.20 standard deviations across a 5-year interval. Detection of differences of this magnitude as statistically significant (e.g., $p < .05$) with .8 probability in a cross-sectional comparison would require between 300 and 5,000 individuals in each age group!

Sensitivity and statistical power will be greater in longitudinal comparisons because age-related effects are examined in the same people, but the vastly different age ranges in cross-sectional and longitudinal contrasts could still account for some of the apparent discrepancies across the two types of comparisons.

Another statistical issue that has the potential to contribute to some of the discrepancies between cross-sectional and longitudinal age trends concerns regression to the mean. This phenomenon refers to the fact that if the reliability of the measurement is not perfect, which is almost always the case for individual variables, then scores that are somewhat extreme on one occasion are likely to be less extreme on a second occasion. Because extreme scores will tend to regress back to the mean, this regression could be interpreted as change when it is actually a statistical artifact. This type of statistical regression will only distort results in longitudinal studies, and even if the effects were not systematic in the sense that the estimates of change were biased more in one direction than another, they could contribute to low precision in the assessments of change.

Short-Term Fluctuation

Although cognitive abilities are usually assumed to be fairly stable, most people exhibit considerable variation in their performance on different versions of the same cognitive tests from one occasion to another.[6] That is, people do not have identical scores when they perform an equivalent version of a test within a few weeks of the original test. This within-person variability will likely reduce the precision of the estimates of an individual's level of performance in both cross-sectional and longitudinal comparisons. However, the existence of large within-person variability can lead to special problems in longitudinal comparisons because some of what is interpreted as longitudinal change could simply be a manifestation of short-term fluctuation.

True change might be distinguished from short-term fluctuation if multiple assessments are available at each measurement occasion to allow comparisons based on the mean of several assessments, and possibly even evaluate change in terms of shifts of the distributions of a given individual's scores across occasions. For example, in some of our studies the research participants perform slightly different versions of the same test on each of three sessions, which allows us to evaluate change relative to the variability across the three scores at each occasion. A procedure such as this not only provides a more sensitive assessment of change by calibrating change in terms of each person's short-term fluctuation, but it also allows the statistical significance of change to be evaluated within individual participants. Unfortunately, in part because multiple assessments such as these add considerable time and expense to the research, measurement burst procedures have seldom been implemented in longitudinal studies.

Instrumentation

Instrumentation refers to factors associated with changes in the assessment conditions, such as the test version, administration procedures (e.g., paper-and-pencil versus computer, group versus individual assessment), instructions, or scoring method. Even subtle changes in the identity of the examiner, or in characteristics of the testing room, have been reported to have effects on cognitive performance over short intervals. To the extent that factors associated with the assessment condition can affect the level of cognitive performance, it is possible that some of the observed longitudinal change may not reflect maturational changes occurring within the individual, but instead represent changes from one occasion to the next in the conditions of assessment.

Instrumentation is unlikely to be a factor in cross-sectional comparisons if all of the assessments are conducted within a relatively short time period and every individual is assessed in the same manner. However, some of the changes observed in longitudinal comparisons may reflect changes associated with characteristics of the assessment if there are shifts in the nature of the assessment over time. Because numerous influences are probably operating in different directions, instrumentation effects are unlikely to have a systematic bias on the estimates of longitudinal change, but they may contribute to greater imprecision of these estimates.

Selective Attrition

The phenomenon of selective attrition, sometimes known as the "class reunion effect," refers to the fact that the individuals who return to participate on subsequent occasions in a longitudinal study are more likely to be from the most successful members of the original group. That is, people who return for repeated testing frequently have higher initial scores on a variety of cognitive tests than the people who drop out of the study. If the entire sample at the first assessment is compared with only those who return at the second assessment, then some of the observed performance difference will be due to differences in the composition of the samples and would not reflect within-person change. However, even if the comparisons are restricted to people with data at all assessments, the results could be misleading if there is a relation between the initial level of functioning and the direction, or magnitude, of change. For example, the age relations would be underestimated if people with initially higher scores are more likely to continue in the study and the age-related declines in these people are smaller than in people whose initial scores were lower.

Selective attrition is affected by how many people discontinue participation (i.e., the magnitude of attrition) and by how representative they are compared to the people who continue to participate (i.e., the selectivity of the attrition). The four major reasons why people do not return for subsequent testing in longitudinal studies are sometimes referred to as the four M's; motivation, mobility, morbidity, and mortality. As one might expect, these causes of attrition tend to vary in frequency as a function of age. To illustrate, approximately 28% of adults in their 20s in the United States moved their residence between 2002 and 2003, but less than 0.2% of the people within this age range died during that interval. In contrast, only 4% of adults between 65 and 85 years of age moved their residence from 2002 to 2003, but 28% of them died during that period.[7]

The magnitude of any type of attrition is only important as an influence on age trends in longitudinal comparisons of cognitive functioning if it is selective with respect to cognitive ability, such that the people who return for subsequent assessment differ in their rate of age-related decline from those who do not return.[8,9] Individuals who continue to participate in longitudinal studies have frequently been found to have higher initial levels of functioning than the individuals who drop out. However, evidence relevant to whether the rates of change vary according to initial level of functioning has been inconsistent, and therefore the exact impact of selective attrition on estimates of longitudinal change is still unknown.

A recent report by a group of Swedish researchers contains some of the most informative results on the impact of selective attrition on age trends in cognitive functioning.[10] Figure 2.3 displays the initial level of performance on three variables for two groups of people: one group consisting of those who returned for another assessment 5 years later, and a second group consisting of people who did not return for subsequent testing. It can be seen that although the average levels were lower for those who did not return, the cross-sectional age relations at the first measurement occasion were similar for the dropouts and returnees. The implication from these results is that analyses restricted to those individuals who continue in the study will likely have higher absolute levels of performance than the total sample, but that the relative age trends will be similar.

It is worth noting that something analogous to selective attrition could also be operating in cross-sectional studies if there is a relation between level of cognitive ability and the likelihood that adults of certain ages would participate in the study. However, an influence of this type in a cross-sectional study would be manifested as nonequivalent groups rather than selective attrition because it is not meaningful to refer to attrition when there is only one attempt to assess the participants.

Selective attrition could be an important factor contributing to the discrepancy between cross-sectional and longitudinal comparisons because

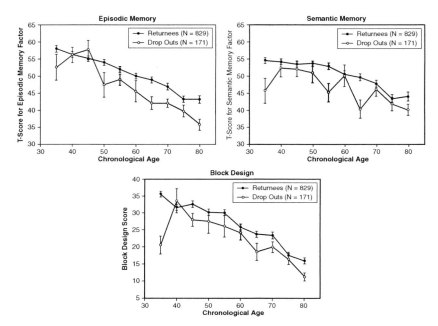

Figure 2.3. Means and standard errors of performance on three different cognitive variables for returning participants and dropouts as a function of age. Data from Ronnlund et al. (2005).

it only operates in longitudinal studies, and the direction of the influence would likely minimize the estimate of age-related decline. Unfortunately, there are few reports of selective attrition in adults under about age 60, where the largest discrepancy appears to exist between cross-sectional and longitudinal age trends.

Retest Effects

Retest effects refer to influences on performance that are attributable to prior assessments. An extensive literature documents better performance on a subsequent assessment of a cognitive test across intervals ranging from a few days to several years. For example, a recent meta-analysis of short-term practice effects in cognitive tests estimated that performance improved approximately 0.46 standard deviation units with a subsequent test containing identical items[11]. In general, retest effects appear to be larger for process variables than for product variables, and for younger adults than for older adults. Furthermore, one study found that retest effects can be detected for at least 12 years after the initial assessment for adults under 60 years of age.[12]

Two basic methods have been used to investigate retest effects in longitudinal research. One method involves comparing the performance of adults of the same age who either were, or were not, tested before. Although seemingly very straightforward, this contrast is complicated because the comparisons need to be adjusted for selective attrition to rule out the possibility that the second-tested individuals may have differed from the first-tested individuals in their initial level of performance.

A second method of investigating retest effects involves statistical decomposition of the longitudinal changes into components associated with maturation and with retest. These two aspects cannot be distinguished in a typical longitudinal study in which everyone is retested at the same interval because there is a perfect correlation between the increase in age and the increase in test experience. However, the two aspects can be distinguished in at least two conditions. One is if there are multiple retests and cumulative test experience is postulated to operate in a discrete step-like manner, but age is postulated to operate in a continuous manner. The second condition in which maturation and test experience effects can be separated is if the retest intervals vary across people such that the increase in test experience is no longer perfectly correlated with the increase in age.[13]

Although the methods are based on different assumptions and analytical procedures, a consistent finding with each of these methods is that the retest effects are almost always positive such that retest-adjusted longitudinal age relations tend to resemble the cross-sectional age relations. In particular, age-related declines are usually larger, and occur earlier, when longitudinal comparisons are adjusted for effects associated with prior test experience. Furthermore, the analyses have revealed that the magnitudes of the retest effects can be quite large and equivalent to what might be expected in cross-sectional comparisons of people differing by 10 or more years of age.

It is not yet clear exactly what is responsible for retest effects because they can occur even when the tests contain different items, and they can persist over relatively long intervals, which suggests that memory for specific items is unlikely to be responsible for all of the effects. Some of the retest benefits could be related to sensitization to particular types of problems, heightened awareness of unfamiliar problems, or reduced anxiety, but the relative contributions of these factors have not yet been determined.

Retest effects only influence longitudinal comparisons because cross-sectional comparisons do not involve testing the same individuals again. Furthermore, because most of the effects are likely to be in the positive direction, retest influences will tend to result in a systematic positive bias on longitudinal changes. Retest effects are therefore a promising candidate for explaining at least some of the discrepancy between cross-sectional and longitudinal results.[14,15]

Period Effects

Period effects can be defined as influences associated with factors in the physical or social environment that affect performance at the time of measurement. They are occasion-specific influences that could have an impact on everyone, and they may include factors such as the state of the economy in a study of political preferences or the occurrence of a famine in a relatively obscure country in a study of geographical knowledge.

Results from cross-sectional comparisons are unlikely to be distorted by period effects because all of the assessments are typically completed within a relatively brief time interval. Because longitudinal assessments occur at different periods in time, some of the performance changes observed in longitudinal comparisons could be due to occasion-specific characteristics. However, period effects are not necessarily systematic in one direction or another, and thus they are likely to contribute to increased noise, or imprecision, rather than to a systematic bias.

Nonequivalent Groups

The most frequently mentioned interpretation of the discrepancy between cross-sectional and longitudinal age trends in cognitive performance is that people in cross-sectional comparisons who differ in age also differ in numerous other characteristics, and that some of those other characteristics contribute to the observed performance differences. This interpretation is intuitively plausible because it is likely that people of different ages are also different in a number of characteristics besides age that could influence level of cognitive functioning. Because longitudinal comparisons involve the same people followed across different ages, influences on age trends attributable to differences across people do not operate in longitudinal studies. To the extent that people who differ in age also differ in other respects that could affect their level of cognitive performance, cross-sectional results may not accurately reflect maturational influences in cognitive functioning.[16]

Some variant of the nonequivalent groups position is probably the most widely accepted explanation for the discrepancy between cross-sectional and longitudinal cognitive aging trends. However, because the critical factor that is presumed to differ as a function of age is seldom specified, this explanation is vague and unsatisfying. If the critical factor was postulated to be something that could be quantified, such as amount of education, composition of one's diet, frequency of physical exercise, number or severity of chronic diseases, etc., then its role could be investigated. That is, variation in the other factor could be controlled, either by matching or by statistical means, to determine whether the cross-sectional age relations were altered, and the discrepancy between cross-sectional and longitudinal age trends eliminated. As will be discussed in Chapter 4, relatively little alteration in the cross-sectional age trends has been found for several factors that have been mentioned as possible contributors to the cross-sectional age differences. Until the critical factor(s) are identified, therefore, the simplest version of the nonequivalent groups interpretation does not appear to be amenable to rigorous investigation, and consequently it may not be scientifically meaningful.

Cohort

A special case of the nonequivalent groups interpretation attributes the discrepancy between cross-sectional and longitudinal age trends to cohort effects. In the context of research on aging, cohort effects refer to influences shared by people growing up in a particular time period that persist as the individual ages. For example, people who grew up during the Great Depression might have similar attitudes toward monetary saving at every period in their life, and people who were exposed to particular methods of learning and memorization during their school years might have different approaches to remembering throughout their lives.

Although frequently mentioned as a factor in studies of aging[17], there are at least four concerns that can be raised about the role of cohort influences as a possible determinant of cognitive aging. First is the lack of systematicity. As just noted, the term *cohort* is often used to refer to potentially enduring effects of early life experiences. However, if cohort effects are unique to a particular combination of age and period, then there is no reason to expect them to be orderly and progressive, in which case they are unlikely to be responsible for the systematic patterns apparent in the relations between age and cognitive performance. In other words, any differences that might exist between successive cohorts may be more qualitative than quantitative, and consequently it is not obvious why a succession of cohorts would necessarily result in a progressive increase (or decrease) in level of cognitive performance.

A second concern about cohort influences is lack of uniformity. That is, the cohort concept might have limited usefulness if the heterogeneity among members of a given cohort is large relative to that between different cohorts. For example, if people who were teenagers during the Vietnam War differ among themselves in attitudes toward war, trust in the government, and various other attributes, then it may not be meaningful to group them together as though they shared a single perspective. Merely because people were born within a certain period does not mean that they share all, or even most, experiences or attitudes with other people growing up at the same time. Rather than assuming that people share critical characteristics because they were born within a particular interval, a preferable strategy would be to measure the relevant characteristics and investigate their influences directly.

The third concern about cohort influences in cognitive aging is lack of mechanism. That is, the cohort concept may not be meaningful in studies of cognitive functioning until there are theoretical mechanisms to link the presumed characteristics of the members of a cohort to performance on a particular cognitive task. Moreover, any mechanisms must presumably be specific to certain aspects of cognitive functioning because, as will be reported in Chapter 4, the same samples of people who exhibit substantial cross-sectional declines in cognitive functioning frequently have little or no relation between age and their average levels of different personality traits or measures of chronic mood.

A fourth concern about attributing the discrepancy between cross-sectional and longitudinal age trends to cohort differences is that the discrepancies are apparent over very narrow age ranges and short time intervals, and thus the critical determinants of cohort variation would have to operate extremely rapidly. For example, the results in Figure 2.2 indicate that different cross-sectional and longitudinal age trends have been found over intervals as short as 3–5 years, which implies that whatever is responsible for cohort effects would have to change very quickly in order for the effects to be manifested in this time interval. Cohort effects are often conceptualized as operating gradually over a period of decades, but with large samples cross-sectional differences can be detected between people differing in age by only a few years.

Systematic and Progressive Change

It is indisputable that there has been rapid social and cultural change over the past 100 years, as well as enormous alterations in the physical and biochemical environment. Because it is clearly possible that an individual's level of cognitive performance is influenced by aspects of his or her environment, it is reasonable to ask how much of the observed age differences in cognitive functioning are attributable to extrinsic changes in the social or physical environment rather than to intrinsic maturational changes.

At the risk of further complicating matters, it may be useful to propose another category of developmental influence corresponding to systematic and progressive changes in the physical, cultural, and social environment that impact cognitive performance. Examples might be amount of toxic chemicals in the air or water, composition of one's diet, and various health practices. The influences of these factors could be cumulative, widespread, and affect people of all ages, although not necessarily at the same rate or to the same degree. However, they are not generation-specific like cohort, or occasion-specific like period, and because they could be orderly and progressive, they might be systematic enough to account for the frequently linear cross-sectional age differences in measures of cognitive functioning.

Before it is plausible to view this category of influence as a potential contributor to the discrepancy between cross-sectional and longitudinal age trends in cognitive functioning, there must be evidence of systematic increases in level of cognitive test performance over historical time. The simplest way to investigate this question is with time-lag comparisons in which performance is compared in people of the same age who are tested at different points in time. Results from comparisons of this type have revealed clear evidence of historical shifts, usually in the positive direction, in the average level of cognitive performance.

One of the first reports documenting this kind of historical increase in cognitive test performance involved a comparison of scores from a sample of WWII recruits (tested in 1943) with the scores from WWI recruits (tested between 1917 and 1919) on a broad cognitive test battery, the Army Alpha[18]. Surprisingly, the individuals tested in 1943 had an average score at the 83rd percentile of the distribution of scores from the 1917–1919 sample. Several comparisons of different generations of college freshmen administered the same cognitive test have also revealed that later generations performed at higher levels than their earlier counterparts.

The most extensive documentation of this time-lag phenomenon was reported by James Flynn[19]. Most of his results were based on one of two types of comparisons. One type involved examining scores of the same people on tests that were normed at different periods in time. The reasoning in this case is that if the same individuals score higher on an old test than on a new test, and if the samples used to establish the norms for each test were equally representative of the populations when the normative data were collected, then one can infer that the levels of ability in the population increased across the interval between the two test standardizations.

A second type of comparison consisted of examinations of the levels of performance on the same tests administered to similar groups of people at different points in time. The rationale is that if the groups at each time are equally representative of the population, and the scores are higher at later times, then one can infer that the average ability level in the population has increased.

Some of the most convincing results reported by Flynn were based on data from European countries on the Raven's Matrix Reasoning test (see Figure 1.2 in Chapter 1). For example, a version of this test was administered to nearly the entire population of 18-year-old males in Belgium when they registered for the draft each year from 1958 to 1967. The mean scores increased as much as 0.25 standard deviation units across this 9-year interval. On the basis of a number of comparisons of this type, Flynn estimated that scores on various cognitive tests increased about one standard deviation from 1932 to 1978 in the United States. Flynn's results have been so compelling that the phenomenon of higher levels of performance on cognitive tests in more recent generations is sometimes known as the Flynn effect.

As an aside, it is interesting that the pattern of higher scores in more recent generations is inconsistent with fears that technological advances such as television, calculators, and computers might lead to a decrease in level of cognitive abilities because of disuse. Alarmist views such as these have apparently always been expressed; for instance, in *Phaedrus,* Socrates is quoted as saying that the discovery of the alphabet "will create forgetfulness in the learners' souls, because they will not use their memories; they will trust to the external written characters and not remember of themselves."

Perhaps the simplest view of what is responsible for the generational improvements in average level of performance on cognitive tests is that the higher scores reflect greater access to information, resulting in greater amounts of knowledge among members of more recent generations. However, one of the surprising aspects of the Flynn effect phenomenon is that the historical gains have often been found to be largest for variables representing efficiency of processing rather than for variables representing amount of acquired knowledge.

Among the most frequently mentioned causes of the increased test performance are greater test sophistication, improved health and nutrition, and higher quality of education. Physical and cultural changes in the environment that could affect cognitive performance include air and water quality, diet and exercise patterns, child care and family size, access to ideas and technology, migration from rural to urban areas, and environmental complexity. Unfortunately, little is currently known about the relative contributions of these different factors to the time-lag improvements in cognitive test performance.

Regardless of its causes, the phenomenon of historical increases in cognitive test scores could be relevant to the interpretation of the discrepancy between cross-sectional and longitudinal age trends, and thus it is important to consider possible implications of the phenomenon for cognitive aging trends. There are at least two quite different interpretations of the historical improvements in cognitive test scores. One possibility is that the time-lag improvements primarily operate in the period of childhood, with little or no influences after the individual has reached maturity. For example, if the effects are due to early nutrition or to quality of education, then the impact might be expected to occur primarily in the period from birth to about age 25. From the perspective of adult age differences in cognition, influences that operate predominantly in childhood might be considered somewhat analogous to the phenomenon of obsolescence. To illustrate, consider comparisons of new and old computers. Newer models are generally faster and more powerful than the older models, but the older models may still operate as effectively as when they were new. Contrasts of models of different vintages would therefore reveal differences in various measures of performance, but the differences would be attributable to obsolescence and would not reflect decline occurring within individual computers.

This interpretation can be made more concrete by examining one index of computer power, namely, central processing unit clock speed, as a function of historical time. The top panel in Figure 2.4 reveals that there have been

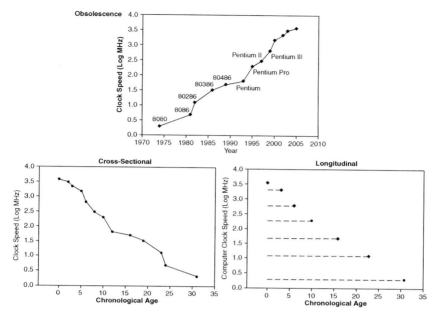

Figure 2.4. Schematic illustration of the obsolescence interpretation of historical improvements in cognitive functioning. The top panel portrays computer clock speed as a function of the year when the computer processor was introduced, the lower left panel portrays speed as a function of chronological age, and the lower right panel illustrates the hypothetical longitudinal trajectories.

dramatic increases in the speed of personal computers over the last 25 years. The lower left panel illustrates that a strong negative relation is evident between computer age and computer performance when computer speed is plotted as a function of computer age. Furthermore, this relation could occur even if there was no change in the capacity of individual computers over time. That is, the lower right panel indicates that there would likely be little evidence of any longitudinal decline if computer clock speeds were compared when the computers were new and in 2010.

The key assumption of this interpretation of the historical improvements in cognitive test scores is that a large proportion of the observed cross-sectional age differences is a reflection of obsolescence in that successive generations achieve progressively higher asymptotic levels, with little or no within-person change in cognitive functioning. The primary implication of the obsolescence interpretation in the current context is that *cross-sectional comparisons* of cognitive aging are misleading because they focus on age-related differences that reflect generational differences.

However, an alternative interpretation of the improvements in level of cognitive performance over historical time is that they are not attributable to influences restricted to the period of childhood, but instead reflect determinants that have a continuing impact on the performance of adults at all ages. According to this perspective, the phenomenon of historical increases in level of cognitive performance may be somewhat analogous to the effects of inflation on salaries, in that comparisons at different points in time are only meaningful after adjustments are made for historical trends.

This interpretation can be made more concrete with data from the U.S. Census on salaries at different ages and in different years. The top panel in Figure 2.5 illustrates that median salaries increased from 1950 to 2000 for males of all ages. However, because adults of all ages received higher average salaries in more recent years, the lower left panel reveals that the cross-sectional relations between age and salary in different years were nearly parallel. Finally, if the same birth cohort was followed over time, analogous to what is done in a longitudinal comparison, then salary would be found to increase as a function of age, as portrayed in the bottom right panel.

The primary implication of the inflation interpretation of the historical increases in test scores is that *longitudinal comparisons* would be misleading as reflections of maturational aspects of aging because some of the observed

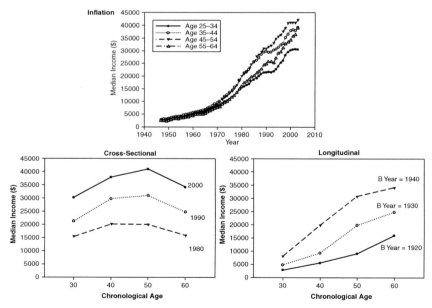

Figure 2.5. Schematic illustration of the inflation interpretation of historical improvements in cognitive functioning. The top panel portrays income as a function of year for adults of different ages, the lower left panel represents a subset of these data as a function of chronological age at three time periods, and the right panel illustrates the longitudinal trajectories for people born at the same time.

changes from one assessment period to the next may be attributable to changes occurring in the sociocultural environment rather than to changes within the individual. That is, just as the longitudinal relation between age and salary might not be interpretable as a reflection of effects associated with aging until adjustments are made for inflation, so might the longitudinal relation between age and cognitive test performance not be meaningful until adjustments are made for historical gains in average level of performance.

Both the obsolescence and inflation interpretations could account for the well-documented time-lag improvements in cognitive test performance because the trends in the top panels of Figures 2.4 and 2.5 are consistent with the Flynn effect of higher levels of functioning in more recent years. Furthermore, both interpretations of increased test scores could account for the discrepancy between cross-sectional and longitudinal results, but they have radically different positions with respect to the source of the discrepancy. The obsolescence interpretation maintains that cross-sectional designs confound obsolescence with maturation, whereas the inflation interpretation asserts that longitudinal designs confound "inflationary" increases with maturation.

It is not yet clear whether the obsolescence or inflation interpretation of the historical increases in level of cognitive performance is more realistic. However, until the inflation interpretation can be unequivocally ruled out, the existence of higher test scores in more recent generations should not necessarily be considered evidence that cross-sectional comparisons are misleading with respect to actual maturational influences because it is possible that it is the longitudinal comparisons that are distorted.

Relative Age Trends

Although across-time improvements in the absolute level of cognitive functioning are interesting, an important question for the interpretation of cognitive aging results is whether the relations between age and cognitive functioning have changed over time. Some researchers have been so impressed by time-lag effects and what they felt was the transient and culturally specific nature of age differences that they claimed that "the search for normal aging phenomena was a Sisyphean task."[20] However, the validity of this claim would be challenged if it were found that the relations between age and cognitive performance have not changed substantially over a long period of time. In fact, qualitatively similar age trends have been reported from the earliest systematic studies, dating at least since the beginning of the last century.[21]

Perhaps the best available across-time age comparisons are those based on the performance scales from the Wechsler test batteries (WAIS, WAIS-R, WAIS-III, WAIS-IV). The scales are not exactly the same because some of the items have changed across successive versions of the tests, but they are nevertheless very similar. Results in Figure 2.6 indicate that the age trends

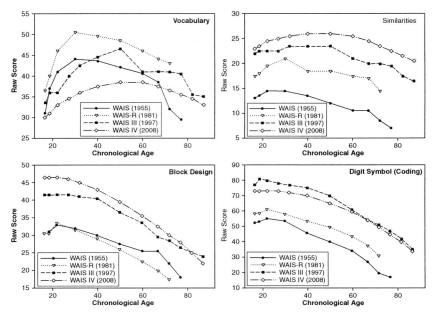

Figure 2.6. Raw scores on four cognitive tests from the Wechsler battery as a function of age and year of data collection. Note that only the relative age trends are meaningful because the absolute values of the scores are not directly comparable due to changes in the number and nature of the items in different test versions.

in the performance scale have been nearly parallel over the more than 50-year interval between the standardizations of the different test versions.[22]

   Regardless of any increases in the average level of performance, therefore, results such as these suggest that the relative pattern of age differences in cognitive test score has not changed appreciably over historical time. Because the current cognitive aging trends resemble those obtained in the past, it seems reasonable to expect that patterns in the future will resemble those at the current time. Contrary to some speculations, the phenomenon of cognitive aging does not appear to be a transient reflection of a particular set of physical and cultural conditions.

Animal Research

Another type of evidence relevant to the role of sociocultural changes on cross-sectional age trends in cognitive functioning involves comparisons of nonhuman animals. Because many animals have short life spans and can be raised in controlled environments, age comparisons in these species are unlikely to be contaminated by historical changes in the quality or quantity of education, amount of social or cultural stimulation, patterns of television viewing, family structure, etc. Smaller, or later, cross-sectional age differences might therefore be expected in nonhuman animals if changes in the social and cultural environment are contributing to some of the age-related differences apparent in cross-sectional comparisons of humans. Given the relevance of research with nonhuman animals for evaluating the influence of cohort effects and other time-lag factors on age trends in cognitive functioning, it is surprising that this literature is almost completely ignored by researchers focusing on cognitive aging in humans.

Of course, several limitations of animal studies for the purpose of examining cognitive aging phenomena should be recognized. First, many of the studies can be criticized because the sample sizes were small, which means that the age trends are not very precise and statistical power to detect moderate-sized effects was fairly low, and there is seldom much concern with measurement reliability, which sets an upper limit on the magnitude of relations a variable can have with other variables, including age. It is becoming more common in human cognitive aging research to report an estimate of reliability for each variable, and sometimes to focus on the relations between age and the reliable variance that several variables have in common, instead of the relations between age and a single variable. However, practices intended to evaluate, or increase the level of, reliability are still infrequent in nonhuman research.

Second, the same animals are sometimes used in multiple studies, which could result in the older animals participating in more research projects than younger animals, with the consequence that age is confounded with amount of testing experience. Furthermore, in a few cases the same animals were included in drug studies prior to the behavioral studies, and therefore some of the observed results could be at least partly attributable to the prior pharmacological experience.

Third, in some species increased age is associated with an increase in body weight that could affect the mobility of older animals relative to young animals. This would not necessarily be a problem in human cognitive research, but it can be a complication when most of the behavioral testing requires running or swimming on the part of the animal.

And fourth, comparing results from nonhuman studies with those from human studies can be complicated because of ambiguity about the meaning of age in different species. That is, what are the ages in a mouse or a monkey that correspond to periods of young adulthood, middle adulthood, or old age in humans? Age of sexual maturity could be used as a possible calibration point in comparisons of different species, but it reflects only one system within the body, and other systems might develop and age at different rates. Another possible reference is the life expectancy of the species, which corresponds to the age at which 50% of the individuals have died. This is not ideal because life expectancies can vary across laboratories even for the same species, and life expectancies can be modified with interventions such as caloric restriction. Nevertheless, it is useful as a first approximation in comparing results from human and animal studies.

Another critical issue is how cognitive functioning is assessed in animals. There are clear limits in the range of cognitive tests that can be administered to animals, but age comparisons have been reported in an impressive variety of tests.[23] One of the simplest cognitive tests is classical conditioning, and a large number of studies have reported age differences in the rate of acquisition and extinction of classically conditioned responses. Age differences have even been reported in animals as simple as fruit flies (*Drosophila melanogaster*), which have a life expectancy of about 50 days.[24] For example, fruit flies have been conditioned to withhold extending their proboscis (a feeding tube somewhat similar to an elephant trunk) by exposure to bitter quinine solution. Both the acquisition and extinction of this conditioned response have been found to decline progressively across groups of flies ranging from 7 to 50 days of age. Fruit flies have also been reported to exhibit age-related differences in the efficiency of learning to avoid one arm of a maze.

A considerable number of studies have investigated age differences in eye blink conditioning.[25] Rabbits, which have a life expectancy of about 8 years, are frequently used in this type of research because they are very docile and have a large eyelid that allows easy measurement of a blink response. The procedure often consists of the presentation of a tone followed by a puff of air, and then measuring the frequency of blinks to the tone in the absence of the air puff. The top left panel in Figure 2.7 illustrates age-related decline in the average number of conditioned responses in rabbits across delay, trace, and long-delay conditions in one study.

Rodents such as mice and rats are probably the most frequently used laboratory animals in behavioral studies of aging. The life expectancy of rats is about 24 to 30 months, and therefore young animals are between 4 and 10 months, and old animals range from 18 to 30 months of age. One task used to study age differences in learning in rodents is a passive avoidance task in which the animal initially receives an electric shock in one chamber, and the time to return to the shocked chamber when placed in the apparatus again is used as a measure of memory.[26] Because older animals return sooner, they have been inferred to have poorer memory.

Another commonly used task with rodents is the Morris Water Maze, which consists of a pool of water with one or more submerged platforms.[27] The animal is placed in the pool, which is often made opaque with styrofoam pellets, powdered milk, or some other substance, and it has to swim to the platform to get out of the water. A condition in which the platform is raised and visible is also frequently administered to assess the animal's ability to swim. Many possible measures of performance can be obtained in this task, including the time to reach the platform, the total distance traversed, and the proportion of time spent in the region of the platform. In most of the

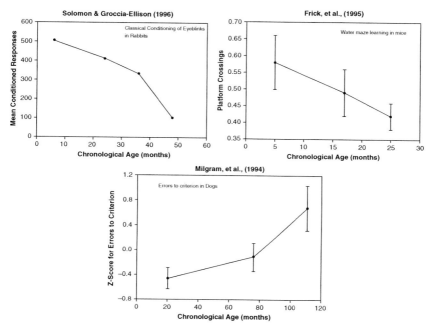

Figure 2.7. Illustrations of cross-sectional age trends for different measures of cognitive functioning in nonhuman animals raised in controlled environments.

measures older animals have been found to perform worse than young animals. The upper right panel of Figure 2.7 portrays results of a maze learning measure in mice of three ages from one of these studies.

Still another task used to investigate learning and memory in rodents is a radial maze task. This is a special type of maze in which between 4 and 12 arms radiate from the center. Food is initially placed either in some or all of the arms, but the critical feature is that the food is not replaced when it is consumed. The animal must therefore remember not to return to the arm that does not contain food, or to the arm in which the food was already consumed. Older animals have been found to return to the empty arm more often than young animals, indicating poorer memory.

Cognitive aging research has also been conducted with dogs.[28] Beagles, who have a life expectancy of 12 to 13 years, are often used in this type of research because they have similar neuropathologies to humans. The dog can respond by using its nose or a paw to displace an object to obtain a food reward such as a piece of meat. A wide variety of tasks have been used in age-comparative studies, such as object discrimination in which a reward is delivered when the animal identifies the object that contains the food, object reversal in which the location of the rewarded object is changed after a certain number of trials, and delayed nonmatching to sample in which the animal first sees a single object and then is presented with two objects and must select the new object to receive the food. Age differences favoring young dogs have been found in each of these types of tasks. The lower panel in Figure 2.7 portrays the average z-score for the numbers of errors across three tasks, discrimination learning, reversal learning, and delayed nonmatching to sample, in three age groups. The correlation between age and this measure was .50.

Squirrel monkeys have an average life expectancy of up to 21 years, and thus young to old animals would range from about 4 to 17 years. In one recent study[29], 31 monkeys within this age range were trained to learn to reach for food when the box opening was in a particular orientation, and then to shift when it was in a different orientation. The correlation between age and errors in this task was .59.

Rhesus monkeys, who have a life expectancy of 20 to 25 years, have been used in a wide variety of tasks in which the paw is used to displace the object, and the reward consists of pieces of apple, raisins, or peanuts. An advantage of primates is that the behavioral repertoire is more similar to humans than other animals. One project administered several tasks, including delayed nonmatch to sample, and spatial and object reversal learning[30]. The first principal component, a statistical measure that represents what the variables from different tasks had in common, was found to be correlated -.74 with age among monkeys ranging from 4 to 30 years. Age differences favoring young primates have also been reported in conceptual set shifting tasks similar to the Wisconsin Card Sorting Test used in neuropsychology.

Comparisons between humans and nonhuman animals are not exact because of the different age ranges, and the more limited variety of tasks that can be administered to animals. Moreover, the precise nature of the age trends in animal studies, and exactly when they begin, can only be crudely estimated from the available data because most of the samples have been small, and relatively few studies have included a complete range of ages. Nevertheless, the phenomenon of age differences in measures of cognitive functioning is clearly evident in nonhuman species, and the available evidence suggests that the age-related influences occur continuously across adulthood rather than beginning only in old age. The phenomenon of cognitive aging is therefore not uniquely human, and of particular importance in the present context, it can occur in the absence of major sociocultural shifts or environmental changes. Because age-related cognitive decline has been found in animals raised under controlled, and presumably nearly constant, environments, it is unlikely that all of the cross-sectional age differences observed in humans can be attributed to as-yet-unspecified changes in aspects of the sociocultural environment.

Another noteworthy finding from animal research is that several studies have reported smaller age differences in measures of cognitive functioning with longitudinal comparisons than with cross-sectional comparisons.[31] Because influences related to cohort differences or changes in the environment are probably very small in comparisons involving nonhuman animals, the discrepancy between the cross-sectional and longitudinal age trends in these studies is most likely attributable to retest effects distorting the longitudinal contrasts.

Reappraisal of Cross-Sectional and Longitudinal Designs

The preceding sections indicate that many factors besides maturation could contribute to the relations between age and cognitive functioning. Cross-sectional age differences likely represent a mixture of maturational influences and differences in miscellaneous characteristics other than age. Longitudinal comparisons can also be assumed to represent a mixture of several different types of influences. In particular, a number of recent studies have provided convincing evidence for the existence of moderately large retest effects and selective attrition influences that can lead to underestimation of negative age trends in longitudinal comparisons. Other influences, such as instrumentation effects, period effects, and short-term fluctuation likely contribute to imprecise assessment, and the impact of this added noise will be greater in the measurement of change in longitudinal research than in single measurements used in cross-sectional research.

Both cross-sectional and longitudinal research designs are informative in determining the relations between age and level of cognitive functioning. It is sometimes claimed that only longitudinal research is relevant to understanding aging, or that the primary goal of researchers concerned with aging should be to explain within-person changes in functioning.[32] However, it may be short sighted to define a phenomenon in such a way that deliberately neglects a major body of potentially relevant research, particularly since the relative contributions of nonmaturational influences in each type of research design have not yet been definitively established. Furthermore, if one is interested in eventually eliminating age-related differences in cognitive functioning, then it is important to understand the mechanisms responsible for both cross-sectional age differences and longitudinal age changes.

Interpretation of Change

An undeniable advantage of longitudinal comparisons is that they provide measures both of initial level of performance and of the rate of age-related change, instead of a single measure that incorporates both aspects as in cross-sectional comparisons. Although change from younger ages is assumed to be an important factor contributing to the observed age differences in cross-sectional comparisons, change is not observed directly. Only if the same individuals are followed over time, as in a longitudinal study, is it possible to directly observe change. Nevertheless, several issues need to be considered when interpreting measures of change in longitudinal studies.

First, as discussed above, any observed change likely represents a complex mixture of several different types of influences, and only a few studies have attempted to distinguish the contributions of maturation, selective attrition, retest effects, and time-lag influences. Longitudinal changes cannot automatically be assumed to provide purer reflections of maturational processes than cross-sectional differences until the contributions of these other determinants have been taken into consideration. Stated somewhat differently, merely because change is observed in the same individuals does not mean that the change reflects maturational aspects of aging.

Second, it can be difficult to interpret relations with measures of change if the average amount of change is close to zero because there are at least two quite different reasons why the mean amount of change might be close to zero. One possibility is that the distribution reflects chance variation around a mean of zero, and none of the individuals in the sample have any true change. A second possibility is that the distribution of change is composed of a mixture of some individuals exhibiting reliable declines, some exhibiting reliable improvements, and some remaining stable. A mixture distribution such as this might occur if multiple mechanisms, such as maturation and retest influences, were contributing to the changes, and the balance among the mechanisms differed across people. Only in this second case would one expect the measures of change to be reliable and related to other variables, but unless the various types of influences were distinguished the nature of the relation might be ambiguous. For example, correlations of the change measure with another variable might primarily reflect differential retest effects among individuals with positive changes, differential maturational declines among individuals with negative declines, or various combinations of the two effects in the same, or different, people.

Third, different methods can be used to estimate change, and the methods do not necessarily yield the same values or the same magnitude of correlations with other variables. For example, a recent study examined several different measures of change, including the linear slope from simple regression, the difference between the last score and the first score divided by the number of years intervening between the measurements, and an estimate of change derived from a statistical (random effects) model, and found that they differed in a number of respects.[33] A better understanding of the reasons for these discrepancies is therefore needed before one can have confidence in the interpretation of any particular measure of change.

And fourth, few longitudinal studies have reported information about the reliability of the measures of change, which is unfortunate because reliability sets limits on the relations the change measure can have with other variables. Reliability is usually assessed in one of two ways. Internal consistency is estimated by the relations of different parts of the test to one another. This form of reliability is inferred to be high when the scores on the parts of the test have moderate to strong relations with one another, such that people are rank-ordered in a similar way across different parts of the test. Another type of reliability is test-retest (or parallel forms) reliability, which is assessed from the correlation of scores on the same, or a parallel, test administered at different times. This form of reliability is also inferred to be high when there is a similar ordering of the individuals on each assessment.[34]

Both methods of evaluating reliability are based on the variability across people in different parts or versions of the tests, and thus the reliability estimates will be low if there is little variation across people in the relevant scores. The magnitude of individual differences in change is therefore a key factor affecting the reliability of measures of longitudinal change. Although it is often assumed that there are large individual differences in rates of cognitive aging, it is rather surprising that the evidence in support of this assumption is not particularly consistent.

One type of indirect evidence relevant to the issue of individual differences in rates of change is the magnitude of between-person variance at different ages. The rationale is that if some people remain stable whereas others decline, the differences among people would be expected to become larger with increased age. However, Figures 1.12 through 1.15 in Chapter 1 indicate that the standard deviations are often remarkably constant across most of the adult age range. This does not mean that between-person variability would not increase with increased age in other, potentially more comprehensive, samples. Nevertheless, the simple expectation that large individual differences in rates of change would result in greater between-person variability at older ages has not been supported in several large data sets.

Another form of indirect evidence relevant to individual differences in cognitive change is based on the correlations between the scores obtained at different test occasions. These stability coefficients reflect the similarity of the rank ordering of people at different times (and at different ages). High values would imply that people maintain nearly the same relative position over time (and age), and hence that individual differences in the amount of change are presumably fairly small. That is, high stability coefficients indicate that a large part of the variability in the later score is associated with variability in the early score, and consequently that a relatively small proportion of the variance in the second assessment could be attributed to individual differences in rates of change. However, the absolute magnitudes of the stability correlations are not necessarily informative by themselves because they are seldom perfect (i.e., 1.0) even with short retest intervals. In order to provide a meaningful reference, the stability correlations can be evaluated relative to immediate retest correlations (i.e., across intervals of a few days to a few months). To illustrate, if the immediate retest correlation is .8, then correlations across an interval of 5 or 10 years must be substantially lower than that value to infer that people exhibit much variation in the rate of change over this interval. Furthermore, one might expect the correlation between the scores at the two assessments to decrease as the interval between assessments increased because there would be more opportunity for change in the age trajectories to be manifested. Unfortunately, very few systematic comparisons of test-retest correlations in measures of cognitive performance as a function of the length of the retest interval have been reported.[35]

A third type of indirect evidence about reliability and variability of change is based on statistical models of change, such as latent growth models. Many of these models not only provide an estimate of the average rate of change, but they can also indicate whether there are significant individual differences in the estimated rates of change. Several studies using these analytical methods have failed to find significant individual differences in the estimates of cognitive change[36], and virtually every study has reported that the between-person variability in the parameters representing level of performance was much greater than in the parameters representing change in performance. These latter results indicate that the differences among people in their initial levels of performance are nearly always much larger than the differences in the rates at which they change over time.[37]

Very few direct estimates of the reliability of longitudinal change have been reported. A simple estimate could be based on correlations of changes observed in different parts of the test (e.g., on odd-numbered items compared to even-numbered items) or on parallel versions of the tests. This method involves minimal assumptions, and it is close to how reliability is computed with single assessments. However, it has apparently been used in one project, and then only in a demonstration manner.[38]

If the change is assumed to be uniform over time, it might be possible to obtain an estimate of reliability from correlations computed between the changes across different intervals. This procedure is based on the assumption that the intervals are parts of the same overall change, and thus correlations among these "parts" might be used to estimate consistency, or reliability, of change. However, four or more assessments are needed to ensure independent assessments of change (e.g., Time 1 to Time 3 to provide one change assessment, and Time 2 to Time 4 to provide another change assessment), and the assumption of constant change across all of the intervals is very strong and would need to be carefully justified before results with this procedure could be interpreted with confidence.

One approximation to estimating the reliability of change involves application of a formula to estimate the reliability of a difference from the reliability of the score at each occasion and from the correlation across occasions:[39]

$$\text{rel}_{12\text{Diff}} = \{[(\text{rel}_1 + \text{rel}_2)/2] - r_{12}\}/(1-r_{12})$$

Inspection of this formula reveals that estimated reliability of the change from time 1 to time 2 (i.e., $\text{rel}_{12\text{Diff}}$) depends on the relation between the reliability of the assessments at each occasion (i.e., rel_1 and rel_2), and the stability coefficient (i.e., r_{12}). For example, if the reliability at each occasion is .8 and the stability coefficient is .7, then the estimated reliability of the measure of change would only be .33. This formula has not been widely used in cognitive aging research, but it is noteworthy that estimated reliabilities of the change measures obtained in this manner would likely be low because stability coefficients are often close in magnitude to the reliabilities at each assessment.

Certain statistical models of change, such as latent difference or latent growth curve models, are sometimes assumed to provide reliable estimates of change because the change estimates are based on latent constructs that are theoretically free of measurement error. However, it is important to distinguish absence of measurement error in a particular analysis from replicability of the results. That is, merely because an estimate of change based on a particular set of measures and occasions does not include measurement error does not necessarily mean that the resulting estimate will be perfectly correlated with an estimate of change based on a parallel set of measures or occasions.[40]

The preceding discussion indicates that a major unresolved issue in cognitive aging concerns the reliability of measures of change. Single occasion assessment can be very reliable, which allows meaningful interpretation of correlations. However, evidence of the reliability of measures of changes in cognitive functioning is still very limited, particularly for change in adults under about age 60.

Does It All Go Together When It Goes?[41]

A particularly interesting issue concerning cognitive aging is whether changes in different cognitive variables are correlated or independent of one another. Although seemingly straightforward, this issue is complicated because the examination of correlated change can be carried out at several different levels of analysis. To illustrate, one possible reference for the interpretation of change involves comparisons of the changes in different variables for the same individual. A question from this perspective might be whether, for a given individual, the change in grayness of hair occurs at the same time as the change in muscle strength. Unfortunately, it is difficult to investigate correlated change within single individuals without a very large number of observations of multiple variables over a period of years, and the availability of analytical procedures that can quantify the degree of time-related coupling of changes in different variables in the same person.[42] Although this is likely what many people are thinking of when they ask whether different variables change at the same time, there have apparently been no published reports with this type of information.

Instead, nearly all longitudinal analyses have been based on comparisons of different people, in which the change on one variable for a given person is compared with the average change on that variable across all of the people in the sample. The reference for interpreting change in a given individual is therefore what happens on the relevant variables in other people, and changes are inferred to be positively correlated if people with greater than average change in one variable also have greater than average change in other variables.

Most cognitive variables are positively correlated with one another, and as reported in Chapter 1, many variables are negatively correlated with age in cross-sectional comparisons. Furthermore, as will be discussed in the next chapter, the strength of the cross-sectional relations of age on one variable are often substantially reduced after controlling the variability in other variables, which is consistent with the idea that the age-related effects on different cognitive variables are not independent of one another. Cross-sectional results such as these might therefore lead to the expectation that longitudinal age changes in different cognitive variables would be related to one another.

However, it is important to recognize that relations evident in comparisons across different people at the same point in time may not be apparent in comparisons within the same individuals at different points in time, and vice versa. For example, variables such as weight and height are likely to be moderately correlated with one another among adults who are all within 20% of their optimal body weight, but a within-person change in weight in this sample would probably not be associated with a change in height. In contrast, there might not be a between-person correlation between weight and a measure of self-esteem in a sample of this type, whereas a within-person change in weight might well be associated with a within-person change in self-esteem. Whether longitudinal changes in different aspects of cognitive aging are correlated should therefore be viewed as an open empirical question that cannot be answered from cross-sectional results.

Significant correlations among longitudinal changes in different cognitive variables have been reported in several studies, which suggests that people who have large declines in some cognitive variables tend to have larger than average declines in other cognitive variables.[43] However, these results need to be interpreted cautiously because several of the studies likely included adults in early stages of dementia and thus some of the declines reflect disease processes rather than normal aging, none contained information about the reliabilities of the change measures that can affect the magnitude of correlations, very few attempted to distinguish how much of the correlation was attributable to correlations among the various components of change, such as maturation and retest, and nearly all only involved adults above about 60 years of age, and thus little is known about whether changes are related when they are first beginning.[44]

Does It Matter When the Changes Occur?

Figure 2.8 illustrates another complication in the interpretation of change, namely, that the relations between the change in two variables, X and Y, could have different meaning depending on when in adulthood the assessment occurs. Notice that change in variable X precedes change in variable Y during the interval between T1 (time 1) and T2 (time 2), but only variable Y is changing during the T5-T6 interval. Both variables change from T3 to T4, but the rate of change during this interval is not necessarily informative about which variable started changing first. In the situation portrayed in this figure, only the T1-T2 interval might be relevant if the researcher is interested in investigating the hypothesis that change in X causes a change in Y. Once both variables are changing (as in the T3-T4 interval), the relative rates of change in the two variables may not be informative about the causal sequence in the variables. Furthermore, intervals when one of the variables has stopped changing, such as in the T5-T6 interval, also may not provide any information about which variable started changing first.

Figure 2.8 suggests that it might be useful to think of the phenomenon of cognitive aging as somewhat analogous to an avalanche in that the relation between cognitive variables and age might be like rocks falling down a mountain.[45] It may be impossible to determine which rocks precipitated the avalanche by only examining the progress of rocks in the middle of the mountain because much movement has already occurred, and the movement is not necessarily uniform at each point along the mountain. Moreover, observations near the bottom of the mountain could be completely misleading with respect to which rocks started

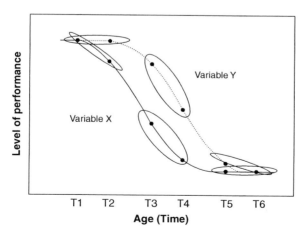

Figure 2.8. Schematic illustration of hypothetical trajectories for two cognitive variables as a function of age (or time).

moving first. The study of changes at any particular region along the mountain can still be interesting and could also be informative about the relations among the elements at that point. However, those results are not necessarily informative about causal influences operating elsewhere, and particularly at the top of the mountain where the rock movement may have originated. For analogous reasons, researchers should be cautious in making inferences about the nature and causes of age-related change from observations within a restricted range of ages, and particularly from a range beyond when the phenomenon is first apparent. The avalanche metaphor can be misleading because it may not be realistic to assume a one-time, ballistic influence rather than continuous and dynamic influences, but it nevertheless serves to emphasize the importance of being explicit about one's assumptions regarding the time course of age-related changes in cognitive functioning when designing and interpreting research.

Conclusions

Longitudinal information is extremely valuable because it allows direct assessment of change. However, maturation is only one of many possible determinants of change, and few studies have controlled more than one or two of the possible determinants when analyzing longitudinal change in cognitive functioning. Until adjustments are made for influences such as nonequivalent groups, selective attrition, period effects, and retest effects, it will be difficult to determine the extent to which results from either cross-sectional or longitudinal comparisons provide the most accurate reflections of maturational influences on the mean levels of cognitive functioning.

Two important observations are relevant to the interpretation of cognitive aging phenomena. First, similar relative age trends have been reported from the earliest systematic studies dating from the 1920s, and second, patterns of cognitive aging in nonhuman animals closely resemble those found in humans. These findings indicate that the phenomenon of cognitive aging can be inferred to be at least somewhat generalizable across specific historical contexts and different species.

It is understandable, but nevertheless unfortunate, that the vast majority of longitudinal studies have been restricted to adults over about the age of 60. This feature makes it impossible to identify causes or consequences of changes that may be occurring earlier, and any conclusions from that research may only be applicable to regions in adulthood after a large amount of change has already occurred.

There are still many questions about the phenomenon of cognitive aging, but a number of variables used to assess cognitive ability have been found to have similar relations to age in both cross-sectional and longitudinal comparisons, particularly after adjusting for retest effects that only influence longitudinal comparisons. Historical improvements in level of performance in cognitive tests are well documented, but depending on how it operates, the impact could primarily affect cross-sectional (obsolescence) or longitudinal (inflation) comparisons. Finally, very similar patterns of cognitive aging have been observed in animals raised in nearly constant environments, which indicates that changes in cohorts or socioeconomic environments cannot account for all cognitive aging phenomena.

3

Approaches to Investigating Cognitive Aging

Major issue: What approaches can be used to investigate cognitive aging phenomena, and what are their strengths and weaknesses?

Related questions: How can the validity of hypothesized processes or components in a cognitive task be investigated? How many separate explanations will likely be needed to account for age differences in cognitive functioning? What are the best methods of determining whether the age-related differences in different cognitive variables are independent of one another? How can the nature of relatively general age-related influences be investigated?

Two broad research approaches have been applied in cognitive aging research over the last 20 years. The approaches differ in what they assume should be explained to account for cognitive aging phenomena and in the analytical methods that have typically been employed.

The dominant approach, at least as reflected by the number of published articles in the field, can be considered to be an extension of mainstream cognitive psychology. That is, this approach relies on theories and procedures developed within cognitive psychology to try to characterize, and ideally explain, age differences in cognitive functioning. In order to better understand this approach, some of the research within a particular domain of cognition—memory—will be reviewed in the next section. The section is by no means a comprehensive review of this voluminous literature. Instead, it is intended to indicate how sources of hypotheses for the locus of age differences in cognition have often been based on models and metaphors in cognitive psychology, and to provide an overview of a selected subset of the phenomena in this area.

Subjective Memory

The perception that there is a decline in memory with increased age is clearly widespread, and as early as 1928 it was stated that "Adults perhaps complain oftener concerning their ability to memorize than concerning any other."[1] However, it is noteworthy that people's reports of their own memory functioning are often only weakly related to objective measures of memory performance, and are frequently more closely related to aspects of mood than to actual memory performance. This pattern of relations is evident in Table 3.1, which contains correlations based on responses of our research participants to various questions about their memory. [2]

Table 3.1. Correlations of Cognitive Abilities and Various Mood and Personality Characteristics to Responses to a Memory Functioning Questionnaire (N = 2,223)

	Rating	Problems	Use of Memory Aids
Age	−.19*	.08*	.21*
Gender (male = 1)	−.06	.03	−.25*
Memory	.20*	−.10*	.05
Fluid	.16*	−.09*	−.02
Speed	.18*	−.11*	−.06*
Vocabulary	.01	−.06*	.20*
Depression	−.25*	.27*	−.01
Trait anxiety	−.27*	.28*	−.04
Neuroticism	−.15*	.16*	.02
Extraversion	.07*	−.07*	.05
Openness	.14*	−.08*	.11*
Agreeableness	.03	−.03	.08*
Conscientiousness	.06	−.05	.16*

*$p < .01$.

 Rating is an average across three questions asking the individual to rate his or her memory relative to other people, relative to the best it has ever been, and in terms of the frequency of memory problems. Higher scores indicate a better self–rated memory.

 Problems are the average frequency of memory lapses across 10 situations, such as forgetting a person's name or an appointment. Higher scores indicate more reported memory problems.

 Use of memory aids refers to the frequency of using various memory aids, such as appointment books and grocery lists. Higher scores indicate greater usage.

As one would expect, the average rating of one's memory was lower with increased age ($r = -.19$). The ratings were higher for people who performed better on the memory tests, but the ratings were also higher for people who performed better on tests of fluid ability and perceptual speed, which suggests that the responses to the questionnaire items may not be specific to memory functioning.[3] People with higher levels of depression or anxiety tended to rate their memory functioning as poor, and they also reported more problems with memory. In fact, the relations of the memory ratings to these mood variables were stronger than the relations of the ratings with age. It might be suspected that at least some of the relations between age and the memory ratings were attributable to age-related increases in depression and anxiety. However, this was not the case in these data because there was no relation of age with the measures of either depression or anxiety, and the correlation between age and self-rated memory was actually slightly more negative ($r = -.26$ compared to $r = -.19$) after statistically controlling the variation in both the depression and anxiety measures.

Several other results from the memory questionnaire are also worth noting. For example, reported use of memory aids was more frequent with increased age, among females, and among people with high levels of vocabulary. Perhaps not surprisingly, people who had high levels on the personality trait of conscientiousness also reported using memory aids more frequently than people with lower levels of conscientiousness.

Although complaints about memory are widespread, the results described above, together with similar findings from many studies by other researchers, indicate that self-reports of memory functioning are at least as strongly related to measures of depression and anxiety as to objectively assessed memory performance. Self-reports of memory may therefore be more useful as a symptom of one's psychological state than as an indication of his or her actual level of memory functioning. Nevertheless, as will be described below, research with objective assessments of memory has revealed that increased age is often associated with lower levels of memory performance.

Normal Age Trends

Results from standardized tests of memory reveal cross-sectional age trends that are very similar to those that have been found with other cognitive abilities. To illustrate, age trends from several standardized tests expressed in standard deviation units of a reference group of young adults are portrayed in Figures 3.1 through 3.4.[4] Most of the samples in these analyses were moderately large, and the individuals were selected to be representative of the general population.

The materials in the tests consisted of unrelated words, stories or meaningful passages, figures or shapes, pictures of faces, and pairs of unrelated words or names, and the memory tests occurred either immediately after

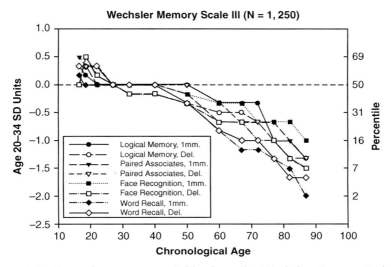

Figure 3.1. Means for memory variables from the Wechsler Memory Scale III as a function of age, scaled in age 20 to 34 standard deviation units. The vertical axis on the right represents the percentile of the reference distribution.

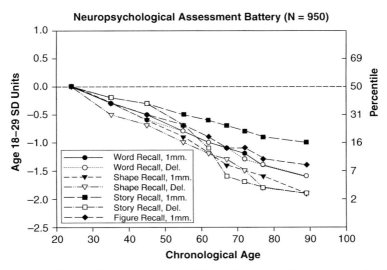

Figure 3.2. Means for memory variables from the Neuropsychological Assessment Battery as a function of age, scaled in age 18 to 29 standard deviation units. The vertical axis on the right represents the percentile of the reference distribution.

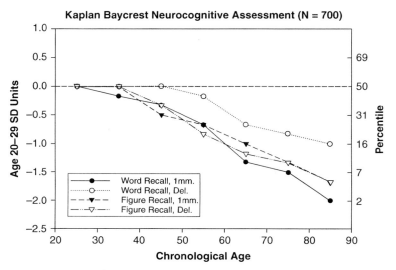

Figure 3.3. Means for memory variables from the Kaplan Baycrest Neurocognitive Assessment battery as a function of age, scaled in age 20 to 29 standard deviation units. The vertical axis on the right represents the percentile of the reference distribution.

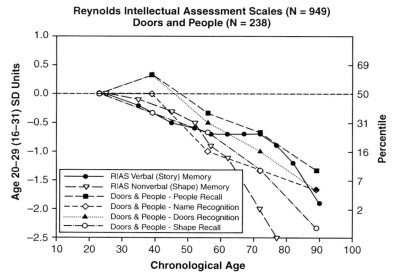

Figure 3.4. Means for memory variables from two test batteries as a function of age, in young adult standard deviation units. The vertical axis on the right represents the percentile of the reference distribution.

presentation of the material or after a delay. There is some variation in the age trends across the variables, but the overall pattern closely resembles that with other cognitive abilities (such as those in Figures 1.5 to 1.8 in Chapter 1), as adults in their 60s and 70s perform at an average level nearly 1 standard deviation below that of adults in their early 20s. Similar patterns of nearly continuous and monotonic age-related decreases in performance with different memory variables have been reported in other research studies involving moderately large samples across a wide age range.[5]

Another way of summarizing research findings on aging and memory is with meta-analyses, which are methods of quantitatively aggregating results across multiple studies. When applied to research on aging, a meta-analysis yields an estimate of the magnitude of the performance difference between young adults (typically with an average age in the early 20s) and old adults (typically with an average age in the 60s or 70s) in units of the average standard deviation.

A few issues need to be considered when interpreting results from meta-analyses in research on aging. First, unlike standardized tests from commercial test batteries, many of the variables from experimental tasks often included in meta-analyses have not had their reliabilities established. Because reliability sets an upper limit on the magnitude of the relations a variable can have with other variables, comparisons of effect sizes across variables can be difficult to interpret without information about the reliabilities. For example, if variable X has lower reliability than variable Y, the estimates of the size of the age-related effects on the two variables could differ for statistical, rather than substantive, reasons. If estimates of reliability are available for all of the variables, the effect size estimates can be adjusted for unreliability, but this type of correction has rarely been done in meta-analyses of age differences in measures of cognitive functioning.

And second, a technical problem with some meta-analyses is that multiple estimates of effects are occasionally obtained from the same samples of individuals, which violates a basic assumption of meta-analysis that all of the values used to derive the estimates are independent. If the non-independence is clearly stated in the original report, then the analyst can take steps to minimize this problem, such as averaging the estimates or using only one of them. However, in some laboratories the same individuals participate in multiple studies that are reported in different articles without any mention of the overlap of the samples of research participants. When this is the case, the results of the different studies are not statistically independent of one another, and the effect size estimates based on these studies could be misleading if the relevant measures of performance are affected by prior research participation.

Although for the reasons just mentioned, results from meta-analyses need to be interpreted cautiously, they can be useful in summarizing results across multiple studies. Several meta-analyses have evaluated age differences in various measures of memory and have revealed effect sizes for differences between young and old adults of about 1.0 standard deviations for word recall, between 0.5 and 0.7 for word recognition, and about 0.7 for prose recall.[6] It should be noted that these values are in the same range as what would be expected from the results portrayed in Figures 3.1 through 3.4. That is, in many of the graphs adults in their 60s and 70s perform at an average level about 0.5 to 1.0 standard deviation below the level of adults in their 20s.

The next several sections contain a brief overview of some of the models and empirical phenomena in research on memory aging. As noted above, this coverage is by no means comprehensive, but rather is intended to convey a sense of the type of theories and phenomena that have guided research in this area.

Metaphors and Models

Speculations about the nature of memory, and possible reasons for age differences in memory, can be traced at least to the time of the early Greeks. For example, Aristotle used a metaphor of a wax tablet to describe the relation of age to memory. He noted that a new (or young) wax tablet is initially soft and makes impressions easily, but as it ages it becomes hard, and although early impressions are retained, it becomes increasingly more difficult to make new impressions.

Another frequently mentioned view of memory is that it is like a limited capacity container, and that "Old people seem more forgetful partly because they have so much more to forget..."[7] This perspective is sometimes expressed in the form of an anecdote about an ichthyologist who became a dean of students. According to the story, the new dean claimed that every time he learned the name of a student he forgot the name of another fish. The idea is that when the capacity of his memory system was reached, a certain amount of old information had to be displaced in order to accommodate new information.[8] However, because there is little convincing evidence of absolute limits on the capacity of information that can be stored in memory, this simple displacement perspective is no longer seriously considered.

Many different ways of conceptualizing memory, and of interpreting age differences in memory, have been proposed over the last 50 years. A few of these conceptualizations will be briefly described in the following section, but more are always being proposed, and thus entire books would be needed to be exhaustive in the coverage of models of memory.

Type of Information

One popular distinction is based on the type of information that is presumed to be in memory. A broad division is between procedural and declarative information, with the declarative category often further divided into episodic and semantic information. Procedural information refers to motor skills and sequences of actions, or more generally to *how* information as opposed to *what, when,* or *where* information.

Episodic information refers to information acquired in specific episodes (i.e., personally experienced past events) in which the individual is often aware of the time and place of the acquisition of the information. Semantic information consists of facts, principles, and rules of general knowledge. Unlike episodic information, semantic information is highly overlearned, with the individual seldom aware of when or where the material was originally acquired. One way of characterizing the distinction among the types of memory is as follows: recalling when you last rode your bicycle is episodic memory, knowing what a bicycle is is semantic memory, and knowing how to ride a bicycle is procedural memory.[9]

The categorization of memory in terms of type of information is of interest in research on cognitive aging because different types of information have been found to have different patterns of age relations. An illustration of these differences from our project is apparent in Figure 3.5, which portrays the age relations in two variables: a measure of paired associates memory performance and a measure of synonym vocabulary performance. In both cases the research participants are asked to determine the best associate of the target word, but the relevant information is recently acquired in the paired associates test, whereas it represents old well-learned information in a vocabulary test. Notice that there is a monotonic decrease with age in paired associates performance, but an increase until about age 60 for synonym vocabulary. These trends, as well as those for measures of episodic memory compared to measures of vocabulary and knowledge in Figures 1.5, 1.6, and

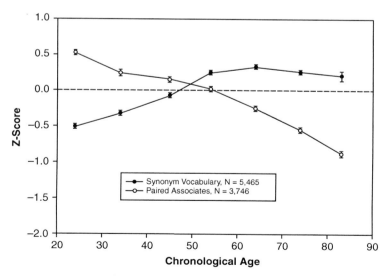

Figure 3.5. Means and standard errors for a vocabulary variable and a paired associates memory variable as a function of age in the Salthouse data.

1.7 in Chapter 1, are consistent with the suggestion that aging is associated with an impairment in the efficiency of learning and remembering new information (episodic), but that it has weaker effects on the retention of highly learned old information (semantic). Much less research has been conducted on age differences in procedural memory, in part because few standardized methods have been developed to assess procedural learning.

Duration of Information

Another conceptualization of memory is in terms of how long the information has been preserved. Memories of varying durations are often assumed to differ in their sensitivity to aging, as is apparent in the following statement from 1927: "The more recent impressions and experiences are the first to be lost; later those of adult life; then those of youth; and finally, those of early childhood."[10] From the perspective of memory research, *short term* refers to durations on the order of seconds, *long term* to durations ranging from minutes to years, and *remote* refers to periods up to decades.

Most studies of memory have involved intervals of seconds to hours. Much less research has been conducted investigating very long-term or remote memory because of problems of verifying the accuracy of the information, controlling the amount of rehearsal since the initial acquisition, and minimizing the role of inference in the memory assessment. To illustrate, consider the situation of an older adult describing details of his or her 4th birthday. It is very difficult to determine whether the reported details are accurate when there is no independent way to verify the information, to ensure that the information dates from age 4 rather than from the last time the story was told, and to be certain that all of the reported information, such as the number of candles on the cake, reflects processes of memory rather than inference.

Several clever attempts have been used to deal with these problems. For example, some researchers have tested memory for songs, faces, news events, and television programs from specific historical periods.[11] Although this type of material has the advantage of allowing the accuracy of the reported information to be objectively verified, there are still problems of how to equate the level of original acquisition and ensure that the information was acquired at the time of the event. That is, some people may never have been exposed to the information, and others may have acquired it later than the original event.

Another approach has focused on assessing memory for information such as names and faces of high school classmates, locations of campus landmarks, and foreign language or mathematics material learned in school. Level of initial acquisition has been evaluated by reports of the original amount of contact with the people or places, or by the grades received in relevant courses, and opportunities for rehearsal have been assessed by asking questions about subsequent exposures with the material.

Similar results have been found for several different types of material with this procedure. In most cases memory accuracy has been found to decline steeply to about 50% or 60% of the immediate level within about 5 years, with the amount of accessible information then remaining remarkably stable for up to 40 years. This pattern of results is consistent with the belief that adults of all ages have relatively good memory for information acquired early in life.

Still another method that has been used to investigate very long-term memory involves prompting the person to report a memory associated with a specific word, and then to indicate how old he or she was at the time of the remembered event.[12] One of the interesting findings from this type of research is that the most persistent and salient memories frequently date from when people were between about 15 and 30 years of age. The reasons for the special salience of memories from young adulthood are not yet clear, but it might be because that is the period when people have the highest levels of cognitive ability, or because that is when most things happen for the first time.

Stages of Remembering

Because remembering something requires that the information be registered, retained, and retrieved, a considerable amount of research has attempted to isolate the role of hypothesized stages of encoding, storage, and retrieval in age differences in memory. For example, in a recall test the research participant has to retrieve or generate the information, but in a recognition test he or she merely needs to select the answer from among a set of alternatives. Comparison across the two types of memory tests has therefore been assumed to be informative about the effects of aging on the retrieval stage in memory.

As noted earlier, meta-analyses often reveal that age differences are smaller with recognition tests than with recall tests. This is also true in age correlations from samples of adults across a wide age range. To illustrate, 657 adults in our research project performed both word recall and word recognition tests. The age correlations were −.39 for the recall test and only −.07 for the recognition test. Results such as these have been interpreted as evidence that part of the difficulty in memory with increasing age is retrieving, or accessing, the relevant information.

However, age differences found with other procedures, such as deciding whether two successively presented complex patterns are the same or different, could be interpreted as consistent with an age-related deficit in registering or encoding the information. No consensus has yet been reached on which hypothesized stage is critical in the age differences in memory, perhaps in part because the stages are intrinsically interrelated and it is difficult to study an effect on one stage independent of effects on other stages.

Processes of Memory

Some memories seem to be automatically available, whereas others require conscious effort or deliberate recollection to be accessed. For example, many adults have immediate associations to the name of John F. Kennedy, but they may have to engage in processes of deliberate recollection to recall when he was first elected as a U.S. Senator.

Controlled or deliberate processing is assumed to be involved in most traditional tests of memory, and consequently special techniques are needed to assess the role of automatic processing. Some of the procedures developed to investigate automatic processing in memory are as simple as asking the participant to classify information that they recognize as "known" or as "remembered." More complex procedures have been based on comparisons of performance with different types of instructions, such as reporting all of the items that can be remembered versus reporting only the items that were presented once but not twice.[13]

There are now quite a few reports of smaller age differences for information that can be accessed automatically compared to information requiring controlled or deliberate processing. These findings have sometimes been interpreted as indicating that a great deal of information is encoded but is simply more difficult to access with increasing age. However, the procedures used to assess automatic processing are often indirect, and not much is currently known about the reliabilities of the measures. This is unfortunate because if reliability is low, then at least some of the smaller age relations could be an artifact of weak measurement rather than reflecting true preservation of that type of functioning.

The preceding are only a small sample of conceptualizations of memory, and they were selected in part because these particular models may be applicable to a variety of different types of memory tasks. Many more models have been proposed to account for performance in specific memory tasks, but because age differences have been reported in a wide variety of memory tasks, most of the models would have to be greatly expanded to account for all aspects of memory aging.

Phenomena

The field of human memory research is notorious for frequent shifts from one experimental paradigm to another as the paradigms, and relevant phenomena, wax and wane in popularity. There is often a great deal of enthusiasm among researchers interested in memory and aging when the initial results with a new procedure appear to suggest that an exception to typical age-related decline has been discovered. The following sections describe a few examples of research on memory aging in which the initial results were considered exciting exceptions to age-related decline, but later research either failed to replicate the original results or led to alternative interpretations. Many more examples could have been selected, but these serve to illustrate the importance of being cautious in the evaluation of new findings, while also providing an indication of the range of memory phenomena that have been investigated in age-comparative studies.

Ecological

It is sometimes claimed that human memory appears to be poor because the tasks used to assess memory in the laboratory do not resemble activities in daily life, and hence are low in ecological validity. Although this argument may appear plausible, it is important to recognize that there is no objective way to evaluate the degree of ecological validity at the current time because ecological validity is a subjective concept. To illustrate, some researchers might consider a task of learning to associate pairs of unrelated words to be artificial and unrealistic, but a case can be made that associative learning is one of the most fundamental processes in all of cognition because the forming of connections between previously unrelated pieces of information is involved in nearly every type of learning. Furthermore, because it is impossible to control all conceivable factors that might influence performance on a cognitive test, the greatest generality might actually be achieved by studying the purest and most abstract form of memory that is least influenced by other factors. When a process is embedded in a specific context, performance may be dominated by influences of a variety of uncontrolled "real-world" factors, with the consequence that the results may not generalize to other contexts where those particular factors are not operating.[14]

Regardless of the merit of arguments about the concept of ecological validity, a considerable amount of research has revealed that age differences in memory are not restricted to abstract, unfamiliar, or meaningless material. For example, age differences favoring young adults have been found in memory for details of movies; news stories appearing in print, on the radio, or on television; musical tunes and lyrics; recipes; eye witness identifications; museum exhibit locations; product warning information; information from physicians; and even one's own golf shots.[15]

Many of these studies had relatively small numbers of participants, and few of the studies reported the reliability of the memory measures. Nevertheless, there is considerable evidence for differences between young and old adults in many types of real-world memory, and therefore it is definitely not the case that age differences are only apparent in artificial and unrealistic situations.

Memory for Activities

Activities or actions that are performed by an individual have been hypothesized to have a special status in memory because of the multiple ways that the information could be encoded—not only by hearing or reading a description but also through various kinesthetic senses as a consequence of performing the activity. Researchers in the 1980s suggested that, possibly because of the rich multimodal encoding of information, little or no age differences might be evident with these types of subject-performed tasks. In fact, several studies did report small to nonexistent age differences in memory for activities or subject-performed tasks.[16]

However, the failures to find age differences were not replicated in later studies with larger samples, in which similar age relations were found for memory of descriptions of actions and memory of performed actions. Although the absolute level of performance is often higher in measures of memory for subject-performed tasks than in measures of memory for descriptions, there currently appears to be no convincing evidence that the age differences for this type of information are appreciably smaller than age differences with other types of information.

Prospective Memory

Prospective memory refers to memory to do something in the future, as opposed to remembering what happened in the past. It is potentially relevant to everyday functioning because in many situations it may be more important to carry out an intended action than to recall something that happened in the past. Early reports of minimal age differences in prospective memory therefore generated considerable interest, particularly since some of the studies suggested that older adults actually did better than young adults in prospective memory tasks such as remembering to make a telephone call or to mail a postcard. However, these findings are now generally interpreted as reflecting older adults' greater use of external memory aids in natural settings, such as calendars and appointment books, rather than a reflection of preserved or enhanced prospective memory.

More recent studies have used a variety of laboratory-based procedures to investigate prospective memory, including asking the participant to perform a particular action whenever a target item appeared while he or she was performing another activity. For example, in one of the studies conducted in my laboratory the research participants were asked to press a specific key whenever a particular stimulus pattern occurred in a concept identification task. Age correlations on measures from four prospective memory tasks in our study ranged from −.21 to −.40, and two recent meta-analyses of age differences in measures of prospective memory reported effect sizes in contrasts of young and old adults ranging from .64 to .85.[17] Both sets of values are similar to those with other memory measures. Contrary to the early suggestions, therefore, it appears that age differences in many measures of prospective memory are nearly the same magnitude as those found with other types of memory tests.

Memory for Emotional Information

The effectiveness of controlling or regulating one's emotions has been postulated to increase with age, and this has led to interest in how emotional material might be remembered by adults of different ages. The role of emotion in age differences in memory has been investigated in a number of studies, but no clear conclusion has yet emerged from this research. Perhaps the simplest prediction is that there would be significant differences in the relations between age and memory for emotional material compared to memory for neutral material, but there are apparently no published studies with this particular outcome. Some studies have reported no age differences in the proportion of emotional material that was remembered, but there have also been studies that did not find this result.[18]

One of the problems with evaluating the role of emotion on the relations between aging and memory is that it is possible to make contradictory predictions. For example, to the extent that increased age is associated with better regulation of emotions, one might expect that manipulations of emotional material would have smaller effects with increased age because the better regulation results in the filtering out of emotionally relevant information that could lead to unwanted emotions. In contrast, if it is assumed that the better regulation is associated with heightened sensitivity to certain types of emotion, then emotional manipulations might be expected to have larger effects at older ages. In either case, the suppression or enhancement could occur for all types of emotional material, or only for positive, or only for negative, material.

Another possible prediction is that if memory for emotional material is related to effective emotion regulation, then the degree of emotion-based processing in memory tasks should be significantly correlated with variables that have been interpreted as reflecting the effectiveness of emotion regulation, such as measures of mood, depression, or anxiety. For example, people with the lowest levels of depression or anxiety might be expected to exhibit the largest differences between memory for emotional and nonemotional material. However, there are apparently no age-comparative studies of memory and emotion reporting these types of correlations.

Stereotypes and Memory

A common stereotype is that increased age is associated with poorer memory, and self-ratings of memory suggest that many older adults believe that they perform worse than young adults on a variety of memory tasks. Interestingly, in the last several decades it has been found that awareness of a stereotype can affect performance on cognitive tests relevant to that stereotype. In particular, social psychologists have reported that performance on some cognitive tests can be affected by an individual's awareness of cultural beliefs or attitudes about the level of functioning of members of his or her group. Because there are well-documented stereotypes that older adults have poor memories, it is possible that activation of this stereotype could affect memory performance of older adults through lower motivation, increased anxiety, ineffective allocation of attention, suboptimal strategies, or some other mechanism.

The primary prediction from the stereotype-threat perspective is that age differences in memory performance should be larger when a negative stereotype about aging and memory is activated compared to when it is not activated. The rationale is that if an older individual believes the stereotype that older adults have poorer memory, he or she identifies with older adults and also perceives the current activity to be a test of memory, then his or her level of performance in the memory task could be low because the stereotype is incorporated into one's thought processes and affects functioning in the task.

Unfortunately, research investigating the role of stereotypes on age differences in memory has yielded complicated, and sometimes inconsistent, results. Some of the studies have only involved older adults, and thus they are not informative about whether the manipulations affected the magnitude of the age differences. Furthermore, several studies failed to replicate the original phenomenon in young adults, which raises questions about its robustness because the phenomenon was initially demonstrated in samples of young adults. Finally, in a few studies manipulations designed to minimize activation of the stereotype resulted in a decrement in the performance of young adults rather than an improvement in older adults, which is inconsistent with a simple stereotype-threat interpretation of the age differences in memory.[19]

Two other issues also need to be considered when evaluating stereotype-threat research applied to memory and aging. First, if one of the mechanisms responsible for activation of stereotypes resulting in lower memory performance is increased anxiety, then older adults would be expected to have higher levels of state anxiety than young adults. However, studies that have included measures of anxiety have often found lower self-reported anxiety in the testing situation with increased age. To illustrate, in our research with 1,648 adults, the average level of state anxiety was slightly, but significantly, lower rather than higher with increased age ($r = -.13$), and level of state anxiety was not related to a composite memory measure ($r = -.04$).[20] Some mechanism other than increased anxiety must therefore be postulated to account for any influences of stereotypes on age differences in memory.

A second issue relevant to the interpretation of stereotype-threat research is that deficits in performance attributable to stereotype threat should only occur when there is evidence of a negative stereotype, and not when no negative stereotypes exist. However, age differences in memory and other cognitive abilities can be detected between adults in their 20s and adults in their 30s and 40s, and it is questionable whether many people within this latter age range would characterize themselves as old, in which case they should not be susceptible to a stereotype threat impairment of performance. Furthermore, there are apparently no negative stereotypes about aging and cognitive abilities such as reasoning or spatial visualization, and yet the age differences in these abilities have been found to be at least as large as those with memory. At minimum, another category of explanation will be needed to account for age relations on abilities that are not represented in negative stereotypes.

New aspects of memory are constantly being discovered, and they are often quickly applied in studies comparing the performance of adults of different ages. These new perspectives often provide valuable information about the nature of memory aging. However, one needs to be alert to the possibility that a constantly shifting focus on currently popular phenomena may distract researchers from what might be considered the primary goal of explaining why age differences are apparent in so many different types of cognitive variables.

Research on other aspects of cognitive functioning has not been as extensive as that on memory, but the research in those areas could also be reviewed in terms of the models and phenomena that have guided the research. However, instead of summarizing past research within specific topic areas, the focus in the following sections shifts to considering the primary ways in which cognitive aging research has been conducted and the implications these practices have for what needs to be explained in cognitive aging.

Micro and Macro Approaches to Cognitive Aging

It is generally assumed that the performance of an individual on any given cognitive task reflects a variety of determinants, but researchers differ in the nature of the determinants assumed to be most important. Some researchers emphasize characteristics of the tasks, such as processes or components hypothesized to be required to perform a specific task. In contrast, other researchers emphasize characteristics of individuals, in the form of cognitive abilities that in various combinations are assumed to determine performance on many different tasks. These two emphases are represented in what can be termed the micro and macro approaches to cognitive aging research.[21] Although these different ways of doing research are sometimes viewed as opposing perspectives, they are not necessarily contradictory and are probably best viewed as complementary, or possibly even with micro considered as a special case of macro. That is, there is no conceptual reason why variables derived from the process-oriented micro approach could not be examined in a broader context with the macro approach.[22]

Another common misconception about these analytical approaches is that they have a one-to-one correspondence with domain-specific or domain-general perspectives about the nature of cognitive aging. That is, theoretical interpretations have been distinguished on the basis of whether the primary mechanisms are postulated to operate at the level of a few specific cognitive tasks or are applicable across a variety of different types of tasks. Although it is probably true that most proponents of domain-specific interpretations rely on the micro approach, it is also the case that it is difficult to discover evidence relevant to domain-general interpretations when the research focus is restricted to a single variable. Only by examining several variables simultaneously, as in the macro approach, is it possible to investigate the independence of age-related influences on different cognitive variables. If there is any correspondence between analytical approaches and theoretical interpretations, therefore, it may be attributable to the fact that domain-general interpretations are not easily investigated within the micro approach.

Micro

The micro approach is most closely associated with the cognitive psychology tradition because it focuses on cognitive processes postulated to be involved in the performance of a task, and not just on the products of those processes. This approach is motivated in part by a dissatisfaction with many measures of cognitive performance because they are assumed to reflect a mixture of different types of theoretical processes that make it difficult to determine precisely what is responsible for a given level of performance. Researchers working within this perspective therefore frequently try to decompose the target task to obtain measures of theoretically interesting processes or components. The decomposition is usually based on theoretical speculations and task analyses, and it often involves the administration of several conditions of a task to obtain measures of each hypothesized process.

As an example, different hypothesized components of word recall might be obtained by examining recall accuracy as a function of the presentation position of individual words to estimate primacy and recency components, as a function of repeated lists of words from the same semantic categories to estimate the accumulation of proactive interference, or after instructions following a word or a list of words to either remember or forget the words to examine efficiency of memory control. The primary assumption in the micro approach is that most measures of cognitive performance reflect a mixture of conceptually distinct processes, and that identification and isolation of these processes may be a key to understanding cognition, and possibly also age-related differences in cognition.[23]

The micro or decomposition approach has several strengths, such as the potential to gain a better understanding of how particular cognitive tasks are performed, and more precise specification of the nature of age-related differences on the tasks. With respect to this latter point, instead of attributing age differences to an undifferentiated mixture of several theoretically distinct components, the decomposition approach attempts to localize age differences to a few critical processes. In light of the potentially valuable information it can provide, together with the fact that decomposition studies can be conducted with relatively small samples of young and old adults, it is not surprising that the micro approach to research on cognitive aging has been very popular.

However, the micro approach has a number of limitations that are not always recognized. For example, questions can be raised regarding the validity of components identified from task analyses. That is, although it is frequently possible to obtain two or more measures from a cognitive task, there is seldom any evidence that the measures actually represent what they are hypothesized to represent. Measures are sometimes inferred to be valid if they are found to be sensitive to particular manipulations in the predicted direction, but this is a limited, task-specific form of validity.

The primary manner in which validity is investigated from an individual differences perspective involves examining patterns of correlations of the target variable with other variables. The rationale is that if a measure of a component from task X represents the same theoretical process as a measure of a component from task Y, then the two measures would be expected to be moderately correlated with each other. A more rigorous investigation of validity involves examining both convergent and discriminant aspects of validity. That is, alternative measures of the same hypothesized component should be moderately correlated with one another to indicate that they converge on the same construct, but they should be only weakly correlated with measures of other hypothesized constructs to establish that different constructs can be discriminated. For example, a measure derived from a particular memory task might be hypothesized to represent effortful memory retrieval. One way to investigate the validity of this hypothesis involves determining whether the measure had moderate to high correlations with measures of the effortful memory retrieval construct derived from different memory tasks, but much lower correlations with measures of other hypothesized constructs such as automatic memory access or memory encoding. Results such as these would provide evidence that the variable of interest represents something that is not merely specific to a particular task, and that it reflects something distinct from other aspects of memory processing. Furthermore, because the analyses are conducted at the level of individual differences, this pattern of results would provide evidence that the hypothesized cognitive processes correspond to dimensions along which people differ from one another. Unfortunately, very little research of this type, in which individual difference information is used to investigate the validity of hypothesized cognitive processes, currently exists.[24]

A second limitation of the micro approach is that estimates of the reliability of the measures of the hypothesized components are seldom reported. There is a long tradition of individual difference research with cognitive abilities, and consequently there has been considerable progress in developing reliable, valid measures of cognitive abilities. Interest in cognitive processes has been more recent, particularly from the perspective of individual differences, and as a consequence much less information is available concerning the reliability of measures of hypothesized cognitive processes. In fact, there is a sense in which the emphasis on robust effects in cognitive psychology may actually have contributed to weak individual difference reliability of measures of cognitive processes. The reason is that a phenomenon is often considered robust when it is exhibited by everybody to nearly the same extent, but if there is little variation across people in the magnitude of the phenomenon, then measures of the phenomenon will tend to have low reliability.

A third limitation of the micro approach with respect to research on cognitive aging is that it is not parsimonious. That is, many different types of cognitive variables have been found to be related to age, and therefore a relatively large number of critical components would presumably need to be postulated to account for all of these effects. Of course, this may eventually prove necessary, but that can only be determined after more parsimonious alternatives have been examined.

A related concern is that the micro approach ignores the possibility of age-related influences that might operate at a broader, or more abstract, level than individual variables. This point can be elaborated by considering two possible groups of researchers. Assume that one group proposed a decomposition of task Y into components $Y1$, $Y2$, and $Y3$ and found that $Y2$ was the only component related to age. These researchers might then concentrate on trying to explain why aging was related to $Y2$. A different group might have proposed a decomposition of task Z into components $Z1$, $Z2$, and $Z3$, and after finding that $Z3$ was the component with the greatest sensitivity to age, they might subsequently concentrate on trying to explain why aging was related to $Z3$. These are quite reasonable research strategies when each task is considered separately. But now consider what would happen if a new group of researchers found that the $Y2$ and $Z3$ measures were highly related to one another, and that the age-related effects on them were not independent. A discovery such as this would likely lead to a shift of at least some of the explanatory focus to trying to account for age-related influences on what was common across two or more different types of tasks.

The majority of research in cognitive aging has investigated one task at a time and has therefore ignored the possibility that a portion of the age-related influences on the variable of interest might be shared with age-related influences on other cognitive variables. This approach has led to separate explanations being proposed for each individual variable, without considering whether at least some of the age-related influences on the variable might operate at broader levels.

One of the fundamental questions in the field of cognitive aging is how many separate explanations are required to account for the age-related effects on different cognitive variables. If the age-related influences on different types of cognitive variables were found to be independent of one another, then separate explanations of the effects of age on each variable would obviously be required. However, even if only a small proportion of the age-related influences on a given cognitive task were found to overlap with age-related influences on other cognitive variables, those influences would need to be taken into consideration to ensure that the proposed explanations are actually accounting for effects specific to the target task.

Macro

The preceding paragraph summarizes the motivation behind the macro approach to cognitive aging, in which age differences on the target variable are examined together with age differences in other cognitive variables. The primary distinguishing characteristic of the macro approach is that it is inherently multivariate rather than univariate, in the sense that multiple variables are considered simultaneously.[25]

Figure 3.6 schematically portrays univariate and multivariate approaches to the study of cognitive aging. The figure employs the convention of using boxes to represent observed or measured variables, and circles to represent latent variables that are not directly observed but are hypothesized to have a causal influence on other variables. Hypothesized causal relations are portrayed with an arrow from the proposed cause to the proposed effect.

The univariate approach is portrayed with an arrow from age to a single target variable, Y, because studies of this type compare people of different ages with respect to a variable from a single task. The variable of age could be represented by a contrast between small samples of young and old adults, or by a relatively large number of people across a continuous range of ages, and the relation to the target variable could be examined with a variety of analytical methods such as t-tests, analyses of variance, or various types of correlation or regression analyses. Several target variables hypothesized to reflect different components of the same task are sometimes included in the analyses, but primarily to obtain measures of different hypothesized components within the same task rather than to examine possible relations across

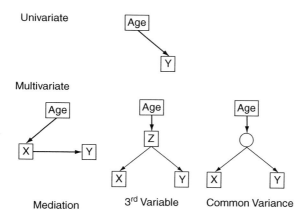

Figure 3.6. Schematic illustrations of the univariate perspective on cognitive aging research (*top*), and three different examples of the multivariate perspective (*bottom*). Arrows in this diagram designate a relation hypothesized to exist between the two variables; observed variables are represented by boxes and hypothesized (latent) variables are represented by circles.

different tasks. Because the univariate approach focuses on a single variable, it implicitly assumes that the age-related effects on different variables and tasks are independent of one another in the sense that interpretation of the age-related influences on one variable is unaffected by consideration of the age-related influences on other variables.

A major advantage of the multivariate perspective is that not only can the independence assumption be investigated but also other possibilities, such as the mediation of age-related effects on one variable through another variable, operation of a third variable that is responsible for age-related effects on both variables, and an influence of age on something the variables have in common. Simple versions of these alternatives are portrayed in the bottom of Figure 3.6. The model in the bottom left postulates that the relation between age and Y occurs because age affects X, which in turn affects Y, and the model in the bottom middle postulates that a third variable, Z, is related to age and to both X and Y. The bottom right panel represents the hypothesis that there is something common to both X and Y that is related to age. This model differs from the one in the middle panel in that in this case the third variable is a theoretical construct that does not necessarily correspond to an observed variable.

Although very simple, the models in Figure 3.6 have quite different implications for the interpretation of relations between age and the target variable. For example, in the bottom left and bottom center panels, the age–Y relation is completely attributable to influences of age on either X or Z, respectively, and in the bottom right panel all of the age-related influences on Y are shared with age-related influences on X because of an effect of age on what X and Y have in common. It is instructive to consider what would need to be explained from the perspective of the different models in Figure 3.6. In the univariate model only the age–Y relation is examined, and hence that is the only relation that needs to be explained. However, with the models in the bottom left and bottom middle of Figure 3.6 either the age-X or the age-Z relation would need to be explained, and in the model in the bottom right an explanation would be needed for the effects of age on what is common to X and Y. These simple examples illustrate that plausible alternative interpretations are neglected when only the univariate model is considered, which could result in incomplete, and perhaps even erroneous, conclusions about the nature of age-related influences on cognitive functioning.

An important issue from the macro perspective is the degree to which age-related influences on different cognitive variables are independent of one another. As used here, independence of age relations on two variables means that knowledge of the influence of age on one of the variables is not informative about the influence of age on the other variable. Three analytical methods that have been used to investigate independence of age-related influences on cognitive variables will be briefly described in the following sections. These methods have primarily been used with cross-sectional data because, as discussed in the previous chapter, correlations among changes in different variables provide a direct method of examining independence of age-related influences in longitudinal data. One analytical method consists of controlling the individual difference variation in one variable when examining age relations on other variables. A second method involves examining age-related influences on a hypothesized structure that represents the organization of cognitive variables, and the third method is a combination of the first two known as contextual analysis.

Variance Control

The simplest method of examining the independence of age-related differences on two or more cognitive variables involves controlling the variation in one variable when examining the relations of age on other variables. For example, assume that both hearing sensitivity and arm strength are related to age, and a researcher is interested in determining the extent to which these two age relations are independent of each other.

One way in which this type of independence can be investigated consists of examining the relation of age to arm strength among people who all have approximately the same level of hearing sensitivity. The reasoning is that if the decrease with age in arm strength among people with the same hearing level is similar to the decrease with age in arm strength in the general population, then age-related effects on hearing ability can be inferred to be independent of age-related effects on arm strength. That is, results such as these would suggest that the people who experience substantial age-related decreases in hearing are not necessarily the same people who experience large age-related decreases in arm strength. An outcome of this type would imply that the two effects were independent because knowing the relation of age on one variable would not be informative about the relation of age on the other variable. In contrast, if the decrease in arm strength with increasing age was found to be much smaller among people who all had approximately the same level of hearing than among unselected people in the general population, it would imply that age-related effects on the two characteristics were not independent of one another. In this case, because the sample of people who experience age-related hearing loss also tend to experience a decrease in arm strength, the age relations on one variable are informative about the age relations on the other variable. Depending on the outcome of the analyses, therefore, interpretations of age differences in hearing sensitivity and in arm strength might require separate explanations to account for age-related effects on the two variables, an explanation for influences that are shared across the variables, or a combination of the two types of explanations.

The basic idea in the variance control procedure is that the independence of age-related differences on two variables, X and Y, can be investigated by reducing or eliminating the variation in one of the variables (e.g., X), when examining the relation of age to the other variable (e.g., Y). Note that the relevant outcome from the analyses is not the level of Y, but rather the strength of the relation between age and Y. The strength of the age–Y relation can be assessed either by the slope of the function relating Y to age, or by the proportion of the variance in Y that is associated with age. Both of these indices are informative because the former indicates how much variable Y changes with each additional year of age, and the latter indicates how precisely the estimated age–Y relation fits the data. For example, two variables might each have a slope indicating a decrease of 2 units for each year of age. However, if the equation for one variable accounted for 75% of the variability in the data, whereas the equation for the other variable was only associated with 25% of the variance, then the variables would differ in the precision of their relations to age.

At least two methods can be used to reduce or eliminate the variation in one variable (X) when investigating relations of age to another variable (Y). One method consists of selecting people from the sample who are all within a narrow range on X. Although clearly possible, this matching procedure is often inefficient because, depending on the strength of the relation between age and the controlled variable, the number of individuals at each age could be quite small. To illustrate, restricting comparisons to participants with scores of 7 or 8 on the Raven's Progressive Matrices variable in our project leaves only 21% of the original sample, and restriction to participants with Pattern Comparison scores of 16 or 17 leaves only 16% of the original sample. In both of these cases, therefore, data from more than 75% of the sample would have to be discarded in order to obtain a reasonable degree of matching. The sample size could be increased by adopting a less stringent matching criterion, but because there is a tradeoff between precision of matching and sample size, this would result in a smaller reduction of the variation in the controlled variable.

An alternative method of minimizing the variation in the X variable involves the use of statistical procedures. One of the most common of these procedures consists of first determining the quantitative relation between the X and Y variables, and then using that equation to remove the influence of X on Y before examining the relation of age on the adjusted (X-matched) Y scores. Because the matching is done statistically, by mathematically adjusting the scores, the data from all participants can be used in the analyses.

Figures 3.7 and 3.8 illustrate the effects of controlling the variation in a reasoning (Raven's) variable and in a perceptual speed (Pattern Comparison) variable on the relations between age and the number of words correctly recalled in a multiple-trial word recall task. It can be seen that both matching and statistical control procedures result in a shallower slope of the function relating the recall variable to age, and in a reduction by about two-thirds of the variance in word recall that is associated with age.

The results in Figures 3.7 and 3.8 imply that the cross-sectional age-related differences on these measures of memory, reasoning, and speed are not independent of one another. In particular, they indicate that samples of adults of different ages who differ in memory also tend to differ in reasoning

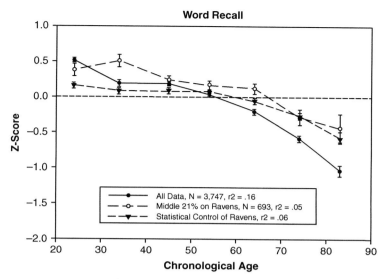

Figure 3.7. Means and standard errors for a word recall variable as function of age when considered by itself, after restricting the sample to participants with similar values on the Raven's matrix reasoning variable, and after statistically controlling the variance in the Raven's matrix reasoning variable.

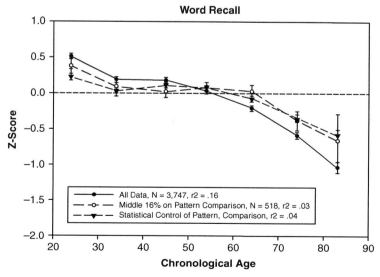

Figure 3.8. Means and standard errors for a word recall variable as function of age when considered by itself, after restricting the sample to participants with similar values on the pattern comparison variable, and after statistically controlling the variance in the pattern comparison variable.

and perceptual speed. Similar findings of a substantial reduction in the relation between age and one cognitive variable after controlling the variation in another cognitive variable have been reported with many different combinations of variables in numerous studies. An important implication of the results of variance control procedures is that it may be misleading to attempt to explain the relation between age and recall without considering the operation of broader influences. In particular, because there is a large degree of overlap of the age differences in this measure of word recall with the age differences in other types of cognitive variables, explanations based on memory-specific mechanisms such as efficiency of encoding, retrieval, or certain types of strategies would likely be able to account for only a small fraction of the observed age differences in the relevant cognitive variables.[26]

It should be noted that although the age–cognition relation is almost always substantially reduced in these types of matching and statistical control analyses, the residual, or direct, age relation is frequently significantly greater than zero. This implies that the cross-sectional age differences in most cognitive variables probably reflect a mixture of general influences that are shared with other variables, and specific influences that are unique to that variable. However, it is impossible to separate the age-related effects on a target variable into portions that are, and are not, shared with other variables when only univariate analyses are conducted. Unless additional variables are included in the analyses, the extent to which the observed age differences reflect influences specific to a particular variable cannot be determined.[27]

Structural Organization of Cognitive Abilities

It has been known for at least 100 years that most cognitive variables are positively related to one another, in that someone who performs well in tests of memory also tends to perform well in tests of other cognitive abilities, such as reasoning and perceptual speed. Because the correlations among the variables vary in magnitude, differences in the strengths of the correlations can be used to organize the variables into structures, with the variables having the strongest correlations located closest to one another in the structure. A variety of different structures have been proposed, but there currently seems to be a consensus that one of the most meaningful organizations of cognitive variables is a hierarchical structure in which observed variables are at the bottom, and progressively more abstract abilities are represented at successively higher levels.

Structures of this type are relevant to research concerned with cognitive aging because they can be used to investigate the breadth of age-related influences across a variety of different cognitive variables. As noted above, when variables are considered separately there is an implicit assumption that each variable has an independent age-related influence. However, when multiple variables are organized into a structure, the degree of independence of age-related influences can be investigated by examining the extent to which age-related influences operate at different levels in the structure. For example, age-related effects restricted to individual variables located at the bottom of the structure would correspond to narrow task-specific influences, whereas influences operating at higher levels in the structure are necessarily broader because they affect what variables or abilities at lower levels in the structure have in common. Depending on how far up in the structure the age-related influences are found to operate, therefore, increasingly broad, or more general, explanatory mechanisms will be required.

This structural approach has only occasionally been applied in cognitive aging research because it requires the availability of many variables from relatively large samples of adults, and the majority of research in the field has focused on single variables in comparisons involving small groups of young adults and old adults. Nevertheless, several studies have revealed a large influence of age on the highest-order, or most general, factor in this type of correlational structure, with additional influences on a few abilities and individual variables.[29]

Figure 3.9 illustrates the results of a hierarchical structural analysis based on aggregate data from approximately 2,800 adults in our project. The numbers next to the arrows are standardized regression coefficients that can be interpreted as representing the strength of the relation between the two variables. When considered separately, each of the variables in the analysis was found to have a significant relation with age, in a positive direction for the

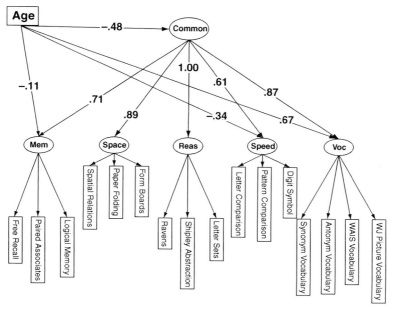

Figure 3.9. Results of an analysis of the influence of age on a hierarchical structure of cognitive abilities in the Salthouse data. The numbers along the arrows are standardized regression coefficients.

vocabulary variables, and in a negative direction for the other variables. However, when the variables were organized into this hierarchical structure, statistically independent influences of age were found on the highest-order factor, which represents what the lower-order factors have in common, and also on first-order factors representing episodic memory and perceptual speed abilities. In addition, there was a positive influence associated with increased age on a construct corresponding to word knowledge. Although not represented in the figure, after taking these higher-order influences into account, the age relations on individual variables were all much smaller than when the variables were examined separately, and for many variables the age-related influences were no longer significantly different from zero.

It is important to emphasize that the outcome portrayed in Figure 3.9 did not have to occur with this type of structural analysis. In fact, analyses of sex differences in the same data revealed that there were no differences between males and females at the highest level in the structure, but males were somewhat lower than females on the first-order memory ability, and somewhat higher than females on the first-order spatial ability.

The implication from structural analyses such as these is that explanations are needed to account for influences of age on what different cognitive abilities have in common, and additionally on speed ability, memory ability, and on measures of word knowledge. Because statistically independent influences of age are apparent on a few individual variables, some task-specific explanations will also be required. However, the existence of age-related influences at higher levels in the structure suggests that a relatively small set of mechanisms may be able to account for a large proportion of the cross-sectional age differences apparent across a wide variety of cognitive variables.

As mentioned in the previous chapter, some studies have examined correlations among longitudinal changes, and the discovery of moderate correlations among the changes in different cognitive factors or composite scores has been interpreted as suggesting the operation of broad age-related influences. Although informative, few of these analyses directly addressed the dimensionality of change because the factors in these analyses were established on the basis of analyses of the level of performance at a single measurement occasion, rather than on the basis of changes among individual variables. In other words, the prior research has focused on evaluating change in existing factors rather than on determining whether changes can be organized into factors.[30]

Contextual Analysis

A recently proposed analytical procedure can be viewed as a combination of the two previous approaches because it involves examining age-related effects on individual variables after statistically controlling influences operating through established cognitive abilities. Figure 3.10 illustrates the framework for this type of contextual analysis. As in the other figures, boxes represent variables that are

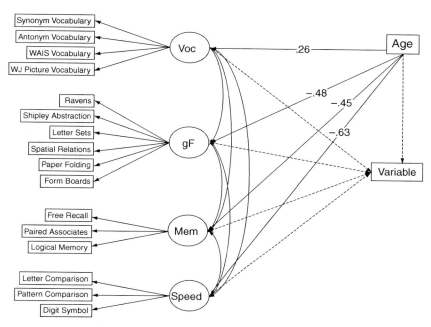

Figure 3.10. Analytical framework for the contextual analysis approach to investigating unique age-related influences on a target variable. The numbers along the arrows are standardized regression coefficients.

actually measured, and circles represent theoretical constructs that are hypothesized to be responsible for the variation in other constructs or variables. Arrows portray hypothesized causal relations, and in this particular figure, solid arrows represent relations that have been established in past research and dotted arrows represent potential influences on the target variable.

The basic assumption in the contextual analysis procedure is that age relations have already been established on many cognitive abilities, and consequently influences of age on new variables should be interpreted in the context of what is already known. A special feature of this procedure is that it ensures that any direct, or unique, age-related effects on the target variables are statistically independent of effects that are already recognized.[31] That is, because the analytical model contains relations from the reference abilities to the target variable, age-related influences on these abilities are taken into consideration when investigating the direct relation from age to the target variable.

Another valuable feature of the contextual analysis procedure is that it helps specify what a target variable represents by providing information about the relative magnitude of relations of different cognitive abilities with the target variable. The rationale is that if people who have high levels of ability *A* perform much better on the target variable than people with low levels of ability *A*, then it can be inferred that the target variable is probably related to ability A. However, if people who have high levels of ability B do not perform differently on the target variable than people with low levels of ability B, then it can be inferred that the target variable probably is not related to ability B. Furthermore, because several abilities are examined simultaneously, the analyses indicate the relations of each ability that are independent of the influences of other abilities.

Table 3.2 contains results from the contextual analysis procedure for a variety of cognitive variables that have been examined across a number of separate studies in my laboratory. The numbers in the table are standardized regression coefficients that represent the influence of one predictor after controlling influences of the other predictors. Although different target variables were examined in different studies, they were evaluated with respect to the same cognitive abilities because all of the research participants performed the same cognitive reference tests. Moreover, the values in the table can be assumed to be relatively precise because at least 200 adults across a wide age range participated in each of the studies.

Among the memory variables that have been investigated with the contextual analysis procedure are several that were selected to represent theoretically important distinctions. For example, measures of recall and recognition memory have been examined, as well as measures of memory for different types of nonverbal materials. Also included have been measures of controlled and automatic processing with the remember/know procedure, directed forgetting, source memory, and prospective memory. The original articles can be consulted for details of the procedures used to obtain the measures, and how the results have been interpreted.[32]

A number of important points should be noted regarding the results summarized in Table 3.2. First, as might have been expected, most of the variables from tasks designed to assess memory were found to be closely related to the episodic memory reference ability. Second, the analyses suggest that memory for nonverbal materials may have closer linkages to fluid ability than to memory ability, which could mean that remembering nonverbal information involves different processes or representations than remembering verbal information. It is also interesting that several measures of memory for the source of the information, as opposed to the information content, were related to fluid ability. These findings raise the possibility that accessing information about context may involve reasoning-like processes instead of, or in addition to, memory processes.

Another noteworthy result in Table 3.2 is that measures of remembering information while carrying out processing of the same or other information, in tasks designed to assess working memory, were more closely related to fluid ability than to memory ability. These findings are consistent with many other reports of strong relations between working memory and fluid ability, and they suggest that memory in the service of cognition, which is one way in which working memory can be conceptualized, may be a critical feature of fluid aspects of cognition.

Table 3.2. Contextual Analysis Results

Variable	Age Total	Age Unique	Gf	Mem	Speed	Voc
Word recall (1)	−.51*	−.21	−.05	.72*	−.01	−.01
Word recall (2)	−.39*	−.20	−.09	.42*	.14	.17
Word recall (3)	−.40*	.02	−.15	.65*	.23	−.07
Word recognition (1)	−.02	.17	−.04	.40*	.10	.13
Word recognition (2)	−.12	.30	.03	.39*	.29	−.03
Word recognition (3)	−.06	.37*	.22	.30*	.15	−.21
Recognition—"remember"	.08	.30*	−.11	.46*	.09	−.04
Recognition—"know"	−.13	−.17	.09	−.08	.00	.21
Directed forgetting						
Words—remember	−.39*	−.20	−.09	.42*	.14	.17
Words—forget	−.10	−.03	−.04	.22	−.03	−.01
Pictures—remember	−.29*	.17	.07	.48*	.27*	−.14
Pictures—forget	.03	.07	−.45*	.44*	.10	.02
Nonverbal memory						
Dot pattern recognition	−.30*	.14	.72*	−.08	.13	−.07
Figure recall	−.48*	−.11	.46*	.16	.02	−.17
Spatial recall	−.40*	.05	.67*	−.06	.16	−.09
Prospective memory						
Running memory	−.32*	−.15	.05	.28*	.06	.09
Drawing classification	−.28*	−.18	.07	.31*	−.09	.08
Source memory						
Color of word	−.24*	.09	.35*	.37*	−.19	−.23
Location of picture	−.50*	−.12	.33*	.18	.06	−.19
Working memory						
Operation span storage	−.33*	.03	.40*	.07	.20*	.03
Symmetry span storage	−.50*	−.10	.71*	−.05	.01	−.13*
Reading span storage	−.22*	−.12	.40*	.05	−.03	.21
Keeping track	−.15*	.08	.55*	.15	−.20	−.09
Running memory letters	−.17*	.24	.78*	−.03	.02	−.12
Running memory positions	−.35*	.15	.81*	.04	.03	−.19
Reasoning						
Analysis synthesis	−.23*	.02	.83*	−.04	−.14	.09
Mystery codes	−.56*	−.21	.73*	−.09	.05	−.02
Logical steps	−.29*	.08	.82*	.10	−.08	.02

*$p > .01$.
Gf, fluid intelligence; Mem, memory; Voc, vocabulary.

Other types of variables have been found to be influenced by different cognitive abilities, with some primarily related to speed, others to fluid ability, and a few to vocabulary knowledge. These results support the usefulness of the contextual analysis procedure in identifying characteristics of people that are important in the successful performance of different types of cognitive tasks. The reference abilities used in these analyses are not necessarily the most primitive or fundamental that could be proposed, but they were selected largely because they correspond to factors identified in the structural analyses as having unique age-related influences.

A particularly interesting outcome of the contextual analyses concerns the estimates of unique age-related influences on the target variables because they represent age-related effects on the variables that are statistically independent of effects on the reference abilities. The discovery that most of the unique age-related influences on the variables were very small suggests that age-related influences on the target variables overlap almost completely with the age-related influences on the reference variables in cross-sectional data. An implication of these results is that an explanation of effects on the four reference abilities will be sufficient to account for effects associated with cross-sectional age differences on a wide variety of cognitive variables. Stated somewhat differently, although a very large number of cognitive variables has been found to differ as a function of adult age, the contextual analysis results suggest that a relatively small number of statistically independent influences may be contributing to those differences.

This brief description of the macro approach to cognitive aging reveals two possible reasons the approach has not been widely used: the data requirements are considerable because multiple variables are needed from many individuals of different ages, and the analytical methods can be somewhat complex. Nevertheless, results from the different types of independence analyses are consistent in suggesting that only a small portion of the age-related differences observed on a given cognitive variable appear to be specific to that variable. The clear implication is that explanations are needed that incorporate mechanisms broad enough to account for effects that are shared across different types of cognitive variables, as well as those for effects that are restricted to particular cognitive tasks. Unfortunately, the analytical methods are primarily informative about the existence of these types of influences, and at the current time only tentative speculations can be offered about the specific nature of any broad mechanisms that might be operating.

Conclusions

Complaints about memory are more frequent with increased age, but research has revealed that those reports are only weakly related to objective measures of memory. Self-reports about one's memory may therefore represent an individual's mood or psychological state as much, or more, than his or her actual level of memory functioning.

Age differences have been documented in many measures of memory in large representative samples, and the magnitudes of the differences appear to be roughly similar across a variety of stimulus materials and retention intervals. The field of memory is a very active area of research, with many models and sets of empirical phenomena. Although there have been numerous speculations about possible exceptions to the general patterns of age differences in memory, some of the initial results with new procedures or paradigms have not proven to be very consistent after additional research has been conducted. Other areas of cognition have not been as extensively investigated as memory, but they are similar in the emphases on task-specific models and the dominance of the univariate approach in age-comparative research.

Both micro and macro approaches have been used to investigate age differences in memory and other cognitive abilities. These different perspectives on how to characterize the relations of age on cognitive functioning each have strengths and weaknesses. For example, the micro approach is valuable in providing a more precise description of what needs to be explained, but questions can be raised about whether different measures truly reflect the hypothesized components, particularly beyond the specific task in which they are measured, and the extent to which the age-related effects on one component are independent of age-related effects on other components and variables.

The primary weakness of the macro approach is the requirement for multivariate data with moderately large sample sizes and multiple variables from each individual. Studies of this type are time consuming and expensive, and thus it is not surprising that they have been much less frequent than univariate studies. However, research from macro studies has not only confirmed that most cognitive variables are moderately correlated with one another but has also revealed that large proportions of the cross-sectional age-related differences on various types of cognitive variables are not independent. These findings therefore raise the possibility that a great deal of the research investigating age differences in specific aspects of cognitive functioning may have been studying somewhat different manifestations of the same phenomenon. An important challenge for future research is to characterize the nature of this broader phenomenon and to explain the mechanisms responsible for it.

4

Mediators and Moderators of Cognitive Aging

Major issue: How can causes of cognitive aging be investigated?
Related questions: What type of information can be obtained from mediation analyses, and what are the limitations of this procedure? What type of information can be obtained from moderation analyses, and what are the limitations of this procedure? What are the likely roles of education, health status, sensory limitations, lifestyle, and personality on the relations between age and cognition?

A key question in light of the strong relations between age and various measures of cognitive functioning documented in the previous chapters is, How can those relations be explained? Stated in abstract terms, if the relevant measure of cognitive functioning is designated as Y, and a potential cause of the age differences in Y is designated as X, a fundamental issue is how can one investigate the hypothesis that X is responsible for, or at least contributes to, the relation between age and Y?

It is widely recognized that the ideal method of investigating cause–effect relationships is a randomized clinical trial in which one randomly selected group of individuals receives a treatment, while another randomly selected group of individuals does not receive the critical "ingredient" of the treatment; but the two groups are identical in all other respects. Among the requirements for a study of this type are the ability to manipulate the critical factor in the treatment, the ability to randomly assign individuals to groups, and the ability to monitor relevant outcomes. Unfortunately, none of these requirements is easily satisfied in research on cognitive aging. First, relatively little is currently known about the causes of cognitive aging, and even if the critical factors were identified, they would likely be difficult to manipulate in humans. Second, studies with random assignment of individuals to treatments to examine effects on the rate of aging are seldom, if ever, practical with humans. Not only are there ethical concerns about the random assignment of people to treatments that could have a major impact on one's lifestyle, but there are practical difficulties of ensuring compliance with a treatment over an extended period. And third, manipulation research of this type is only informative about effects on aging if the individuals are followed over a period long enough to detect possible differences in rates of aging. Many studies have only examined effects of a manipulation on the immediate level of performance, and thus they are not necessarily relevant to the relations between age and cognitive performance. The critical information for studies of causes of cognitive aging is not the difference between control and treatment groups immediately after the intervention, or even at various intervals after the treatment. Instead it is the *relation* between age and measures of cognitive performance, or of the *rate of age-related change* in the variable of interest.

How can the role of X on the age–Y relation be investigated without random assignment to experimentally manipulated levels of X and long-term monitoring? At least two research strategies could be used. One strategy consists of conducting research with nonhuman animals in which random assignment to treatment conditions and long-term monitoring are more feasible. The ability to randomly assign research participants to experimental and control groups is a clear advantage of this approach, but important disadvantages are that not all aspects of cognition can be investigated in other species, and the results might have limited generalizability to humans.

A second strategy that can be used to investigate causes of cognitive aging is based on correlational research with humans. Because this approach tends to rely on naturally occurring variation in the levels of X, it yields only weak inferences about the causal role of X on the relations between age and Y. Nevertheless, two analytical procedures—mediation and moderation—can be informative about potential causes of age–cognition relations. Both are based on the principle that although correlation does not imply causation, in many cases causation does imply correlation.

Mediation

Statistical mediation is an analytical procedure that can be used to investigate the hypothesis that the age relation on variable Y is at least partially caused by, or mediated through, variable X.[1] To illustrate, assume that it is hypothesized that the decrease in hearing sensitivity (variable Y) with increased age is caused, at least in part, by cumulative exposure to noise (variable X). An implication of this hypothesis is that the relation of age to Y should be smaller if there was no variation in X. That is, if the hypothesis is correct, then little or no age-related hearing loss would be expected among people for whom there was no age-related increase in cumulative exposure to noise.

This implication can be investigated by examining the age–Y relation after controlling the variation in X. Even if the value of X cannot be experimentally manipulated, the age–Y relation can be examined among people who have little or no variation in X to determine whether they also exhibit little relation between age and Y. Because the association between two variables, in this case between age and Y, is postulated to be mediated through another variable, X, this type of analysis is known as mediation analysis.

There are three major predictions of mediation analyses of cognitive aging. First, if X mediates the age–Y relation, then the variable of age should be associated with X because X is not meaningful as a mediator of the age relations if it is not related to age. Second, X is predicted to be associated with Y because the hypothesized mediator must be related to the target variable or it cannot function as a mediator. And third, reduction of the variation in X is predicted to result in a decrease in the relation between age and Y. That is, if the causal pathway between age and Y is from age to X, and from X to Y, then eliminating the link through X should reduce, or possibly even eliminate, the age–Y relation. Because it is not the existence of X, but rather variability in the values of X, that is responsible for its relations with other variables, the hypothesized causal link can be broken by eliminating the variation in X. To illustrate, in the example of age, cumulative noise exposure and hearing loss, the relevant comparison sample is not people without any noise exposure, but rather people who all have approximately the same level of cumulative noise exposure. The two primary methods used to reduce the variation in X are matching, which involves comparing people of different ages who are very similar in their values of X, and statistical control, which involves comparing people of different ages who are statistically equated with respect to the values of X.

A relatively large number of studies concerned with aging and cognition have focused on the relations between age and a single variable. Research of this type can be considered primarily descriptive because it does not examine whether the age-related increases on that variable are a potential cause, or consequence, of age-related influences on other variables. Although descriptive research is valuable as a first step, the plausibility of causal hypotheses can be examined with additional information of the type described above.

Mediation analyses address the question of whether people who do not differ on a hypothesized causal variable, X, still exhibit the same relation between age and some other variable, Y, as people who do vary with respect to their values of X. This analytical method can be viewed as a special case of the variance control procedure described in the previous chapter to investigate independence of age-related influences because mediation analyses are based on the assumption that the reason variables do not have independent relations to age is that the effects on one variable are mediated through effects on the other variable. The analyses can be as simple as examining different types of correlations among age and two variables (i.e., X and Y), or they can be quite complex and involve many measures of X and of Y at multiple ages and at multiple time points.

Mediation analyses are fairly straightforward in cross-sectional comparisons. That is, if the hypothesis is that something associated with increasing age causes a change in variable X, which in turn causes a change in variable Y, then the implication is that eliminating the variation across people in X should reduce the cross-sectional relation between age and Y. Given certain assumptions (e.g., that the relations are linear, that the variables are measured reliably, and that no critical variables are omitted), this prediction can be readily tested with cross-sectional data in the manner described above.

However, the longitudinal equivalent of this type of statistical control is not immediately obvious. What might seem to be a comparable prediction is that if there was no change in X, then there would be no change in Y, but in order for this prediction to be tested the temporal relation between changes in X and changes in Y would need to be specified. Because a causal hypothesis implies that change in one variable (e.g., X) precipitates, and therefore precedes, later change in another variable (e.g., Y), the relation between the two changes should be sequential and not concurrent. However, unless the interval between the cause and the effect is known, as well as whether there is a critical temporal window within which the causal influences must operate to be effective, mediational results with longitudinal data can be difficult to interpret.[2]

Unfortunately, almost no information is currently available about the timing of causal events in cognitive aging, or about the interval between change in one variable and change in other variables.[3] Moreover, the analyses will become very complicated if, as seems likely, there are differences across variables and across people in the timing of when the changes occur in each variable, in the intervals between changes in the leading (or cause) and lagged (or effect) variables, and possibly also in the threshold values of X that must be exceeded before a change is triggered in Y.[4]

Finally, a key requirement for meaningful application of mediation analyses is that the measures of change in the X and Y variables are reliable, and as noted in Chapter 2, there is still limited evidence regarding the reliability of measures of longitudinal change. This is particularly true for adults under about age 60, which may be the age range of greatest theoretical interest because this is when many cognitive changes first occur. Although some researchers have interpreted results from analyses of correlated change in longitudinal research as relevant to the causal sequencing of variables, the issues just mentioned suggest that much more information is needed before strong conclusions about causal order would be justified from longitudinal data.

Mediation analysis can be a powerful tool for investigating causal implications, but several issues need to be considered when interpreting mediation outcomes. One issue concerns the logical status of mediation analyses. In some respects the reasoning underlying mediation analysis can be considered analogous to the *modus ponens* argument in logic[5]:

> *If P then Q*
> *P,*
> *Therefore Q,*

with P corresponding to the hypothesis that X mediates the age–Y relation, and Q corresponding to the prediction that the age–Y relation is reduced when the variation in X is controlled. Careful consideration of this argument reveals that only a failure to find Q is informative in evaluating the validity of the hypothesis, and that particular outcome would suggest that the hypothesis was false. That is, a failure to find a reduction in the age–Y relation after controlling the variation in X (i.e., not Q) would be inconsistent with the hypothesis (i.e., P) that X mediates the age–Y relation.

Advocates of the P hypothesis would obviously prefer an outcome of Q rather than not Q, but it is important to recognize that even this desired result does not allow a conclusion that P is valid. In fact, inferring that P is true from an outcome of Q relies on an argument of the form:

> *If P then Q*
> *Q,*
> *Therefore P,*

which is a logical fallacy known as *affirming the consequent*. Reasoning of this type is not valid because Q could occur for reasons other than P. In the context of research on aging, a discovery that the age–Y relation was reduced after controlling the variation in X would not be definitive with respect to the mediation role of X because many factors besides X could be responsible for variations in the age–Y relation.

It may not be surprising that there have been relatively few formal tests of mediation in cognitive aging research because advocates of a particular hypothesis are usually not very motivated to conduct a test that would only be definitive in the negative direction. That is, failure to find the predicted Q outcome would suggest that the P hypothesis was false, whereas a finding of Q would merely be consistent with P and also with many other hypotheses.

A second issue concerning mediation analyses is that the results can vary according to the reliability of the hypothesized mediator, X (or changes in X). That is, if the reliability is low, then the extent of mediation may be incomplete for statistical rather than substantive reasons. This problem can be minimized by using analytical methods that take measurement reliability into account, such as latent variable structural equation models, but these methods have only been used in a few mediation analyses in the area of cognitive aging.

A third issue is that the relations among age, X, and Y may not be linear, in which case the equating by statistical control may be incomplete, and the mediation results potentially misleading. This particular problem need not be serious because procedures are available to examine whether relations are not linear, and analytical methods, such as transforming a variable or adding polynomial predictors to the regression equation, can be used to deal with most nonlinearities.

A fourth issue concerning mediation is that some of the X–Y relations could be induced by relations of age to both X and Y, in which case those variables could be related to one another only because each is related to age.[6] Although spurious relations such as this could clearly occur, they would be detected in mediation analyses because if X is only related to Y because of its relation to age, then the age–Y relation would not be affected by controlling the variation in X. That is, if X and Y are not directly related to one another, eliminating the variation in X would not have any effect on the relation of age to Y. Nevertheless, if a researcher was interested in investigating the extent to which the relation between variables X and Y was attributable to the relation each variable had with age, the X–Y relation could be examined in a sample of adults within a narrow age range, or after statistically controlling the variation in age.

The possibility that X and Y do not represent distinct constructs is a fifth issue that should be considered when interpreting mediation analyses. Variables X and Y must be related to one another in order for mediation to be plausible, but if they are very strongly related then controlling the variation in one of the variables may be equivalent to partialling the variable from itself. For example, if X and Y are both measures of a similar type of cognitive functioning, then it may not be meaningful to examine the role of one of the variables as a potential mediator of age differences in the other variable because the mediator and the target variables might actually be different measures of essentially the same construct.

A sixth issue in mediation analysis is that statistical control procedures essentially equate everyone at the average level of X in the sample, but it is possible that the age–Y relation could be different at other values of X. For example, there may still be age-related hearing loss when everyone has an amount of cumulative noise exposure equal to the average in the sample, but not among only those people who do not have any noise exposure. This possibility can be investigated by examining interactions of age and X in predicting the level of Y with moderation analyses, as discussed below.

This relatively long list of cautionary issues may give the impression that mediation is not a very useful analytical procedure.[7] This is not the case, and in fact, mediational analyses are among the most powerful methods available to investigate implications of causal hypotheses when random assignment is not possible. However, as with nearly any procedure, the results can be misleading if the method is applied or interpreted improperly.

Moderation

The second correlation-based analytical procedure that can be used to investigate the plausibility of potential causes of age–cognition relations is known as moderation because it examines whether the age–Y relation is moderated according to the value of X. The rationale is that X may be causally involved in the age–Y relation if the strength of that relation varies depending on the magnitude of X. As an example, a finding that the amount of age-related hearing loss (i.e., the age–Y relation) varies according to the amount of cumulative noise exposure (X) would be consistent with the hypothesis that noise exposure is a cause of age-related hearing loss.

Moderation implies the existence of an interaction of age and X in the prediction of Y. That is, if moderation is operating, then people with certain values of X (such as a high amount of education, excellent health, or frequent physical exercise) should have little or no age–Y (age–cognition) relation, whereas strong age–Y relations would be apparent among people with other values of X. There is a sense in which moderation can be viewed as more complex than mediation because in mediation the age–Y relation is postulated to occur because of variation in X, but in moderation the age–Y relation varies in strength according to the value of X. In other words, moderation implies that the age–Y relation is reduced only for certain values of X.

In longitudinal comparisons moderation would be demonstrated if the age-related change in Y was found to vary as a function either of the level of X, or of the age-related change in X. Some of the same complications in tests of mediation apply in tests of moderation, namely, unknown reliability of change scores, uncertain time course of the changes in the two variables, and limited data from adults under about age 60. Nevertheless, a finding that the age-related change in Y varies as a function of the level or change in X would be evidence that some aspect of the change in Y is related to X.

The primary moderation prediction is that the age–Y relation varies as a function of the level of X, perhaps in the direction of a small age–Y relation at low values of X and a large age–Y relation at high values of X. Equivalently, the interaction could be manifested as variation in the X–Y relation as a function of age.[8] For example, the X–Y relation could be small at young ages and large at old ages. In the case of the noise–hearing example, a weak relation between cumulative noise exposure (X) and hearing loss (Y) might be expected in young adults, but because of their greater cumulative noise exposure, the relation would be expected to be stronger in older adults.

It is important to recognize that the existence of moderation of age–cognition relations cannot be determined without examining individuals across a wide age range. People of different ages are clearly needed to allow age–Y relations to be compared, and several ages are also needed if the researcher is interested in examining the X–Y relation at different ages. This point may seem obvious, but the existence of moderation has some-times been inferred, at least implicitly, from the presence of an X–Y relation in a sample consisting of only older adults within a limited age range. Because evidence is needed that the relation varies in magnitude across different ages to infer that moderation exists, one cannot conclude that the age differences are moderated when the comparisons involve a single age group.

Ideally, both mediation and moderation should be examined when investigating possible causes of age–cognition relations because the combina-tion of the two procedures is more informative than either method by itself. For example, there could be evidence of partial mediation if X is related to both Y and age, and controlling the variation in X is found to reduce the age–Y relation. However, it would be misleading to infer that X is responsible for the relation between age and Y if it were also found that the age–Y relations were all significant, and similar, at each level of X (i.e., that there was no evidence of moderation).

What Level of Analysis?

Mediation and moderation predictions can be examined with outcome vari-ables at several different levels of analysis, including measures of performance in individual tasks, or even measures of specific theoretical processes if they are available. A somewhat more abstract level consists of analyses conducted on a combination of several variables hypothesized to represent the same theoretical construct, such as a particular cognitive ability. Advantages of this latter level are that reliability and generalizability tend to be higher, and validity will also often be greater because aggregation across variables will tend to cancel task-specific influences and emphasize the contribution of whatever is common to all variables.

Because our project contains considerable data on four cognitive abil-ities, results of mediation and moderation analyses will be reported for composite variables created by averaging z-scores for the three to six variables that represent each of the four abilities. These composites are broader and more reliable than individual variables, but it is important to note that the patterns for individual variables were very similar. Age relations for the composite variables in the complete sample of approximately 2,500 adults

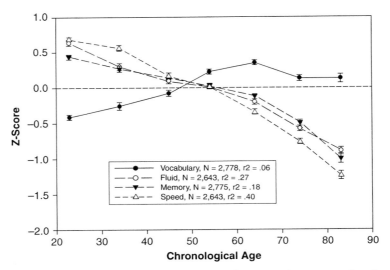

Figure 4.1. Means and standard errors of composite scores for four cognitive abilities as a function of age. Note that the composite scores are based on four vocabulary variables, six fluid ability variables, three memory variables, and three speed variables.

are portrayed in Figure 4.1. It can be seen that the patterns closely resemble those in the figures from Chapter 1, with an increase until about age 60 followed by a decrease for vocabulary, and nearly linear decreases for the other abilities.

The factors examined in the following sections are obviously not all of the possible causes of age differences in cognitive functioning, but they represent some of those that are most frequently mentioned, and they serve to illustrate how mediation and moderation methods can be applied and interpreted with cross-sectional data. In the terminology described earlier, Y is the composite cognitive variable, and X is a measure of the potential cause. Mediation analyses involve examining the age–Y relation before and after statistical control of X, and moderation analyses involve examining the interaction of age and X when predicting Y. Outcomes of all of the analyses are summarized in Table 4.1, with results relevant to mediation in the top panel and results relevant to moderation in the bottom panel. The values in the top panel of the table are proportions of variance in the composite cognitive variable associated with age before (top row) and after (subsequent rows), controlling the variance in the hypothesized mediator. Values in the bottom panel are the proportions of variance associated with the interaction of age and the hypothesized moderator variable. Figures are also presented for some of the variables to portray the age–Y relations after statistical control of the variation in X, and at values corresponding to the 75th and 25th percentiles of the distributions of the X variable.

Table 4.1. Mediation and Moderation Results with Composite Variables

Mediation—Proportion of Variance Associated with Age

	Vocabulary	Gf	Memory	Speed
Without any control	.06	.27	.18	.40
After control of:				
Education	.03	.32	.21	.43
Health composite	.09	**.17**	**.13**	**.26**
Visual acuity	.06	**.13**	**.10**	**.19**
Cognitive stimulation	.06	.27	.18	.39
Physical exercise	.07	.27	.18	.39
Need for cognition	.07	.25	.17	.38
Neuroticism	.06	.28	.18	.40
Extraversion	.06	.28	.18	.41
Openness	.05	.29	.19	.42
Agreeableness	.06	.29	.18	.41
Conscientiousness	.06	.28	.18	.41
Satisfaction with life	.06	.31	.20	.42
CES–depression	.06	.28	.19	.39
Trait anxiety	.05	.29	.18	.39
State anxiety	.05	.30	.19	.42
PANAS positive mood	.07	.26	.17	.40
PANAS negative mood	.05	.30	.19	.41
All variables	.04	.13	.09	.16

Moderation—Proportion of Variance Associated with Interaction

	Vocabulary	Gf	Memory	Speed
Interaction of age and:				
Education	.01	.01	.01	.00
Health composite	.00	.00	.00	.00
Visual acuity	.01	.00	.01	.01
Cognitive stimulation	.01	.00	.00	.00
Physical exercise	.00	.00	.00	.00
Need for cognition	.00	.00	.00	.00
Neuroticism	.00	.00	.00	.00
Extraversion	.00	.00	.00	.00
Openness	.00	.00	.00	.00
Agreeableness	.00	.00	.00	.00
Conscientiousness	.00	.00	.00	.00
Satisfaction with life	.01	.00	.00	.00
CES–depression	.00	.00	.00	.00
Trait anxiety	.00	.00	.00	.00
State anxiety	.00	.00	.00	.00
PANAS positive mood	.00	.00	.00	.00
PANAS negative mood	.00	.00	.00	.00

Boldface indicates that there was a substantial reduction in the age-related variance.
CES-D is the Center for Epidemiological Studies, Depression Scale, PANAS is the Positive and Negative Affect Scale.

Early Speculations

Many potential explanations for age-related cognitive decline have been mentioned beginning with the earliest systematic studies on this topic. To illustrate, a study published in 1933 considered, and rejected, several possible interpretations for the negative relations between age and various measures of cognitive functioning.[9] The hypothesized determinants, and reasons why they were not considered plausible, were as follows: motivation—the tests were designed to be interesting; sensory loss—age differences were not restricted to tests with high visual or high auditory demands; disuse—there was decline in the following directions and common sense tests that assess abilities in frequent use; and speed—there were decreases in the proportion of correct responses and not just in the number of items attempted.

It is noteworthy that some of these same interpretations are still mentioned as potential causes of cognitive aging. Although many factors are likely contributing to the relations between age and measures of cognitive functioning, the challenge is to identify which factors are critical, and to evaluate their relative importance, for different types of cognitive variables. As noted above, one way in which this can be done is to rely on systematic procedures, such as mediation and moderation analyses, that can be informative about the potential role of the hypothesized causal factor on the relations between age and measures of cognitive functioning.

Childhood

Intriguing relations have been reported between measures of early childhood cognitive ability and the level of one's cognitive ability in middle and late adulthood. For example, one project reported a correlation of .63 between the scores on cognitive tests at age 11 and at age 77, and a similar study with an independent sample of participants found a correlation of .66 between scores at age 11 and at age 79.[10] The mechanisms responsible for relations originating in childhood are not yet understood, and no mediation or moderation analyses have apparently been conducted to examine the role of factors operating during childhood on adult age differences in cognitive functioning. Nevertheless, influences on adult cognitive functioning that originate in childhood are potentially important because they could affect the interpretation of results that might otherwise be attributed to processes of aging. To illustrate, if there is a correlation of .6 between the level of childhood cognitive functioning and the level of cognitive functioning at age 70, then 36% of the variability at age 70 can be assumed to be associated with factors that have been present at least since childhood. Ignoring this relation could result in an overestimation of the influence of factors that operate only during the adult years.

Education

Strong positive correlations have often been found between amount of education and measures of cognitive ability. Although this association is well established, its meaning is still controversial. For example, it could be argued that more education is the cause of higher cognitive ability, but it is also possible that higher levels of cognitive ability may be required to gain access to greater amounts of education. Furthermore, many of the influences of education could be indirect and operate through factors that are related to amount of education, such as perseverance, early childhood stimulation, socioeconomic status, exposure to occupational hazards, overall level of health, smoking and alcohol use, nutrition, access to medical care, etc.

Despite these ambiguities, the possibility that amount of education contributes to the relations between age and different measures of cognitive functioning clearly warrants investigation. Inspection of the results of the mediation analyses in our project, summarized in Table 4.1, reveals that statistical control of amount of education led to the relations between age and cognitive variables becoming more negative (e.g., for fluid ability the proportion of age-related variance increased from .27 to .32). Note that this is opposite of the predicted mediation outcome, and it occurs because amount of education in this sample was positively associated both with age and with the measures of cognitive performance. That is, in our project increased age was associated with more years of education ($r = .17$), with adults in their 20s and 30s having an average of 15.1 years of education, and adults in their 60s and 70s having an average of 16.2 years of education. Because eliminating the variation in education made the negative age relations more pronounced, amount of education appears to have been acting as a suppressor variable in these analyses.

Other studies have also reported little or no change in the age–cognition relations after statistical control of amount of education.[11] Although it has sometimes been claimed that education plays an important role in the relations between age and certain measures of cognitive functioning, there is no evidence in these results that amount of education mediates the age–cognition relations apparent in cross-sectional comparisons.

Moderation analyses investigate whether the age–cognition relations vary as a function of amount of education, and in particular, whether the age–cognition relations might be smaller among more people with higher levels of education. The relations between age and composite cognitive scores at different levels of education are portrayed in Figure 4.2, where it can be seen that there was no indication that the age–cognition relations were moderated by amount of education. All of the interactions between age and amount of education in Table 4.1 were very small, and other researchers have also reported nearly parallel age relations at different levels of education.

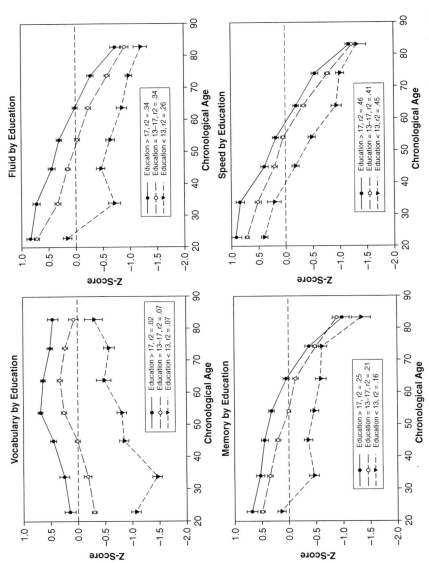

Figure 4.2. Means and standard errors of composite scores for four cognitive abilities as a function of age and at three levels of education.

The available results therefore suggest that although differential amounts of education can influence the magnitude of age–cognition relations when people of different ages vary in their average levels of education, amount of education does not appear to be a major determinant of the association between age and cognition because the relations between age and cognitive functioning are similar among people with different amounts of education.

Health

Certain health conditions and diseases are known to affect cognitive functioning, and their prevalence often increases with advancing age. For example, hypertension, cardiac disease, respiratory disease, and various vitamin deficiencies are all more prevalent with increased age, and each has been reported to be related to at least some measures of cognitive functioning. It is therefore plausible to postulate that health status might be involved in the relations between aging and cognitive functioning.

Unfortunately, health status is a challenging concept to assess because it is almost certainly multidimensional, and yet the specific dimensions of health that are important for different aspects of cognitive functioning are not well understood. Furthermore, comprehensive assessments of health are seldom attempted because they are very time consuming and expensive. Health status was assessed in our project with four self-report questions: ratings of one's overall health; the extent to which one's activities were limited by health; whether any medications were prescribed to control high blood pressure; and the total number of prescription medications currently taken. These are obviously crude questions for the assessment of health, but the results might be expected to be informative because the reports likely incorporate the individual's perception of his or her health in addition to objective health factors, and perceptions of one's health could have effects on cognitive functioning above and beyond any effects associated with actual health status.

Figure 4.3 indicates that there were relatively modest declines with increased age in average self-ratings of health, but fairly substantial increases in the reported number of medications taken per week. Because each health variable had similar relations to the cognitive ability measures, the four variables were combined into a single composite health index by averaging the z-scores, after first converting them if necessary such that higher scores on each variable corresponded to better health[12].

Results relevant to mediation and moderation are summarized in Table 4.1 and in Figure 4.4. Notice that there was a slight increase in the positive relation between age and the vocabulary composite when the variation in the health index was controlled, but that the other age–cognition relations were reduced after statistical control of this health measure. The decrease in

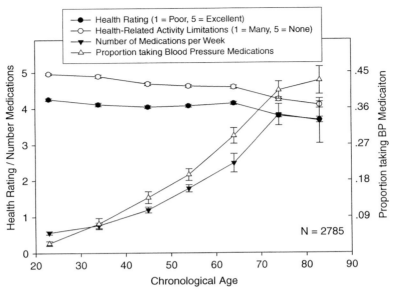

Figure 4.3. Means and standard errors of health ratings and proportion of participants taking medications as a function of age.

the strength of the negative relation is consistent with partial mediation of the age–cognition relation by age differences in health. However, it is important to note that the age–cognition relations for people in the highest and lowest quartiles of the sample on this composite health measure in Figure 4.4 were fairly similar, and there was little evidence in Table 4.1 of interactions between age and health for any of the composite cognitive variables.

Main effects of health status were apparent on some cognitive variables, in each case in the direction of higher levels of cognitive functioning among individuals with better self-reported health. However, this was true to nearly the same extent for people of all ages, and thus the results are not consistent with the hypothesis that the age–cognition relations in this sample were attributable to variations in health status. That is, if X represents health and Y represents cognition, these findings indicate the existence of an X–Y relation, but there was no evidence of moderation because the X–Y relation was no stronger at older ages than at younger ages.

The outcomes of the mediation and moderation analyses involving health are therefore similar to those for education in that the results indicate that age differences in the level of health can distort the relations between age and cognition, but variations in health are unlikely to be the primary cause of these relations because the associations between age and cognition were similar at different levels of health. It is important to emphasize that these results do not mean that health status could not be a factor in the relations between age and measures of cognitive functioning in some samples. What

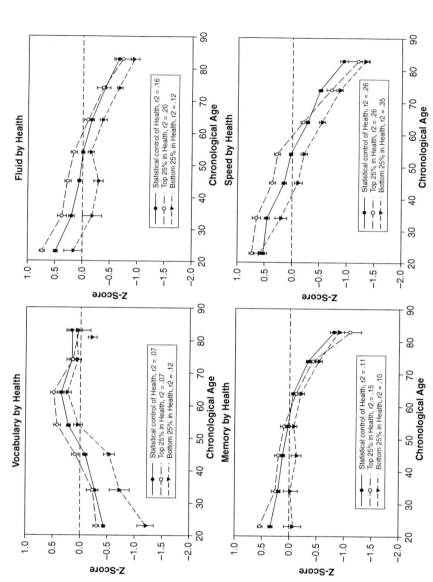

Figure 4.4. Means and standard errors of composite scores for four cognitive abilities as a function of age after statistical control of health, and for adults in the top and bottom 25% of the sample on the health variable.

they do suggest is that differences in health status are probably not the major factor responsible for relations between age and cognition in the types of samples typically studied in research in cognitive aging.

Sensory Limitations

The possibility that cognitive performance is limited by sensory abilities has been mentioned at least since the 1920s and 1930s[13], and it is obvious that if information is never registered then performance on tasks requiring that information is unlikely to be successful. Only one measure of sensory ability was available in our project, and that was the individual's visual acuity at reading distance, measured while he or she was wearing any prescribed corrective lenses. Figure 4.5 illustrates that there was a decrease in corrected visual acuity from an average of about 20/25 at age 35 to an average of about 20/50 at age 55, with smaller decreases after that age. Visual acuity might not have been corrected to the 20/20 level because of failure to update one's prescription for economic or other reasons, or because of an inability to achieve a complete correction due to peripheral or central deficits. Because the first factor is unlikely to be related to age whereas the second factor could be, the age trends in this measure of corrected visual acuity can be tentatively assumed to reflect actual sensory deficits.

Results of the mediation analysis are summarized in Table 4.1, and graphically portrayed in Figure 4.6. Notice that the strength of the age–cognition relations was reduced when the variation in visual acuity was controlled, with a reduction as much as 50% for some cognitive composites. These results imply that that the age–cognition relations in this sample would have been smaller if

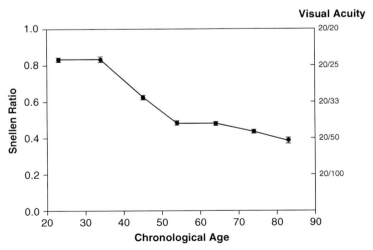

Figure 4.5. Means and standard errors of visual acuity as a function of age.

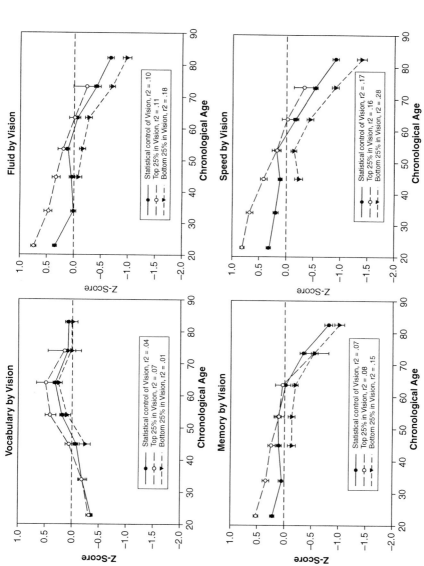

Figure 4.6. Means and standard errors of composite scores for four cognitive abilities as a function of age after statistical control of visual acuity, and for adults in the top and bottom 25% of the sample on the visual acuity variable.

everyone had been compared at the average level of visual acuity. The moderation analyses revealed that people with better visual acuity tended to have higher levels of cognitive functioning than people with poorer acuity, but this was equally true at all ages, and there was no evidence of any interactions of age and visual acuity on the age–cognition relations. (No results are portrayed in Figure 4.6 for young adults with very poor vision, or old adults with very good vision, because of the small numbers of individuals in these categories.)

It is tempting to interpret the mediation results as evidence that decreases in visual acuity may have been responsible for some of the age differences in cognitive functioning. However, it is important to note that eliminating the variation in this measure of visual acuity also reduced the age differences in the composite memory variable based on tests involving auditory stimuli and vocal responses. Because these tests had no visual requirements, the measure of visual acuity in the current project may have been a proxy for some other factor. This interpretation is consistent with several reports of significant relations between measures of cognitive functioning and measures of olfaction, balance, lower limb strength, and lung function.[14] Results such as these have led researchers to question whether sensory differences are the cause of the age–cognition relations, in the sense that sensory factors limit the quantity or quality of information getting into the system, or are merely another consequence of something more fundamental, such as aging of the central nervous system or of multiple systems within the body. If the former is the case, then correction for sensory limitations might be expected to eliminate, or at least greatly reduce, age differences in cognitive performance. In contrast, if the latter is the case, then remediation of sensory deficits should have relatively little effect on the age–cognition relations because the primary limitation is not sensory. Unfortunately, perhaps because of differences in the type of sensory correction and in the nature of processing required in the task, manipulations of sensory factors have yielded mixed results, with some reports of reduced age differences, but other studies finding no alteration of the age differences.[15]

Although there are some uncertainties about the meaning of the measures of sensory function, the mediation and moderation analyses lead to a fairly straightforward conclusion. Namely, visual, and possibly other sensory, deficits may exacerbate age-related declines in cognition, but they do not appear to be responsible for the majority of the age differences.

Physical Exercise

In the last several years there have been a number of reports that the prevalence of dementia was lower among people who engaged in more physical exercise. Positive relations between physical exercise and level of cognitive functioning have also been reported in samples of healthy older adults, with higher functioning among people with more exercise.

Participants in our project were asked about their degree of engagement in several different types of physical exercise. Running and vigorous walking were by far the most frequently mentioned forms of exercise, and thus a single physical exercise variable was created by summing the reported amounts of walking and running per week.

Figure 4.7 indicates that the proportion of individuals reporting no exercise was greater at older ages, which is consistent with the possibility that amount of exercise might mediate age–cognition relations. However, the results in Table 4.1 and Figure 4.8 indicate that there was no evidence of mediation or moderation of age–cognition relations with this running-and-walking measure of physical exercise. That is, statistical control of amount of exercise did not attenuate the age–cognition effects, and the age–cognition relations were similar in people with different amounts of exercise.

Because other forms of exercise were not very frequent, it is unlikely that the weak relations of exercise in our project were attributable to the focus only on running and walking. It is possible that the total amount of time devoted to exercise is too crude a measure, and our assessment might have been more sensitive if we had included intensity information in addition to duration information. Stronger influences of physical exercise might also be found in a sample with a lower average level of cognitive functioning.[16] Alternatively, it may be that what is critical for age–cognition relations is level of physical fitness rather than amount of exercise, and no measure of actual fitness was available in our project. Regardless of the validity of these speculations, however, there is no evidence of a role of exercise in the age–cognition relations with the current

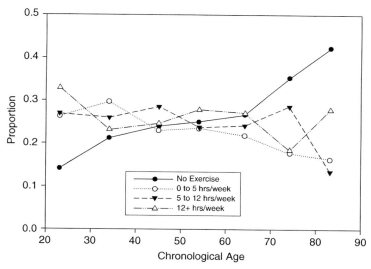

Figure 4.7. Proportions of adults at different ages with different amounts of walking and running exercise.

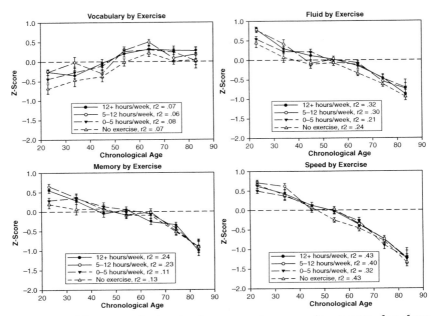

Figure 4.8. Means and standard errors of composite scores for four cognitive abilities as a function of age for adults at four different levels of physical exercise.

data and analyses, and thus any effects of physical exercise on age differences in cognitive functioning that do exist may be rather subtle.

Mental Exercise

The idea that cognitive abilities decline only if they are not used has been very popular, in part because it implies that people have some control over their own cognitive destinies. Versions of this "use it or lose it" idea have been around for centuries, as is apparent in the following quote by Cicero (*De Senectute,* 44 BC): "Old men retain their intellects well enough, if only they keep their minds active and fully employed."

A potential role of cognitive stimulation in the age–cognition relations was also mentioned in the earliest scientific reports in the 1920s[17], and the view that mental exercise affects the rate of cognitive aging is prominent in many books intended for the general public. Advocates of this position frequently refer to an analogy with physical exercise and suggest that just as physical exercise prevents muscle atrophy, mental exercise may prevent brain atrophy.

Research with rodents raised in enriched environments is often cited in support of the mental exercise hypothesis because neurobiological changes after placement in enriched environments have been documented in several studies. However, there have apparently been no reports from these studies of the information that would be most relevant to the mental exercise hypothesis, namely, that age-related declines in measures of cognitive functioning were smaller among animals reared in enriched environments, or that the benefits of enriched environments were larger at older ages.

A recent review of research on mental exercise and mental aging revealed some evidence of a relation between amount of cognitive activity and level of cognitive functioning.[18] However, results such as these can be considered evidence for an overall relation between X and Y, and in order to infer that mental exercise moderated the age–cognition relation there should be evidence that the age–Y relation varies as a function of X, or that the X–Y relation varies as a function of age. The conclusion in the review article was that there is currently little evidence that the relation between age and cognition differs according to an individual's level of cognitive stimulation, or that the effects of cognitive stimulation are greater at older ages.

Objective assessments of the amount or intensity of cognitive activity are not yet feasible in naturalistic settings. Most of the relevant research has therefore relied on self-reports of participation in different activities to assess amount of mental exercise. However, it is difficult to know whether all of these self reports should be viewed as assessing cognitive stimulation because the questions have asked about activities as varied as ballroom dancing, gardening, and participation in clubs. Assessments of mental exercise are likely to be most meaningful when the questions focus on behaviors and activities that might contribute to intellectual maintenance or growth, and not on prior attainments (such as education), or on activities that are primarily social or physical in nature.

The procedure used in our project to assess cognitive activity consisted of asking participants to rate the cognitive demands of each of 22 different activities, as well as estimate the number of hours per week they engaged in each activity. A cognitive stimulation index, created by summing the products of rated cognitive demands and hours of engagement across the 22 activities, was designed to be analogous to assessments of physical exercise that combine duration and intensity in the activity. Evaluations of the cognitive demands of an activity are obviously subjective, which is desirable if they accurately capture true variations across people in the cognitive requirements of the activity, but is undesirable if they reflect extraneous factors that vary from one individual to another. Unfortunately, the relative contributions of these different influences cannot be determined from the available data. However, it should be noted that the mediation and moderation results were very similar when the analyses were repeated with the measure of cognitive stimulation consisting of only the number of hours in the activities, or only the number of hours in the activities with the highest average rated cognitive demands.

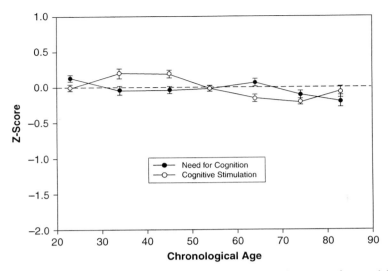

Figure 4.9. Means and standard errors of the self-reported cognitive stimulation variable and the need for cognition variable as a function of age.

Figure 4.9 reveals that age was only weakly related to this measure of self-reported cognitive stimulation. At least among the adults in our project, therefore, there is little evidence of a decrease with age in amount of cognitive stimulation. The entries in Table 4.1 also reveal that there was no evidence of mediation or moderation of the age–cognition relations with this cognitive stimulation index.

Very similar outcomes were found with a self-report assessment of one's tendency to engage in cognitively stimulating activities, known as the Need for Cognition scale. Rather than assessing actual engagement, as in the activity inventory described above, the items in this questionnaire are intended to represent dispositions or preferences. However, the pattern of results was nearly identical to those with the cognitive stimulation index as the scores on the questionnaire were not related to age, and there was no evidence that these dispositions were involved in either the mediation or moderation of relations between age and measures of cognitive functioning.

Currently available assessments of mental exercise have many limitations, but the existing results are not very consistent with the view that age-related decreases in amount of cognitive stimulation contribute to the age–cognition relations apparent in cross-sectional comparisons. Mental exercise could still be important in the relations between aging and cognitive functioning, but better assessment of the type and amount of cognitive activity is needed before strong conclusions can be reached regarding its role in contributing to, or modifying, age-related decline in cognitive functioning.

Personality, Mood, and Anxiety[19]

There is a broad consensus that much of the variation across people in aspects of personality can be captured in terms of five broad dimensions or traits, known as the "Big 5." The five traits are neuroticism (or its converse, emotional stability), extraversion, openness, agreeableness, and conscientiousness, and they are typically assessed by asking people to rate the extent to which various statements apply to them. A numerical value for each trait can be obtained by summing the ratings across the statements considered to reflect each trait.

Figure 4.10 illustrates that there is very little relation between age and the average levels of these personality traits among the nearly 1,900 people in our project who completed personality questionnaires. A slight dip is evident among adults in their 60s and 70s in the level of neuroticism, but the overall pattern is one of remarkable constancy across age in the average level of these traits. Other studies have also reported relatively little cross-sectional age differences in the average level of personality traits, and thus this finding is not unique to the current sample.[20]

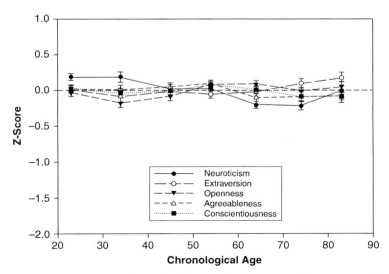

Figure 4.10. Means and standard errors for scores on five personality dimensions as a function of age.

The entries in Table 4.1 reveal that there was no evidence for either mediation or moderation of the age–cognition relations with any of these personality traits. Some of the personality traits were related to certain measures of cognition, as exemplified by a relation between openness and vocabulary ($r = .34$), but there was little change in the age relations after control of the variation in the traits, and there were no interactions of any of the traits with age in the prediction of the cognitive composite scores.

Many of the participants in our project also completed several questionnaires that yield variables that can be broadly characterized as representing either positive or negative affect. The average levels of these variables as a function of age are portrayed in Figures 4.11 and 4.12. The graphs reveal an increase in positive affect, and a decrease in negative affect, among adults in their 60s and 70s.[21] This is a somewhat unusual pattern in research on aging because most cognitive variables have been found to have monotonic age relations beginning from early adulthood. One interpretation of these results is that the happiest period of adulthood appears to be when people are in their 60s and 70s.

Of greatest relevance in the current context was that there was no evidence for mediation or moderation of age–cognition relations with any of the personality or mood variables. Furthermore, very few of the mood variables were related to the cognitive variables. For example, although depression has sometimes been reported to be related to memory, there was no relation (i.e., $r = .02$) between our measure of depression (CES-D) and the composite memory score in this sample.

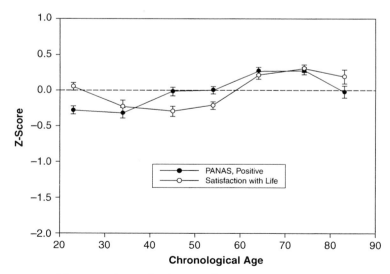

Figure 4.11. Means and standard errors for scores on a measure of positive mood and on the satisfaction with life scale as a function of age.

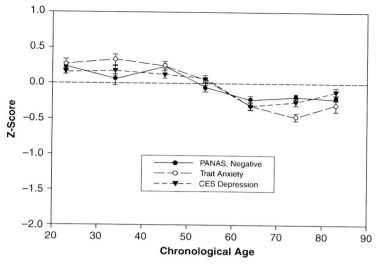

Figure 4.12. Means and standard errors for scores on a measure of negative mood and on anxiety and depression questionnaires as a function of age.

Neurobiology

Because all determinants of cognitive functioning can be assumed to have neurobiological substrates, a complete explanation of cognitive aging will eventually have to include neurobiological variables as potential causal factors. However, because behavior can also influence the brain, lifestyle factors will need to be considered along with aspects of molecular biology and genetics when trying to determine why neurobiological variables change with age.

Some neurobiological variables have an ambiguous status in mediation and moderation analyses because they could function as the X variable (potential cause) or as the Y variable (another reflection of cognitive functioning). The boundary between the two roles is often blurred, but one way of thinking about the distinction is to consider that the goal of an intervention designed to investigate causal influences is to determine how the relations of age and Y are affected by changes in X. Now consider how a particular type of neurobiological variable, such as a measure of brain activation obtained in a study of functional neuroimaging, might be interpreted within this framework. Because it is unlikely that one would intervene to change the locus or level of neural activation, whereas interventions could attempt to target what is responsible for the patterns of activation, functional neuroimaging data might be most meaningfully viewed as representing another type of behavior, albeit behavior more directly reflecting activity of the brain than more overt forms of behavior. From this perspective, therefore, the status of measures of brain activity may be similar to that of hypothesized cognitive processes in that they have the potential to provide a more precise description of what needs to be explained, but they should not be considered a cause or an explanation by themselves. However, other neurobiological variables, such as the quantity of neurotransmitters or measures of the integrity of myelin, might be reasonable targets for intervention, and are thus more analogous to X variables in the current framework.

One neurobiological variable that has frequently been linked to cognitive functioning in adults is brain volume. Many studies have reported that the sizes of certain brain regions shrink with age, or that there is an enlargement with advancing age of the ventricles that contain cerebral spinal fluid rather than white or gray matter. Numerous studies have also reported significant relations between either global or regional measures of brain volume and measures of cognitive performance. Unfortunately, few studies have reported mediation analyses with measures of global or regional brain volume as the hypothesized mediator of age–cognition relations. Furthermore, there is little evidence that the strength of the volume–cognition relation varies as a function of age, as would be predicted if brain volume served as a moderator of age–cognition relations.

Measures of brain volume are relatively crude, and not much is currently known about the specific factors responsible for reductions in brain volume. That is, the extent to which the volume loss reflects neuron death, deterioration of synapses, dendrite or cell body shrinkage, reduction in the number of support cells like glia, alteration in vasculature, or something else, is not yet clear. Unfortunately, these other characteristics are more difficult to measure in living humans than regional or global volume. Although it is often claimed that brain aging is attributable to loss of neurons, early estimates of neuron counts were imprecise because they were based on rather crude quantification procedures, and relatively small numbers of research participants at each age. The initial estimates may also have been inaccurate because they were based on assessments of density, and it has been discovered that younger brains have greater shrinkage of tissue (particularly amount of dendritic branching) after death, resulting in the appearance of higher density. Until there is a better understanding of why volume decreases with increased age, it may not be possible to identify the mechanisms involved in relations among age, brain volume, and cognitive functioning.

Age-related decreases in the quantity or effectiveness of different types of neurotransmitters responsible for propagating neural signals between neurons is another promising candidate that might account for some age–cognition relations. A particularly interesting neurotransmitter is dopamine because it is hypothesized to modulate other neural activity, especially in the frontal lobes. Although it is not yet possible to measure the quantity of dopamine in living humans, indirect estimates can be obtained by using special types of neuroimaging to measure the number of dopamine receptor sites in particular brain regions. This form of imaging is very expensive, and consequently the sample sizes in this type of research have been quite small. Nevertheless, the available results are intriguing because these indirect estimates of dopamine quantity have been found to be related both to chronological age and to the level of several different types of cognitive functioning.

Another potentially important neurobiological determinant of age–cognition relations is alteration in the integrity of myelin. Myelin is the sheathing around axons, and it is largely composed of fat, which is responsible for its white appearance. Myelinated fibers are associated with faster transmission of neural signals, which enhances communication across distributed networks and likely results in more precise temporal coding. Loss of myelin may therefore disrupt the synchronization of impulses, which could lead to functional disconnection. Furthermore, the impact of myelin degradation may be greatest for tasks requiring the most communication across different brain regions.

Integrity of myelin can be assessed by the presence of abnormalities known as white matter hyperintensities, which are abnormal formations of myelin that are assumed to reflect deterioration of myelination. Diffusion tension imaging (DTI) is a special type of magnetic resonance scan that can detect the orientation of water molecules. When the myelinated fibers are intact, water molecule motion is primarily in the direction of the fiber tract, but as the fiber deteriorates the orientations of the molecules become more diffuse. Increased age has been found to be associated both with a greater number of white matter hyperintensities and with DTI evidence of myelin degradation. These measures have also been linked to a variety of cognitive variables, and thus changes in myelin are plausible as a potential mediator or moderator of age-related declines in cognitive functioning.

Relatively little mediation or moderation research has been conducted with neurobiological measures, and the analyses that have been reported have typically been based on very small samples.[22,23] The small samples are understandable because it is often expensive to measure these types of neurobiological variables, but a consequence is that the results can only be viewed as suggestive. The lack of more mediation and moderation research is unfortunate because these types of analyses could be informative about the plausibility of hypotheses concerning age–cognition relations. That is, as with other types of variables, a neurobiological variable (X) would not be plausible as a potential cause of age–cognition relations unless *(1)* it is related to age (Age–X), *(2)* it is related to the criterion cognitive variable (X–Y), *(3)* control of the variable is found to reduce the age–cognition relation (Age–Y controlling X is smaller than Age–Y), and *(4)* there is little relation between age and Y at some levels of the X variable.

Conclusions

There is still little definitive information about the causes of cognitive aging, at least in part because ideal studies, with random assignment to different levels of the hypothesized causal variable and monitoring for decades to examine rates of age-related change, are not feasible in humans. Most of the relevant research has therefore been based on approximations in which age–cognition relations are examined at different levels of the hypothesized causal variable (moderation), or after controlling the variation in the hypothesized critical variable (mediation).

Results from mediation and moderation analyses with cross-sectional data have been informative in suggesting that some hypothesized causes, such as amount of education, health status, sensory ability, amount of physical or cognitive exercise, and level of personality or mood, do not appear plausible as major determinants of the relations between age and cognitive functioning. Some variables, such as amount of education, health status, and sensory ability have been found to influence the age–cognition relations, but they do not appear to be primary causes because substantial relations between age and measures of cognitive functioning are still evident at every level of these variables. Longitudinal research investigating moderation or mediation of age–cognition relations has been very limited, and primarily restricted to the period of late adulthood. Furthermore, issues of the sensitivity and reliability of measures of change and the timing of causes and consequences have not yet been resolved, and consequently the currently available longitudinal results need to be interpreted cautiously when trying to reach conclusions about causes of age-related changes.

5

Normal and Pathological Cognitive Aging
in Late Adulthood

Major issues: How is normal cognitive aging distinct from pathological aging?
Related questions: How early before dementia is diagnosed are symptoms
  apparent? Which categories of risk factor research are likely to be most
  informative in identifying potential causes of cognitive decline and
  dementia? What are the major risk factors associated with cognitive decline
  and dementia, and what are the relevant mechanisms?

The focus in the current chapter is on cognitive functioning in late adulthood.
Because the results discussed in the previous chapters were based on people
who report themselves to be in good to excellent health, who live independently in the community, and who are generally functioning at high levels in
their daily lives, the findings can be considered to reflect normal (or perhaps
even supra-normal) cognitive aging. Those results are informative in their
own right, but it is natural to wonder if, and how, the age-related cognitive
differences apparent in young and middle-aged adults might be related to the
pathological aging conditions that become progressively more common after
about 70 years of age. If such relations were found to exist, a question of
particular interest would be what is responsible for some people continuing
on the same trajectory as in early adulthood, and others experiencing more
rapid cognitive decline associated with pathology. Unfortunately, because
there is almost no research relating age-related changes in young and

middle adulthood to normal and pathological changes in late life, those questions cannot be answered at this time. Instead three related topics are discussed in this chapter. The first topic is dementia, the second is the preclinical phase of dementia, and the third topic concerns risk factors for cognitive decline and dementia.

Dementia

The term *dementia* literally refers to loss (de-) of cognitive or mental (-mentia) abilities. Dementia is a particularly devastating condition because decline of memory and other cognitive abilities results in the loss of one's sense of identity. It is therefore not surprising that a recent survey indicated that dementia is the most feared disease among Americans above 55 years of age.[1] In fact, this fear is sometimes termed "alz-ism," as though worry about developing the disease was a separate disease itself.

Several different types of age-related cognitive pathologies, or dementias, have been identified, with Alzheimer disease (AD) the most common. Alzheimer disease accounts for about 60% to 70% of dementia cases, with vascular dementia (also known as multi-infarct dementia) estimated to account for between 15% to 20%, Lewy body disease accounting for about 10% to 20%, and frontotemporal dementia accounting for approximately 5% of dementia cases. However, because it is sometimes difficult to distinguish among types of dementia, and because more than one type can occur simultaneously, it is important to recognize that these frequency estimates are only approximate.

Prevalence and Incidence of Dementia

Prevalence refers to the number of individuals who have a disease at a particular time, regardless of how long they have had the disease, whereas incidence refers to the number of new cases that occur within a specified time period. Estimates of both the prevalence and incidence of dementia differ across research studies because of variation in the types of samples examined (e.g., random selection of individuals from the community versus people referred to a memory disorders clinic), and in the criteria used to classify individuals as demented. Classifications can be crude, such as when they are based on the score on a screening test like the Mini-Mental Status Examination (MMSE), or they can be more formal and based on detailed neuropsychological assessments, including structured interviews with the patient and an informant such as a close friend or relative. However, the most definitive diagnostic evaluations require confirmation by the presence of a particular neuropathological pattern in an autopsy, which obviously does not occur until after the patient has died.

Although the absolute numbers vary, there is considerable agreement regarding the relative age trends in the incidence and prevalence of dementia. Incidence rates tend to range from less than 1% per year for people between 65 and 69 years of age, to almost 5% per year for people between 85 and 89, and prevalence estimates range from about 0.8% between 65 and 69 years of age, to between 30% and 50% for adults over age 85[2]. It is clear that both the number of new cases, and the total number of cases at any given time, increase dramatically with increased age. These numbers are sometimes interpreted as reflecting a recent dementia epidemic, but the major reasons dementia is more common now than in the past are probably because it has only recently been recognized as a distinct disease, and more people are living to the age of greatest susceptibility.

The annual costs related to dementia in the United States are enormous, with one recent estimate for both direct and indirect expenses of approximately $148 billion per year. Because of the strong relation of age to incidence and prevalence of dementia, it has been estimated that delaying the onset by 1 year might result in nearly 210,000 fewer prevalent cases after 10 years, and at a cost per patient of $47,000 per year, this delay could represent a savings of $10 billion/year after 10 years. Dementia is therefore a major concern not only for individuals and families but for all of society.

Characteristics of Alzheimer Disease

Clinical diagnosis of AD is based on impairment of memory and disruption of at least one additional ability, such as aspects of language, identification of objects, control of motor actions, or abstract thinking and judgment.[3] Two additional defining characteristics of AD are that other causes must be ruled out, and the impairments must be severe enough to interfere with one's daily life.

The most important behavioral criteria that distinguish dementia from normal aging are a decline from one's prior state, and interference with daily activities. In other words, the current level of functioning must be lower than one's earlier level, and the individual's work or daily life must be affected. Unfortunately, both of these criteria can be difficult to evaluate because decline is only definitively established with longitudinal data, and very few sensitive measures of daily functioning are currently available.

An informal way of characterizing the symptoms associated with dementia is with the acronym JAMCO because the most prominent behavioral attributes are problems with: judgment, affect, memory, comprehension, and orientation. Of course, more systematic systems for diagnosing and classifying AD and other dementias are also available. One of the most widely used is known as the CERAD battery because it was developed by the Consortium to Establish a Registry for Alzheimer Disease.[4] This battery of tests was designed to assess the principal cognitive manifestations of AD in the form of memory, language, praxis, and general intellectual status. Among the tests in the battery are immediate and delayed recall of 10 words, copying line drawings, naming pictured objects, and naming as many animals as possible in a fixed period of time.

As noted above, a definitive diagnosis of AD is based on the presence of brain pathologies apparent in an autopsy. The most prominent pathological characteristics are plaques and tangles. Plaques are extra-neuronal β-amyloid proteins surrounded by glial cells and degenerating neural processes, and they are thought to cause oxidative injury and inflammation by the release of free radicals. Neurofibrillary tangles (tau) are tangled bundles of fibers inside the cell bodies of neurons that are sometimes considered markers of neuron death. In specialized Alzheimer Disease Research Centers, the diagnosis of AD based on clinical examinations, interviews, and neuropsychological assessments is quite accurate, as the diagnoses have been confirmed by autopsy in over 90% of the cases.[5] However, diagnostic accuracy is likely lower in other settings that rely on crude instruments like the MMSE, or that may not even use cognitive assessments to reach a diagnosis.

Treatment

Although there are no cures for AD at the current time, as of 2008 two categories of medications have been approved for use by the U.S. Food and Drug Administration on the basis of safety and efficacy studies in clinical trials. One class of approved medication is known as cholinesterase inhibitors because these drugs inhibit the action of an enzyme that breaks down the acetylcholine neurotransmitter, such that the transmitter remains at the synapse longer and potentially enhances neural communication. Medications in this category, with the commercial name in parentheses, are Tacrine (Cognex), Donepezil (Aricept), Rivastigmine (Exelon), and Galantamine (Reminyl). The second category of FDA-approved AD medication, Memantine (Namenda), is most often used for more advanced AD. It is intended to reduce the action of the glutamate neurotransmitter because AD has been found to be associated with excess release of this neurotransmitter.

The evidence based on randomized clinical trials indicates that these medications slow the progression of the disease, but that they neither stop nor reverse it. In fact, a recent summary of the drug research on AD claimed that the drugs "temporarily slow worsening of symptoms for about 6 to 12 months, on average, for about half of the individuals who take them."[6] Although results such as these might not seem very impressive, even a delay of 6 months until placement into a nursing home could result in sizable financial savings and substantial benefits in the quality of life for the patient, caregiver, and family members.

No truly effective treatment for AD is available at the current time, but it is widely accepted that treatments will likely be most beneficial if they are administered in the earliest stages before the disease has progressed to a state of irreversible damage.[7] One of the contributions of cognitive aging research could therefore be to develop and apply cognitive assessments to identify the earliest stages in the disease.

Detection of Impending Alzheimer Disease

Implicit in the criteria for dementia is that the decline in cognitive performance is more severe than what occurs in normal aging. There is still some controversy about whether the distinction between dementia and normal aging is qualitative or quantitative, but dementia clearly involves more profound deficits than those that occur in normal aging. One informal way of characterizing the relative severity of the deficits in the two conditions is as follows: it is normal to have problems remembering where you placed your keys, but you should be concerned if you do not recognize what keys are when you are holding them in your hand.

As noted in Chapter 1, assessments of normal aging involve tasks such as remembering lists of 12 or more unrelated words, identifying rules that relate sets of geometric patterns, imagining the configuration of holes that would result from folding a piece of paper and punching a hole through the folded surface, and so forth. In contrast, because dementia is typically associated with severe impairments of cognitive functioning, the initial screening for dementia is often based on relatively crude global evaluations of cognition.

One of the most frequently used dementia screening tests is the MMSE. It includes items such as remembering three words, drawing two overlapping shapes, and following a three-step command (e.g., take the paper in your right hand, fold it in half, and put it on the floor). The maximum score on the most commonly used version of this test is 30, and the vast majority of healthy normal adults under age 85 with at least 12 years of education tend to have scores of 27 or higher.

Figure 5.1 portrays the age relations on the MMSE for participants in our research project, together with the age relations on several cognitive tests. Notice that in contrast to most of the earlier figures, the vertical axis in this figure represents the proportion of the maximum score at any age. This figure reveals that the same individuals who exhibit little or no age relation on the MMSE exhibit nearly continuous age-related declines on sensitive cognitive tests beginning fairly early in adulthood. Similar discrepancies between the age trends on various dementia screening instruments and the age trends on sensitive cognitive tests have been found in other studies with moderately large samples of adults across a wide age range.[8]

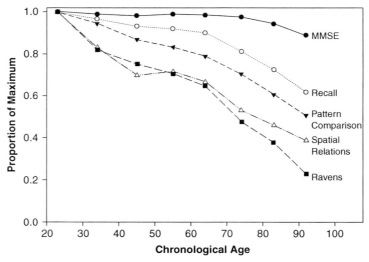

Figure 5.1. Proportion of the maximum score on the Mini Mental Status Exam (MMSE) and on four cognitive tests as a function of age in the Salthouse data.

Another way of illustrating the distinction between the cognitive declines in normal aging and those in dementia is portrayed in Figure 5.2. This figure illustrates the relations of age to performance on a word recall test from a standardized test battery that is often used in assessing dementia.

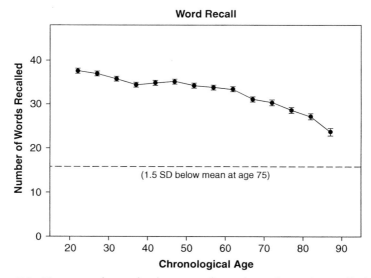

Figure 5.2. Means and standard errors of number of words recalled as a function of age and the performance level corresponding to 1.5 standard deviations below the mean at age 75.

Notice that although substantial age-related decline is evident in normal adults, even at old ages the absolute level of performance is still much higher than the level that might be considered a threshold between normal and abnormal functioning, namely, 1.5 standard deviations below the mean at age 75.

The results in Figures 5.1 and 5.2 indicate that there is a considerable difference in the level of functioning of presumably healthy older adults and demented individuals. Nevertheless, one of the most interesting findings from studies in which samples of adults were followed longitudinally is that there appears to be a long preclinical phase of AD. Specifically, differences in mean level of performance between individuals who will and will not eventually develop AD have been found up to 7 or 10 years prior to the clinical diagnosis. Moreover, several studies have reported that rapid decline is evident only in the 1 to 4 years immediately prior to the diagnosis. Figure 5.3 illustrates these patterns in a schematic form for the MMSE, but similar results have been reported with more sensitive cognitive measures.[9]

The pattern of results portrayed in Figure 5.3 suggests that people who develop AD may have had relatively low levels of cognitive functioning for many years, in addition to experiencing pronounced decline in the 2 to 3 years before they reach the stage at which AD is clinically diagnosed.[10] This period before formal diagnosis of the disease has been of considerable interest because it could be a primary target for interventions intended to delay, or prevent, the progression to dementia.

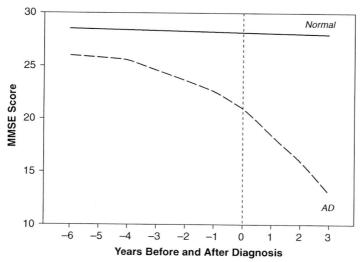

Figure 5.3. Schematic portrayal of the age relations for healthy normal adults and for adults who develop Alzheimer disease for the years before and after diagnosis. MMSE, Mini Mental Status Exam.

Two different approaches have been used to investigate the earliest signs of dementia: the clinical perspective in which the stage prior to formal diagnosis is postulated to correspond to a distinct diagnostic category, and the predictive perspective in which the focus is on identifying cognitive variables that might predict subsequent development of dementia. These approaches are briefly summarized in the following sections.

Preclinical Dementia as a Separate Diagnostic Category

Many terms have been proposed to describe the hypothesized transition state prior to formal diagnosis of dementia. For example, the term *age-associated memory impairment* (AAMI) was intended to refer to memory problems in otherwise healthy adults age 50 and older. The specific criteria for AAMI were as follows: the individual was at least 50 years of age, he or she reported memory loss, and his or her performance was at least 1 standard deviation below the mean of young adults on one or more memory tests. However, these particular criteria have been criticized as unrealistic because they could apply to as many as 90% of adults over the age of 50.

Other terms for this hypothesized transition phase are *benign senescent forgetfulness, age-consistent memory impairment, late-life forgetfulness, aging-associated cognitive decline, age-related cognitive decline, mild cognitive decline, limited cognitive disturbance, mild cognitive disorder, mild neurocognitive decline,* and *cognitive impairment no dementia* (CIND).[11] The most popular term at the current time is *mild cognitive impairment,* or MCI. A consensus report in 2004 proposed the following criteria for MCI[12]: "*(1)* person is neither normal nor demented; *(2)* there is evidence of cognitive deterioration shown by either objectively measured decline over time and/or subjective report of decline by self and/or informant in conjunction with objective cognitive deficits; and *(3)* activities of daily living (ADLs) are preserved and complex instrumental functions are either intact or minimally impaired." As noted earlier in the chapter, the acronym JAMCO is sometimes used to refer to the symptoms of dementia. In a similar manner, the acronym SOUND has been proposed to characterize the symptoms of MCI[13]: subjective memory complaint; objective memory deficit; unaffected overall cognition; normal capacity to perform ADLs; and dementia criteria not met.

One of the original definitions of MCI referred to impairment of a single cognitive function, usually memory, at a level more severe than what would be expected for the person's age, often defined as more than 1.5 standard deviations below age-specific norms, and without signs of dementia such as attention and language deficits. However, three subtypes of MCI were later distinguished: amnestic (memory), multiple domains slightly impaired, and single non-memory domain impaired.[14] The distinctions are potentially important because there is some evidence that only the amnestic category may be strongly related to the subsequent development of AD.

Regardless of the label or the specific criteria, all of these transition-state proposals refer to something different from normal aging that may correspond to the earliest stages of a pathological condition. People in this category have been found to have a high probability of converting to AD, with conversion rates of 10%–15% per year compared to rates of 1%–2% for normal adults. To illustrate, one study found that over a period of 4.5 years 55% of individuals classified as MCI progressed to dementia, but less than 5% of those classified as normal progressed to dementia. However, in some studies a substantial number of individuals have been found to revert back to the normal category after several years, and therefore the status of MCI as a distinct diagnostic category is still somewhat controversial.[15,16]

Prediction of Dementia

The second approach to investigating early dementia is not concerned with whether a separate diagnostic category exists, but rather with identifying variables that have the strongest prediction of later dementia and discovering the mechanisms that might be responsible for these predictive relations. Advantages of this approach are that it does not require an a priori definition of the transition category, it can provide an unbiased description of the period preceding dementia, and it is informative about the duration of the preclinical period.[17]

Some relations with late-life cognitive functioning and dementia have been found many decades before any signs of decline are apparent. For example, a finding from the Nun Study has received a considerable amount of publicity in the popular media.[18] The specific result was that the nuns whose autobiographical essays, written when they were in their late teens and early 20s, were rated low in idea density had a higher prevalence of late-life dementia compared to the nuns whose essays were rated higher in idea density. This relation is intriguing, but it is not yet clear exactly which aspects of cognitive functioning contribute to idea density in written language, and therefore the mechanisms involved in these relations have not been identified. It is possible that the language measures may reflect aspects of general cognitive ability because relations between late-life dementia and a measure of general cognitive ability have been reported at even younger ages. For example, two reports based on separate samples of individuals from the Scottish Mental Survey found that higher cognitive ability scores at age 11 were associated with lower risk of late-onset dementia, but interestingly, not for dementia that occurred before age 65.[19]

The discoveries that measures of cognitive functioning in childhood and in early adulthood were related to cognitive functioning and the likelihood of developing AD in late life were very surprising, and they have led to a number of speculations about the reasons for these relations. One possibility is that factors that contribute to individual differences in cognitive ability in childhood, such as perinatal influences and early environmental conditions, may also contribute to susceptibility to dementia that occurs in late adulthood. That is, there may be a common cause for both phenomena. A second possibility is that childhood cognitive ability may shape various types of health and lifestyle behaviors throughout life, some of which could be related to the likelihood of dementia. And third, because higher childhood ability is related to higher cognitive ability in late adulthood, the relations from early life may simply reflect the fact that it is more difficult to detect early stages of dementia among individuals who are functioning at high cognitive levels.

Only a few studies have investigated AD relations from early life, and most of the research investigating predictors of late-life cognition and dementia has been based on prospective studies in which adults in their 60s or older were assessed longitudinally. Although memory ability might be expected to exhibit the greatest decline prior to the diagnosis of dementia because it is frequently the first aspect of cognitive functioning to be severely impaired in dementia, this does not always seem to be the case. In fact, a recent meta-analysis found that several different types of cognitive variables, including global cognition, speed, and executive functioning, all had effect sizes comparable to episodic memory in distinguishing between individuals who did and did not go on to develop dementia. The authors of this report emphasized this point in their conclusion, where they stated that "episodic memory does not have a unique status among categories of cognitive markers for identifying forthcoming AD."[20]

The research on early predictors has revealed that, compared to people who do not develop dementia, not only do people who go on to develop dementia have a lower average level of performance on many cognitive tests at least several years prior to diagnosis, but in addition they appear to experience rather precipitous decline of functioning within about 3 years of diagnosis. Although these patterns have been reported multiple times and therefore can be considered robust, very little is currently known about the mechanisms responsible for these early signs of impending dementia. Stated somewhat differently, it seems clear that some cognitive differences can be noticed prior to formal diagnosis, but there are still many questions about their exact nature, how early they occur, and whether it is meaningful to refer to a distinct transition category intermediate between normal aging and pathological aging.

The existence of preclinical cognitive impairments raises the question of the extent of distortion of age trends in what are considered normal samples by inclusion of individuals who will eventually develop dementia but who have not yet been diagnosed. If these individuals are included in the sample, then the mean level of functioning will be lower, and the between-person variance will be higher, than in a sample of truly healthy adults. Moreover, to the extent that norms do not just represent normal people but also some people in a preclinical phase of the disease, detection of dementia will be impaired. The problem of mixing preclinical dementia cases with normals clearly complicates the interpretation of age trends among adults over about age 70. One proposed solution to this problem is the use of "robust norms" based on data from individuals who are followed for several years to ensure that they do not develop dementia within a specified time period.[21] Contamination of norms by inclusion of preclinical dementia cases is assumed to be less of a problem at younger ages because of the much smaller incidence of dementia at those ages. However, because relations with late-life dementia have been reported in children as young as age 11, truly robust norms might require that individuals be followed across their entire life span to rule out combining those who eventually will and will not develop dementia from the sample.

Identification of Risk Factors for Cognitive Decline and Dementia

Because many of the same risk factors are relevant both to late-life cognitive decline and to dementia, and because the same data sets are sometimes used to investigate both outcomes, they will be considered together in this section. However, this joint focus should not be interpreted to mean that the same risk factors are necessarily involved in normal aging and in dementia, but rather it simply reflects the convenience of discussing the two outcomes together.

Risk factors for a disease are often identified from epidemiological studies in which people with and without the disease (or other attribute of interest) are compared on a large number of characteristics. Variables found to differ between the groups are considered risk factors if they are associated with higher incidence or prevalence of the disease, and they are considered protective factors if they are associated with a lower incidence or prevalence.

Risk factor results from a single study often receive a great deal of attention in the popular media because of the considerable interest in the topics of age-related cognitive decline and dementia. Although some of the findings eventually turn out to be genuine, many of the results could simply be chance occurrences, and they may not be replicated in subsequent research. Initial results concerning a specific risk factor from a single sample or data set might therefore best be viewed as the basis for a hypothesis that should be investigated, and confirmed, in other data sets before the association is considered established. Another point to recognize about risk factor research is that although it is valuable for indicating the presence or absence of an association, it seldom provides evidence about the nature of the relevant mechanism(s). Other types of research methods are therefore typically needed to discover why an association exists.[22,23]

Finally, it is important to emphasize that risk factor research is inherently correlational, and therefore all of the well-recognized limitations of correlational data apply (e.g., possibility of a third variable affecting both X and Y, and ambiguous causal direction). Despite the reliance on correlational data, inferences based on risk factor research are sometimes phrased in causal terms, as in statements that "Engagement in cognitively stimulating leisure activities has recently been reported to *reduce the risk of Alzheimer disease* ...," or that "... a modification to lifestyle, namely the frequency with which persons engage in cognitively stimulating activities, may *lower the risk of cognitive impairment* in old age (italics added)."[24] These claims imply a causal linkage because they suggest that if there were random assignment to conditions involving engagement in cognitively stimulating activities, a significant difference would be found in the rate of age-related cognitive decline or in the incidence of dementia. Inferences of this type may eventually turn out to be valid, but it is important to recognize that they do not necessarily follow from the mere discovery of a risk factor relation.

Before discussing results with specific risk factors it is instructive to consider strengths and weaknesses of different categories of evidence relevant to the investigation of risk factors. The following discussion will be rather abstract, and it will refer to one variable (Y) as an outcome measure reflecting cognitive performance or risk of dementia, and a second variable (X) as a potential risk factor. However, the various categories can be made a little more concrete by considering a measure of performance on a memory test as Y, and a measure of engagement in cognitively stimulating activities as X. Six categories of research that differ according to the nature of the relevant X–Y relation are listed in Table 5.1. For the purpose of this discussion we will assume that the measures of the changes in X and Y are both sensitive and reliable, but it should be noted that this may not always be the case. The taxonomy is most applicable when Y is a continuous variable such as level of cognitive functioning, but many of the predictors (in the left column) will also be relevant when Y corresponds to a dichotomous variable such as presence or absence of dementia at a particular time.[25]

The first category in Table 5.1 portrays a simple cross-sectional relation between variables X and Y at a single point in time. This is the weakest type of evidence for a causal relation between X and Y because when both variables are measured at one point in time relations attributable to changes in one or both variables cannot be distinguished from pre-existing relations between the variables, and causal direction is ambiguous. In more concrete terms, both memory performance and engagement in cognitively stimulating activities could be influenced by some aspect of the environment in early childhood, and the relation might be attributable to greater engagement in cognitively stimulating activities contributing to better memory, or it might reflect the possibility that participation in these activities is only feasible in individuals with high levels of memory. Stronger inferences from X–Y relations might be possible if it is hypothesized that the current levels of X and Y are due to prior changes in X, because in this case examination of the X–Y relation at different ages would provide relevant information. That is, the relation might be expected to be weaker at young ages, before there has been much opportunity for change to occur in X.

Table 5.1 Possible Relations between a Potential Causal Variable (X) and an Outcome Variable (Y)

Category Relation
1. $X_i - Y_i$ Are variables X and Y related at time i?
2. $X_i - \Delta Y_{ij}$ Is the value of variable X at time i related to the change in variable Y from time i to time j?
3. $\Delta X_{ij} - \Delta Y_{ij}$ Is the change in variable X from time i to time j related to the change in variable Y from time i to time j?
4. $\Delta X_{ij} - \Delta Y_{jk}$ Is the early change in variable X (e.g., from time i to time j) related to later change in variable Y (e.g., from time j to time k)?
5. $\Delta X_{ij}.X_i - \Delta Y_{ij}.Y_i$ Is the change in variable X after controlling the value of X at time i related to the change in variable Y after controlling the value of Y at time i?
6. $\Delta X_{ij}.X_i - \Delta Y_{jk}.Y_i$ Is the early change in variable X after controlling the value of X at time i related to the later change in variable Y after controlling the value of Y at time i?

Category 2 research is an improvement over Category 1 research because change is directly observed in one of the variables. A possible example of this type of research would be when a researcher investigates whether people with higher levels of cognitive engagement at the initial assessment have a smaller decline in memory from the first to the second assessment. Although Category 2 research is more informative than Category 1 research, it still provides a relatively weak basis for causal inferences because the critical factor responsible for the relation with the change in Y might not be X, but any variable that is related to X. In other words, declines in memory could be influenced by anything that is associated with cognitive engagement at a given point in time, such as childhood environment, education, general cognitive ability, or a lifetime of cognitive engagement.

Category 3 research can be more informative than Categories 1 and 2 because change is examined in both the X and Y variables. That is, because relations between two sets of changes are examined in Category 3 research, the results may be more likely to represent coupled influences on change rather than relations of pre-existing influences. A possible example of this type of research is when a researcher investigates whether change in the amount of engagement in cognitively stimulating activities (ΔX) is related to change in the measure of memory (ΔY) across the same interval. To illustrate, a researcher might be interested in determining whether people who have greater increases in their level of cognitively stimulating engagement from age 65 to 75 have smaller memory declines over that age range than people with smaller changes in their level of engagement. A discovery that the changes in the two variables are coupled would strengthen the inference that they are linked, but it is still possible that some other factor is responsible for both changes, such as a decline in health affecting changes in both activity and cognition.

The rationale for Category 4 research is that if the X–Y relation is truly causal, then the change in X would be expected to precede the change in Y. The focus in Category 4 research is therefore on lagged relations, in which the hypothesized cause precedes the hypothesized consequence. A possible example of this type of research is when a researcher asks whether a change in the amount of engagement in cognitively stimulating activities from age 65 to 75 (ΔX_{early}) is related to the change in memory performance from age 75 to 85 (ΔY_{late}). Category 4 research has the potential to be more informative than the preceding categories, but it can be difficult to implement without detailed knowledge of the time course of relevant influences. For example, the temporal relation between change in X and change in Y could be missed if the spacing of the observations is greater than the interval between the leading (cause) and lagged (consequence) events.

Category 5 research controls pre-existing influences on X and Y when examining relations between changes in the variables. This additional control is desirable if the initial value of either X or of Y might be related to the amount or direction of change in X or Y, because to the extent that this is the case then some of the relations among the changes could be indirect reflections of influences on the initial values of X and Y. A potential example of Category 5 research might be if a researcher examines the relation between changes in level of engagement in cognitively stimulating activities, after controlling the initial level of engagement, and changes in level of memory functioning, after controlling the initial level of memory performance. Finally, Category 6 research is similar to Category 5, but with the addition of lagged relations analogous to the difference between Category 3 and Category 4 research.

Although the preceding taxonomy might seem fairly comprehensive, another factor that needs to be considered in risk factor research is that, as noted in Chapter 2, the relation between the changes in two or more variables could vary according to the position of each variable is in its own developmental trajectory. In particular, if all of the observations are collected during the period of later adulthood, one or both variables may have already experienced considerable change, and thus the dynamics of the relations among variables could be quite different than earlier in adulthood when changes in the variables are just beginning.

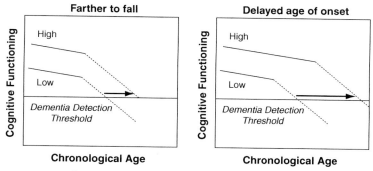

Figure 5.4. Hypothetical functions illustrating the possibility that a risk factor could have an indirect effect by altering the level of cognitive functioning (*left*) or a direct effect by altering the age of onset of the disease.

Finally, the specific nature of the influence on the outcome variable also needs to be considered when interpreting risk factor research. Figure 5.4 illustrates two possible patterns when a variable is found to be related to incidence (or age-specific prevalence) of dementia. The left panel portrays an indirect relation because the risk factor variable is associated with a different level of functioning, and therefore an outcome of later age of onset merely reflects the fact that more time must elapse from the beginning of decline until the diagnosis threshold is reached when the initial level of functioning is higher. In contrast, the right panel illustrates a direct relation to the outcome in that the risk factor variable is associated with an actual delay in the age of onset of decline. Although the second possibility might be more informative than the first in identifying mechanisms responsible for the risk factor relation, the two alternatives are seldom explicitly distinguished.[26]

Most epidemiological research concerned with risk factors for cognitive decline and dementia has involved what would be classified as Category 1 and Category 2 research. There have been a few reports of Category 3 relations, but the most informative categories are 4, 5, and 6, and there is apparently no published risk factor research with this type of evidence. Category 4 research and Category 6 research are both difficult to conduct because little information is currently available about the critical lag between the beginning of changes in X and the beginning of changes in Y, and the data collection and analyses would be further complicated if this interval varied across people. Category 5 research is more feasible, but some researchers may be reluctant to control the initial values of X and Y when examining changes in X and Y because the initial values of X and Y might be assumed to reflect meaningful changes in those variables that occurred before the beginning of the observations. However, evidence relevant to this assumption could be derived from a contrast of the results of Category 5 (with control of the initial values) research and Category 3 (without control of the initial values) research.

Intervention studies can be considered to be similar to research in Categories 3 and higher in that the focus is on changes in Y after a change has been introduced in X. However, they are different in that rather than relying on naturally occurring variations in the change in X, one or more randomly assigned groups receives an experimentally induced change in X. Research of this type provides the strongest basis for causal inferences, but its application in aging has been limited by the practical difficulty of following the individuals over an extended time period. Nevertheless, there have been a number of interventions with short-term follow-ups, and some of these will be discussed in Chapter 6.

Risk Factor Results

A recent consensus report identified 52 factors associated with risk (increased prevalence) or protection (reduced prevalence) for cognitive decline and dementia[27] Among the major risk factors were increased age, hypertension, diabetes, history of strokes, and low mood. Factors with the strongest evidence for a protective role were better baseline cognition, more education, higher socioemotional status, emotional support, and higher levels of physical exercise. Another recent review of major epidemiological risk factors for dementia identified protective effects for stronger social networks and more physical activity or mental activity. Some of these factors were considered as potential mediators or moderators of age-related decline in Chapter 4, but they will be briefly reviewed here with a focus on their role as risk factors for dementia and cognitive decline in the period of late life.

Genetics

Although genetic influences on AD have been clearly established, specific gene mutations seem to account for a relatively small proportion of the total cases of AD. For example, it has been estimated that about 7% of early-onset AD (i.e., diagnosed before age 65), but less than 1% of late-onset AD (i.e., diagnosed after age 65) is caused by known inherited factors. However, the role of genes in AD is somewhat controversial because a recent population-based twin study concluded that both the probability, and the timing, of AD were highly heritable.[28]

The greatest amount of research investigating genetic influences on AD has focused on the Apolipoprotein E (ApoE) gene located on chromosome 19.[29] The relation of this gene to AD was discovered in the mid-1990s, and it has been hypothesized to be involved in plaque formation and efficiency of neuronal repair. There are three versions, or alleles, of the ApoE gene, which are designated e2, e3, and e4. Base rates for single copies of these alleles in populations of European ancestry are approximately 78% for e3, 14% for e4, and 8% for e2. Presence of the e4 allele has been identified as a risk factor for AD because the odds of AD relative to someone with two copies of the e3 allele are 1.2 for e2e4 (i.e., one e2 and one e4 allele), 2.7 for e3e4, and as high as 12.5 for e4e4. The influence of e4 seems to be greatest for people around age 60, which suggests that the e4 allele may affect the age of onset as much, or more, than the probability of acquiring the disease. However, it is important to realize that the influence of the e4 allele is only probabilistic, and not deterministic, because about 30% of AD patients do not have an e4 allele, and about 50% of the people with the highest risk factor of two copies of the e4 allele do not have AD by age 80. It is largely because of this probabilistic nature that a consensus committee recommended against testing for this gene because the presence of the risky allele is not definitive with respect to the eventual presence of AD, and yet information about its presence could lead to increased anxiety on the part of the patient, and possibly expose him or her to discrimination from health insurers or potential employers.[30]

Although the presence of the ApoE gene does not change with age, there has been considerable interest in determining how early in life cognitive differences associated with ApoE might be detected.[31] Unfortunately, the evidence regarding an influence of ApoE on cognition prior to about age 65 has not been very consistent. Some studies have reported impaired cognition among e4 carriers among children and middle-aged adults, but other studies found no relations. One factor that may be contributing to the inconsistencies is that ApoE effects may only be apparent in some variables, perhaps primarily those reflecting aspects of learning and memory rather than other types of cognition.

Education

Because most formal education is completed relatively early in adulthood, the bulk of the research evaluating education as a risk factor for cognitive decline and dementia corresponds to Category 1 or Category 2 research within the taxonomy of Table 5.1, in which education is a static variable assessed at a single point in time. A number of studies have found that higher levels of education were associated with a lower age-specific prevalence, or later onset, of AD.[32] A few studies have also found more education to be related to slower rates of cognitive decline, but there are also a number of failures to find this pattern, and thus the nature of the relation between education and cognitive decline is still controversial.

If a true relation between education and AD or cognitive decline did exist, among the factors that could be contributing to the relation are that amount of education may reflect innate differences in cognitive abilities, education may be indicative of early life factors such as socioeconomic status which could affect both education and AD risk, education may be related to better health practices throughout life that serve as a protective factor which minimizes the consequences of other risk factors, or education may reflect exposure to high levels of mental stimulation during a critical period of one's life that has protective effects with respect to AD. Unfortunately, very little research has been conducted that would allow these possibilities to be distinguished.

Physical Activity

Quite a few studies have identified physical activity as a protective factor with respect to the prevalence or incidence of AD. However, neither the exact nature of the relation nor the mechanism that might be responsible is yet known. For example, it is not clear whether more physical activity actually delays the onset of the disease, or whether early stages of the disease merely limit one's level of physical activity (i.e., reverse causation). Careful examination of the research also reveals that some of the effects are extremely small and were likely only detected because of very large sample sizes. As an example, one study reported a difference in average decline of only about 0.04 MMSE points per year between women who walked a median of 7 blocks per week and women who walked a median of 175 blocks per week.

Furthermore, although there is agreement at a broad level, the results are less consistent when similar measures of physical activity, physical fitness, and cognitive functioning are considered across studies. To illustrate, the study referred to above was published in 2001 and found that older women with a greater level of physical activity at baseline experienced less cognitive decline over a 6-to-8 year interval. This finding of a smaller rate of cognitive decline among people reporting more physical exercise at baseline was replicated in a study published in 2004. However, another study published in 2001 found this relation held only for women and not for men, and a study published in 2006 found a relation between exercise and incidence of dementia only for men and not for women. No relation between reported physical activity at baseline and cognitive decline was reported in a study published in 2003, but that study did report a relation between cardiorespiratory fitness and cognitive decline. Little or no relation between initial level of physical activity and cognitive decline was found in two studies published in 2004, but in one study there was a significant relation between physical activity and the incidence of dementia, and in the other study there was a relation between change in physical activity and change in cognitive functioning. One study only found a relation between physical activity and cognitive decline for individuals without the e4 allele, but another study found the opposite pattern, with a relation between physical activity and cognitive decline only for e4 carriers. Finally, no relations between any measures of physical activity and cognitive decline or incidence of dementia have been reported in other studies.[33]

This brief review reveals that although there are many reports of some type of relation between physical exercise and cognitive decline or risk of AD, there are surprisingly few direct replications. Until the inconsistencies among the studies are resolved it is difficult to reach a definitive conclusion about the specific relation between physical activity and either the magnitude of cognitive decline or the risk of developing dementia.

Cognitive Stimulation

A number of studies have found smaller rates of cognitive decline, and lower rates of prevalence or incidence of AD, for people who report greater levels of cognitive stimulation or mental activity.[34] Furthermore, a recent meta-analysis of 22 studies found that adults reporting more engagement in cognitive activity were almost 50% less likely than adults with little or no cognitive engagement to develop dementia. Unfortunately, as with physical activity, the research literature on this topic is deceptively complicated. In the case of cognitive activity, it is compounded because of variations in the type of activities assumed to be cognitively stimulating, in how activity involvement and cognitive functioning are measured, and in the many different ways in which relations between activity and cognitive decline or incidence of AD have been analyzed. To illustrate, assessments of cognitive stimulation have been based on reports of participation in book discussion clubs, learning a foreign language, and on the frequency of watching television or gardening, and assessments of amount of involvement have ranged from the number of different activities performed at least once in 6 months to the number of hours devoted to "intense" engagement in multiple activities. One of the difficulties of conducting research in this area is that no objective assessments of cognitive stimulation are currently available, and therefore nearly all of the research has relied on self-reports of the number or frequency of various activities as the index of cognitive stimulation. Unfortunately, it is not yet possible to quantify the amount of cognitive engagement in daily life with something analogous to a pedometer that records the number of cognitive "steps" executed during daily activities.

Although many relations between some measure of cognitive activity and some measure of cognitive functioning have been reported, there are few direct replications in which the same measures of activity and the same measures of cognitive functioning have been examined in different samples of participants. Furthermore, most of the research investigating cognitive activity as a risk factor in cognitive decline has been Category 1 or 2 research from the taxonomy in Table 5.1, and as noted above, the most convincing type of research would be from Categories 4, 5, or 6. For example, a finding that individuals who were similar in amount of engagement in cognitively stimulating activities and in their levels of memory performance at one point in time, but differed in their later change in memory as a function of their earlier change in cognitive activity, would provide stronger support for the interpretation that change in activity is a potential cause of change in level of cognitive functioning.

A number of important questions about both cognitive and physical activity engagement also need to be considered when interpreting any relations they might have with cognitive decline. For example, is it the activity itself, or the people who choose to engage in the activities, that is critical in the relation? Also, if it is the activity, does it matter when in one's life it occurs, or are the effects cumulative in nature such that the critical factor is how much activity has occurred regardless of when it occurred? And finally, if an individual already engages in a moderate level of activity, will further increases be beneficial? The fact that we know almost nothing about the answers to these questions is an indication of the impoverished level of understanding of the role of physical and cognitive activity on cognitive decline and incidence of dementia.

Miscellaneous Risk Factors

Many other variables have been examined in terms of their relations with cognitive decline and incidence of AD, but few strong relations have emerged. To illustrate, mixed results have been reported with respect to influences of smoking and alcohol use on the rate of age-related cognitive decline and on incidence of AD, with some studies finding positive relations and some studies finding no relations[35]. Effects of major surgical operations involving general anesthesia on measures of cognitive functioning have been reported in a number of studies.[36] In fact, the effects on cognition are so common that the syndrome of impaired cognitive functioning after surgical operations has been referred to as post-operative cognitive disorder, or POCD. The mechanisms responsible for cognitive effects of major operations are not yet fully understood, but they may be attributable to a reduction in blood pressure during the operation, or to emboli released during surgery. Although little information is currently available about age and POCD, cognitive consequences of major operations could be more frequent at older ages either because older adults have more operations, or because the effects associated with any given operation are more severe.[37]

There is also research indicating that people with larger or closer social networks have a lower incidence of AD, and possibly also a slower rate of cognitive decline.[38] However, there are apparently no published studies linking changes in social support to changes in either the rate of cognitive decline or dementia incidence (i.e., research in Category 3 or above).

Because women stop producing estrogen after about 52 years of age, another factor that has received considerable attention as a potential influence on cognitive functioning is estrogen supplements in females.[39] Estrogen is plausible as a determinant of cognitive functioning because it is important in maintaining cholinergic neurons, stimulation of acetylcholine activity, and formation of synapses and dendritic spines. Better cognitive performance among women receiving estrogen replacement therapy has been reported in some studies, but other studies have reported no effects. One possible factor that could be contributing to this inconsistency is that estrogen may only be important during a critical period close to menopause, and there might be little benefit on cognitive functioning if the estrogen supplements are delayed. Regardless of the validity of this speculation, there is apparently no evidence at the current time that estrogen supplements alter the rate of age-related cognitive decline.

Dietary supplements are also often mentioned as potential cognitive enhancers. As with many other factors postulated to affect cognition, little or no research has been reported assessing the rates of change in cognitive functioning in adults who are, or are not, taking supplements. Furthermore, two recent reviews of dietary supplements, one concentrating on gingko biloba, reached similar conclusions about effects on cognitive functioning. The group considering all dietary supplements concluded that "All in all, we believe that the current data do not allow strong scientifically based recommendations for any of these memory nutrients." The conclusion from the group specifically evaluating gingko biloba concluded, "We found evidence supporting the view that gingko enhances cognitive functions, albeit rather weakly and with considerable variability, under some conditions. However, our overriding impression after seeing the available studies is that there is not enough information to say that ginkgo does or does not improve cognition."[40]

Conclusion about Risk Factors

Although there is a large and growing literature on risk factors for cognitive decline and dementia, there are very few published reports with the most definitive type of evidence from the taxonomy in Table 5.1. The most commonly reported relations are also the least informative, and therefore only tentative conclusions are currently possible about the specific factors that affect the rate of cognitive decline, or the probability of developing dementia.

Cognitive Reserve

One of the puzzling results concerning dementia is that although neuro-pathological characteristics are used to establish a definitive diagnosis of AD, there are a number of reports of individuals who at autopsy met the neuropathological criteria for AD but who did not have any behavioral deficits while they were alive. At least two different interpretations could account for this discrepancy between the behavioral observations and the brain indicators. One possibility is that the behavioral measures currently used to diagnose dementia are rather crude and might not be sensitive to some neurobiological changes. This interpretation therefore attributes the discrepancy to insensitive behavioral assessments.

A second interpretation of the brain–behavior discrepancy is that some people may be better than others at tolerating neuropathology. In other words, there may be individual differences in the strength of the coupling between brain and behavior. One speculation, known as the cognitive reserve hypothesis[41], postulates that factors such as initial level of cognitive ability, amount of education, degree of cognitive or physical activity, etc., change the brain so that it has more cognitive or neural reserve, and as a consequence they allow the individual to perform at levels above dementia thresholds despite significant amounts of neuropathology.

The basic assumption underlying the cognitive reserve hypothesis is that something is needed to account for the weaker coupling of brain pathology and cognitive functioning or dementia among some individuals compared to other individuals. Although the hypothesis attributes the weaker coupling between existing brain and behavior measures to the concept of cognitive reserve, at the current time the term is primarily descriptive rather than explanatory, and the specific neurobiological characteristics associated with this construct remain to be identified.

Conclusion

Dementia, and AD in particular, is characterized by severe impairment in cognitive functioning. It is a particularly devastating disease because it destroys one's sense of self, and there are currently no effective treatments to prevent or even delay the disease. Because when interventions are developed they are likely to be most effective if applied before the disease has progressed very far, researchers in cognitive aging have been interested in studying the earliest stages of the disease.

Research has revealed differences in cognitive performance between individuals who will and will not develop the disease several years prior to the eventual diagnosis. However, what is responsible for these relations and whether it is meaningful to refer to a distinct diagnostic category are still controversial issues. A vast and rapidly increasing literature exists on risk factors, but much of the evidence can be considered relatively weak because many alternative interpretations have not been ruled out. Because risk factor research is inherently correlational, one cannot conclude that an individual will necessarily experience benefits in the outcome variable by changing to a lower risk category.

6

Practical Consequences and Potential
Interventions

*Major issues: Why are there not greater consequences of age-related cognitive
declines in everyday life? What can be done to prevent, or remediate, these
declines?*

*Related questions: What are the relative contributions of different factors in
circumventing age-related cognitive limitations in everyday activities? What
factors need to be considered when evaluating the efficacy of cognitive interventions? Should the primary goal of an intervention be to improve the immediate
level of cognitive functioning or to alter the subsequent rate of cognitive aging?*

Assuming that the phenomena described in earlier chapters are accepted as
robust and valid, two questions are often asked: *(1)* Why are there not greater
consequences of these cognitive declines in everyday life, and *(2)* What can be
done to prevent, or remediate, these declines? These are the two major topics
addressed in this chapter.

Why Are There Not Greater Consequences?

Even though the research evidence suggests that they may be performing at
lower levels than the average 20- or 30-year-old adult on a variety of cognitive
tests, many people over 65 years of age function at very high levels. Because

the age trends are approximately parallel across different initial levels of ability, it seems unlikely that all of these high-functioning people are special cases, who are somehow exempt from any age-related cognitive decline.[1] Instead, many of these individuals are probably functioning at high levels in their everyday activities *despite* some declines in basic abilities.

One of the key questions in the field of cognitive aging is how this is possible. That is, what is responsible for the sometimes dramatic discrepancy between the phenomena observed in the laboratory and the level of functioning observed outside the laboratory? Among the likely reasons, which will be briefly discussed below, are that people seldom need to perform at their maximum levels; effects of age likely vary across tasks or activities; there are large individual differences in the level of cognitive functioning at each age; cognition is not the only important factor associated with success in most activities; increased age is often accompanied by greater amounts of experience, which may minimize negative consequences of declining abilities; and people may accommodate to declining abilities in a manner that could minimize any effects on real-world functioning.

Seldom Need to Perform at One's Maximum

It is informative to compare the physical demands of daily life with the capabilities of an elite athlete. Age-related declines are well documented among highly skilled athletes in a variety of different physical capacities, such as running, lifting, and throwing. However, most people seldom, if ever, need to perform at their physical maximum and are quite capable of carrying out their normal activities. Substantial physical aging can therefore occur with little or no limitation in daily functioning, and the same is probably true for cognitive aging.

Some researchers have distinguished between typical and maximal performance.[2] This distinction is relevant in the current context because although cognitive tests are designed to assess maximal performance, very little of what is done in daily life requires one to perform at his or her maximum. Furthermore, the physical and cognitive demands in most daily situations have been minimized through the design and modification of aspects of the environment to accommodate a wide range of ability.

Variations across Activities

Effects of age on a specific type of functioning can be expected to depend on the relative importance of knowledge and of efficiency of processing in the activity. For example, if the activities are novel, with high demands for controlled or deliberate processing, then the age effects will likely be large and negative. However, smaller or even positive age effects might be expected with familiar activities because as experience increases, performance can be assumed to become less dependent on novel problem solving and more dependent on acquired skills and knowledge. Furthermore, within a given domain, what one already knows may often be more important for effective functioning than how efficiently new knowledge can be acquired. Because most of the situations that are encountered in daily life are familiar, there is rarely a need to deal with novel problems that are completely unrelated to past experience, and it is these latter situations that tend to be most susceptible to negative age effects. Detailed inventories of the actual activities performed in daily life, and the cognitive demands of those activities, are not yet available. Nevertheless, it seems reasonable to expect that activities requiring consciously controlled processing of the type needed for maximum functioning are only a small part of most people's daily lives.

Individual Differences

As mentioned in Chapter 1, there is considerable variation in cognitive performance at each age, such that some older individuals perform at levels higher than the average young adult, and some young individuals perform at levels lower than the average older adult. This variability is apparent in Figure 6.1, which contains a scatter plot of the scores on the matrix reasoning test (cf. Figure 1.2) for 968 adults who all had more than 16 years of education. Although college graduates obviously comprise a very select group, it is important to note that even within this sample a number of 60-and 70-year-olds are in the top 25% of the overall distribution, and a

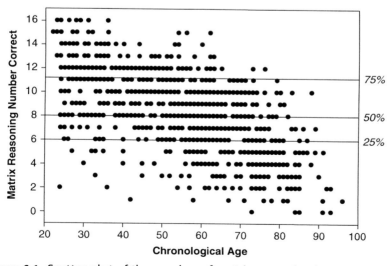

Figure 6.1. Scatter plot of the number of matrix reasoning items correct as a function of age for a sample of college graduates in the Salthouse data.

number of 20- and 30-year-olds are in the bottom 25% of the distribution. Because of the enormous variability of performance within each age range, it is difficult to make predictions about the performance of any given individual. Therefore, even though the phenomenon of cognitive aging is clearly evident at the group level (i.e., in these data the correlation with age was–.59), it is not necessarily apparent in every individual.

There Is More to Life Than Cognition

Another factor that may be contributing to the lab–life discrepancy with respect to the inferred capabilities of older adults is that assessments in the laboratory attempt to focus exclusively on cognition, whereas activities outside the laboratory have numerous other determinants. Many potentially important characteristics are not assessed with cognitive tests, such as the ability to persuade and control people; traits such as dependability, cooperativeness, energy, promptness, and ambition; and attributes such as energy, physical and mental health, and physical appearance. Cognitive tests may also have relatively little to do with how effectively one applies his or her abilities or with how well one's abilities are integrated with knowledge acquired through past experience.

Multiple determinants of functioning have long been recognized in the research literature concerned with work and job performance. To illustrate, one researcher proposed that there are three major determinants of job performance: cognitive ability ("can do"), interest or conscientiousness ("will do"), and experience ("have done").[3] Although the first determinant may decline with age, the second either may not be related to age or might increase with age, and the third determinant is likely to be greater with increasing age.

Industrial-organizational psychologists frequently refer to KSAOs as important factors affecting work performance. In this scheme, *K* refers to knowledge (i.e., factual and procedural knowledge relevant to the performance of one's job), *S* refers to skills (i.e., physical and cognitive procedures acquired through experience that are relevant to the performance of specific jobs), *A* refers to abilities (i.e., physical or cognitive abilities that might affect acquisition of knowledge or skills and are relevant to functioning in novel situations), and *O* refers to other (i.e., miscellaneous factors that affect job performance such as motivation, morale, loyalty, seniority, connections, and chance). Although there is clear evidence that many abilities decline with increasing age, knowledge is often greater, job-specific skills are related to experience which frequently increases with age, and some aspects within the "Other" category may also increase with age.

Benefits of Experience

As experience increases, more aspects of behavior become automatic and habitual, which has the benefit of freeing up cognitive resources for other activities. Over 100 years ago, William James referred to habit as the enormous fly wheel of society because when activities become automatic, they no longer need conscious and deliberate control. Moreover, because tasks requiring conscious and deliberate processing tend to exhibit the largest negative age effects, at least some benefits of experience might be greater with increased age if previously demanding tasks become automatized and no longer require conscious control.[4]

It is also possible that although experience may not prevent decline, it could serve to obscure some of the manifestations of decline. That is, age-related decline might occur among people at every level of experience or expertise, but if more experience is associated with higher levels of cognitive performance, then the greater experience often accompanied by increased age may functionally offset some of the declines associated with aging.

Two examples from research in my laboratory will be briefly described to highlight the importance of experience in comparisons of adults of different ages. The first example is from a research project on transcription typing. Individuals of different ages, but who as a group had no relation between age and overall typing proficiency, were recruited to participate in a research project designed to determine how people of different ages were able to achieve nearly the same level of proficiency in typing. The project involved administering several typing tasks on a computer. In one task the number of characters visible on the display was varied to determine the effect on rate of typing. Another task involved blanking the display screen containing the to-be-typed text at random points while the research participant was typing to determine how many characters could continue to be typed after the disappearance of the material.[5]

The major finding in the project was that older typists achieved the same typing speed as younger typists by greater anticipation of the to-be-typed material. The expanded eye–hand span was not only apparent in the moving window procedure, in the form of older adults requiring a greater number of visible characters than younger adults to type at their normal rate, but also by the older adults typing a greater number of characters after unexpected blanking of the screen. This research on typing is a simple illustration of how experienced older adults appear to circumvent some of their limitations by relying on a different approach to the task. However, it should be noted that the generalizability of this type of compensation is not yet known because it has been difficult to identify other activities in which increased age is associated with lower functioning in some components of an activity but higher functioning in other components of the same activity.

A second example of the role of experience on age differences in cognitive functioning is apparent in a research project in which the age trends were compared on two challenging tasks that each required finding solutions that would simultaneously satisfy multiple constraints. Illustrations of portions of the two tasks—analytical reasoning and a crossword puzzle (with the actual puzzle taken from a weekend edition of the *New York Times*)—are portrayed in Figure 6.2.

Crossword Puzzle

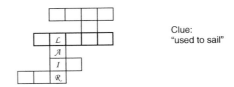

Clue:
"used to sail"

Analytical Reasoning

Jason and Jessica are planning a dinner party and have invited six guests: Mark and Meredith, Christopher and Courtney, and Shawn and Samantha. Their table seats three people on each side and one at each end. In planning the seating arrangements they need to:
> have Jason and Jessica sit at opposite ends of the table
> place Christopher at a corner with no one on his left
> not have Mark seated next to Samantha
> have Courtney seated next to Meredith

Which of the following is a possible arrangement of the diners along one side of the table?
(A) Jason, Samantha, Mark
(B) Christopher, Jessica, Shawn
(C) Mark, Courtney, Samantha
(D) Meredith, Shawn, Courtney
(E) Shawn, Christopher, Meredith

Figure 6.2. Illustration of two types of problems that require satisfaction of multiple constraints. The top panel portrays a portion of a crossword puzzle, and the bottom panel illustrates a problem from an abstract reasoning test.

It was postulated that a critical difference between the two tasks is the amount of knowledge relevant to successful performance, which is high for crossword puzzles and low for analytical reasoning. That is, cognitive tasks can be assumed to primarily involve information retrieval when knowledge is critical to performance, but a considerable amount of effortful problem solving may be required when the task is less dependent on prior knowledge.[6] Figure 6.3 reveals that the crossword puzzle and analytical reasoning tasks had dramatically different age trends in the same individuals. The analytical reasoning task exhibited age-related declines similar to those found in many measures of process cognition, but performance on the knowledge-dependent crossword puzzle task increased until about 60 or 70 years of age. These results are intriguing because many of the situations people encounter in their daily lives may be more like crossword puzzles than analytical reasoning in that effective functioning is heavily dependent on one's relevant knowledge. It is therefore tempting to view the contrast between these two tasks as a microcosm of the lab–life discrepancy with respect to age differences in cognitive functioning.

Although there is currently little relevant evidence, it is also possible that not only is there an age-related shift in the levels of various determinants of cognitive functioning but also a shift in the importance of these factors. That

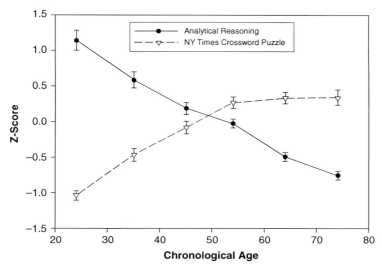

Figure 6.3. Means and standard errors for measures of performance in the crossword puzzle task and the analytical reasoning task as a function of age.

is, in domains in which they are experienced, older adults might not only have higher levels of knowledge than young adults, but they might also rely more heavily on that knowledge. In the terminology of multiple regression, increased age could be associated with differences both in the levels of the predictor variables and in the regression weights reflecting the influence of the predictor variable on performance.

Accommodations

In the current context the term *accommodation* refers to changes in what is done, or in how it is done, that have the effect of minimizing the consequences of declining abilities. A phrase by B. F. Skinner in his book *Enjoy Old Age* illustrated a common form of accommodation, "in place of memories, memoranda."[7] In other words, an older adult might accommodate to declining memory by increasing his or her reliance on various types of memory aids. In fact, in our project we found that increased age was associated with more use of appointment books and various types of lists (Table 3.1). A similar pattern is also apparent in research on prospective memory (i.e., remembering to do something in the future), in which older adults are sometimes found to perform better than young adults because they use external reminders such as calendars and notes, and in research on medication adherence in which older adults tend to make fewer errors than young adults because they set timers and link the taking of medication to rituals such as brushing one's teeth.[8] This greater reliance on external memory aids can be considered an example of accommodating to memory losses.

Another example of accommodation is in the area of driving. Although crash rates are higher among adults over age 60 compared to adults in their 30s, 40s, and 50s, older adults actually have fewer crashes than one might predict based on their levels of sensory, motor, and cognitive abilities. A likely reason for the better-than-expected driving behavior of older adults is that good strategic and tactical decisions offset age-related reductions in operational capacity[9]. Examples of optimal strategic decisions are not driving in rush hour, at night, in bad weather, or on unfamiliar routes, and examples of tactical decisions when driving are avoiding left turns or driving in fast lanes, and maintaining an adequate following distance. It seems plausible that these changes in how one drives may minimize the consequences of age-related ability declines, and that the rates of vehicle crashes and injuries involving older drivers might be much larger without these accommodations.

An interesting finding relevant to age differences in driving is that fatal crashes when a passenger is present are more frequent for drivers under the age of 20, but they are less frequent for drivers over the age of 50.[10] This may be another instance of accommodation, in this case involving sharing of responsibility for monitoring some aspects of driving. Of course, this result could also reflect effects of distraction or peer pressure in the case of teenage drivers, and thus it can only be considered suggestive and by no means definitive.

Summary on Consequences

Research results are unequivocal in establishing that increased age is often associated with lower levels of performance on many cognitive tests. However, these age-related declines do not necessarily have a large impact on an individual's functioning in daily life for several reasons. First, cognitive tests are designed to evaluate an individual's maximum level of performance, but we are seldom required to perform at our maximum levels. Second, many attributes important for successful functioning are not assessed with currently available cognitive tests. Third, performance is often much better with greater experience, and amount of experience typically increases with advancing age. And fourth, many people can accommodate to cognitive declines to minimize much of the negative consequences of those declines in their daily lives.

How Can Decline Be Prevented or Remediated?

A question of great interest to many people, and one that is a frequent topic in the popular media, is whether age-related cognitive decline can be remediated, or prevented, by behavioral interventions. Not only is this question of considerable practical interest, but it is also important from a theoretical perspective because the most convincing evidence that the causes of a phenomenon are understood are results establishing that the phenomenon can be manipulated through interventions.

Although the idea that an intervention might remediate cognitive decline is very appealing, a number of issues need to be considered when thinking about the results of interventions.[11] Some of these are widely recognized in the literature on cognitive interventions, but others may be specific to attempts to remediate age-related cognitive decline.[12]

As an example, complications exist even in something as seemingly simple as interpreting the size of intervention effects. That is, outcomes of interventions are sometimes expressed relative to the amount of normal age-related decline observed on a target variable, as when an intervention is claimed to have an effect as large as 10 years of normal aging. Comparisons with other types of effects can be a meaningful way of expressing the magnitude of intervention results, but this particular contrast has the potential to be misleading if the intervention is interpreted as having reversed age-related decline by altering the same mechanisms that were responsible for the declines. For example, visual functioning in someone who can no longer focus on near objects might be improved by the use of corrective lenses, but this is accomplished without any reversal of the reduction in lens flexibility that was responsible for the decline in focusing ability. In a case such as this, therefore, different mechanisms are involved in the "loss" and "recovery" of the functional outcome, and hence it may be more accurate to refer to the interventions as having improved performance by an amount "equal to a particular magnitude of decline" rather than as having "reversed the decline."

It is sometimes suggested that different types of intervention effects (e.g., reversal of decline versus acquisition of new skills) might be distinguished by comparing the magnitude of intervention gains in young and old adults. The rationale is that intervention gains in older adults might be assumed to reflect both remediation of prior decline and some type of new learning, whereas only new learning effects could occur in young adults because there is no decline to be remediated. Unfortunately, it is difficult, if not impossible, to distinguish qualitatively different types of influences simply on the basis of quantitative information. For example, young and old adults might have quantitatively similar intervention benefits if young adults only improved because of new learning and older adults improved primarily because of remediation, or if older adults were somewhat less effective than young adults in new learning but also had some benefits of remediation. The interpretations would likely be less ambiguous if the intervention effects were larger in older individuals than in younger ones. In fact, a few studies in nonhuman animals, with interventions consisting of dietary supplements, scopolamine, or a dopamine d1 agonist, have reported greater intervention effects in older animals compared to younger animals. However, outcomes of this type have seldom been reported in behavioral interventions in humans.

To the contrary, most studies involving multiple age groups have found that younger individuals benefit more from the intervention than older individuals, such that the performance differences between adults of different ages are frequently larger after cognitive training than before.[13]

In the initial stages of research one might simply be interested in whether there is an improvement in cognitive performance after an intervention. However, eventually it is desirable to determine how, and why, the intervention was effective. One approach that can be used to investigate how an intervention operates is based on the selection of relevant control conditions. Some type of control comparison is necessary because merely performing a cognitive test again is often associated with a performance improvement of up to 0.5 standard deviation units, but there is no consensus about which type of control condition is most appropriate for cognitive interventions. A major reason for the lack of agreement is that the type of control condition considered ideal depends on one's assumptions about how the intervention is assumed to operate. A no-contact control condition, in which the individuals in the control group simply receive assessments at the beginning and end of the period in which the experimental group receives the intervention, is the simplest type of control condition, but it is also the least informative about the factors that might be contributing to any benefits observed in the experimental group. Unfortunately, a true placebo condition in which everyone is treated the same except for the presence of the critical ingredient in the experimental group, is seldom possible with behavioral interventions because both the research participants and the investigators are typically aware of the group to which the participants have been assigned. Most control conditions therefore fall somewhere on a continuum between the no-contact and placebo extremes. Designing informative control conditions is challenging because as many potentially relevant factors as possible should be incorporated into the control group to rule out plausible alternative interpretations while still preserving the critical distinction between the experimental and control groups.

A second method that can be used to learn about the mechanisms involved in an intervention involves examining the relation between the amount of change in the directly manipulated aspect of the intervention and the amount of change in the primary outcome variables of interest. The rationale is that if the intervention is working as hypothesized, then individuals exhibiting the greatest proximal effects of the intervention should also have the greatest effects on the primary outcome variables. For example, if an intervention involves training in a particular strategy, then the individuals with the largest intervention-related improvement in effective use of the strategy would be expected to have the largest benefit in the cognitive outcome variables. A failure to find a significant relation between amount of change in the immediate target of the intervention and amount of change in the relevant cognitive outcome variable would lead to questions about whether the intervention is operating as hypothesized. To illustrate, if a study with a physical exercise intervention failed to find that benefits in cognitive performance were related to the intervention-related improvements in a measure of physical or aerobic fitness, the assumption that exercise effects are attributable to improvements in fitness would be challenged. The absence of a relation might instead suggest that any cognitive benefits are associated with improved mood, social interactions with other exercisers, or simply to the addition of a structured event to one's schedule. In fact, a recent meta-analytic review of exercise interventions on cognition found that there was no significant relationship between the effect size of aerobic fitness gains and the effect sizes of cognitive performance improvements, which led the authors to suggest that the empirical literature was inconsistent with the hypothesis that physical exercise affects cognition through improved cardiovascular fitness.[14]

In addition to proximal measures of the hypothesized mechanism, measures of compliance with the protocol are also desirable in intervention studies because it may not be reasonable to expect much benefit among individuals who do not adhere to the treatment program. In many intervention projects the analyses are based on results from all of the participants initially assigned to the treatments, in what are known as intent-to-treat analysis procedures, in part because lack of success due to nonadherence is a potentially informative consequence of the intervention. However, if one is interested in the mechanisms underlying the effectiveness of an intervention, it is desirable to distinguish between lack of improvement attributable to nonadherence and lack of improvement for other reasons.

One of the most important questions regarding interventions concerns the breadth of the intervention effects. This is a critical issue with respect to intervention research because an intervention may not have much practical importance, or theoretical significance, if the effects are very narrow. Generalizability or transfer is a major concern in cognitive intervention research because most cognitive training programs have found benefits of the intervention primarily on tasks that closely resemble the trained task or activity.[15] For example, some interventions have trained participants to detect relations among a sequence of elements and have then tested the ability to identify relations with various types of series completion tasks, or they have trained techniques for remembering words and have then administered tests consisting of a variety of word memory tests. Although these types of comparisons are valuable in establishing that participants can learn the relevant procedures and improve some aspect of cognitive performance, they are not very informative about the potential generalizability of the results. A broad range of cognitive tests is needed to determine if the intervention effects will transfer to different types of tests hypothesized to represent the same ability (e.g., to paper folding after training in mental rotation, to concept formation after training in series completion, to memory of faces after training in memory of unrelated words), and an even wider range of cognitive tasks would be needed to evaluate transfer to different cognitive abilities (e.g., to reasoning ability after training in memory ability).[16]

The limited transfer of previous cognitive interventions has led some researchers to speculate that broader and more generalizable outcomes might be found with interventions that are more diverse, such as learning to act, volunteering in schools, bird watching, quilting, or even shopping.[17] Activities like these can be assumed to involve a number of potentially relevant components, including making decisions, frequent retrieval of information from memory, and sometimes even physical exercise, and thus they might incorporate several possible routes to improvement. Evidence for the effectiveness of broad-based interventions on cognitive functioning is currently very limited, but if these types of interventions were found to be successful it would eventually be important to identify the relevant mechanisms to determine why the intervention was effective, and to allow selection of the most efficient mode of intervention.[18]

Another issue relevant to interventions concerns the most appropriate age at which to intervene. It is understandable that most interventions have focused only on older adults because they are the individuals seemingly most in need of intervention due to their lower average level of performance in many cognitive tasks.[19] That is, the fact that many older individuals may be close to some type of functional threshold implies that any intervention effects for older adults might have considerable practical importance. Even modest improvements could therefore be quite valuable if they serve to increase an older individual's quality of life, perhaps by contributing to the ability to live independently.

However, two points relevant to the target age for intervention should be considered. First, because many of the figures in the previous chapters suggest that age-related cognitive decline appears to begin when individuals are in their 20s, with nearly 50% of the difference from the peak to age 85 apparent by about age 60, interventions should presumably begin in early adulthood if the goal is to prevent decline. Of course, it is possible that different mechanisms may be operating in early and late adulthood, which might require different types of interventions at different periods in life. Nevertheless, if a purpose of the intervention is to maintain functioning at the highest level, which for many cognitive variables is when adults are in their 20s or 30s, then the intervention should probably be targeted at, or even before, those ages.

A second point to consider is that if the functional outcome of the intervention is important and valued in society, ethical issues might eventually arise if an effective intervention is not made available to adults of all ages. In other words, if an intervention was found to benefit people of all ages, it could be argued that it should be available to everyone, and not just to older individuals who have the lowest initial levels of performance. However, if people of all ages were to receive an effective intervention, it is possible that the intervention could increase, rather than decrease, the discrepancy between the functioning of young and old adults. Only if the intervention targets fundamental processes responsible for the age differences would it be likely to reduce, or eliminate, the age differences in relevant measures of cognitive functioning.

A key question relevant to interventions in the context of aging concerns the primary goal of the intervention. That is, is the purpose to improve the level of cognitive performance immediately after the intervention, or is it to alter the subsequent rate of change in cognitive functioning? Judging from the number of interventions that have been reported to be effective in increasing performance of specific cognitive tasks, it appears to be relatively easy to devise an intervention that will result in a higher level of performance on a particular cognitive task immediately after the intervention. Moreover, this seems to be true for adults of just about any age, although the magnitude of the benefits is likely to be smaller with increased age. However, it could be argued that the most relevant question from the perspective of aging is what happens after an intervention has been found to result in an improved level of performance.

Figure 6.4 illustrates that at least four outcomes could occur after an immediate benefit of an intervention has been established. In one case performance remains stable at the same level reached immediately after the intervention, and in another case it declines at the same rate as it would have without the intervention. The former outcome corresponds to a stopping of the age-related decline, and the latter outcome reflects an initial increase in level of performance but with no effect on the rate of decline. The top function illustrated in Figure 6.4 has a slope after the intervention of the same magnitude, but in the opposite direction, as the slope before the intervention; thus, a result such as this could be interpreted as a true reversal of the decline. The fourth possibility portrayed in Figure 6.4 is that there is an

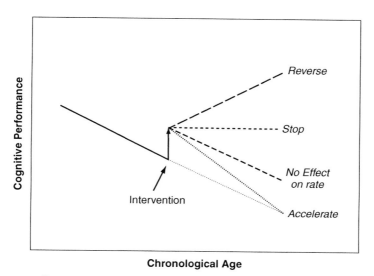

Chronological Age

Figure 6.4. Illustration of potential outcomes of an intervention on the relations between age and cognitive performance.

accelerated rate of decline after the intervention, perhaps because the overall rate of decline represents the combined effects of normal age-related decline and gradual loss of the initial benefits of the intervention.

The outcomes portrayed in Figure 6.4 illustrate an important distinction between what can be termed *plasticity* and *modifiability of age relations*[20,21]. As noted above, there have been quite a few demonstrations that adults of all ages can improve their level of cognitive performance immediately after some type of intervention. The fact that level of cognitive performance is not fixed, but is malleable and can be increased (or decreased) can be considered evidence of cognitive plasticity. Plasticity is interesting and important in its own right, but it should not be interpreted as evidence that the rate of cognitive aging has been, or could be, altered. Instead, the phrase "modifiability of age relations" can be used to refer to changes in the rate of cognitive aging. Although a discovery of plasticity is sometimes used as the basis for inferring that age relations are modifiable, there is no necessary connection between plasticity and modifiability. This point can be seen by inspection of Figure 6.4. Plasticity is apparent as an effect on the immediate level of performance, and the magnitude of plasticity corresponds to the length of the vertical arrow in the figure. In contrast, differences in modifiability correspond to the various outcomes to the right of the vertical arrow because this term refers to effects on the rate of change in performance over time. Note that modifiability can only be examined if the effects of the intervention are monitored long enough to detect possible differences in the magnitude of age-related declines. Moreover, because the rates of age-related changes in cognitive performance are typically small, either very large samples of adults, or long monitoring periods, will likely be required to detect statistically significant differences in rates of aging after the initial phases of an intervention.

In some projects performance is monitored at different intervals after the intervention to determine the persistence of the effects. However, the question of the persistence of intervention effects is not the same as the question of influences on the rate of change. To illustrate, all four of the outcomes in Figure 6.4 have relatively long-lasting intervention effects, and yet the outcomes and implications are quite different. The critical information with respect to effects on rates of aging is therefore not the magnitude of the intervention effect at any particular point after the intervention, but rather the rate at which performance changes as a function of time (or age).

Another issue related to persistence of the effects concerns the duration of the actual intervention. For practical reasons, most interventions have been limited to 100 hours or less over periods of up to 6 months. Although this represents a considerable investment of time from the perspective of a researcher, it is reasonable to ask whether it is sufficient to induce long-term change in an individual's behavior. That is, it could be that major change resulting in an alteration of the rate of cognitive aging requires thousands of hours over many years, in what is equivalent to a substantial change in the individual's lifestyle. Furthermore, if a major lifestyle change is required, the success of lifestyle modifications to reduce weight or stop smoking should be considered, because these programs have been found difficult to maintain even when the short-term effectiveness is well established.

For the reasons just discussed, the best cognitive intervention studies include evaluations of transfer to other cognitive tests and abilities, long-term monitoring, and control conditions designed to investigate alternative interpretations of any effects that might be observed. Tests of transfer are desirable because intervention effects may not be very important or interesting if they are very narrow and specific to what was trained, and extended monitoring is desirable as interventions with only short-term benefits may have limited value. Because many interventions involve adults participating in an unfamiliar activity, often in the company of people not previously known to them, factors such as novelty and social interaction need to be considered in designing control conditions that will help identify mechanisms responsible for any intervention benefits. Both the practical and theoretical implications would be quite different if the critical aspect of an apparently successful intervention was found to be interaction with a group of strangers rather than the factors hypothesized to be relevant to improved cognitive functioning. Unfortunately, very few intervention studies with these characteristics have been reported, and apparently none in studies investigating commercial products that are often claimed to slow or prevent brain aging.

Intervention Examples

Two examples of interventions that have received considerable publicity are briefly described because, despite some limitations, they are among the best in addressing the issues discussed above.

ACTIVE

The ACTIVE (Advanced Cognitive Training for Independent and Vital Elderly) clinical trial was an ambitious multisite study with a large (N = 2,802) diverse sample of older adults, multiple follow-ups, and outcomes ranging from performance on tests nearly identical to those that were trained to functional activities associated with daily living.[22] The participants were initially randomized into four groups: a no-contact control group, and training groups focusing on reasoning, memory, and speed. Each of the three training groups received ten 60-to-75-minute sessions of training focusing on a specific cognitive ability, with initial sessions devoted to demonstration of the training strategies and later sessions focused on practicing the strategies. The reasoning training involved instruction of specific strategies to break the problem into easier steps, identify patterns of relations among elements, etc., and the memory training involved instruction of strategies to form images or associations and organize the to-be-remembered material. The speed training group received computer-administered tests of visual search and divided attention, with the level of difficulty progressively adjusted according to the individual's level of performance.

As expected from prior research, there was an improvement in performance immediately after the training on tests similar to those used in training. The magnitude of the training benefits relative to the gains in the control group were 0.48 standard deviation units for reasoning and 0.25 units for memory, which are 7 to 15 times larger than the expected annual cross-sectional age decline for these abilities. Even larger training gains were found in the speed group, but there are apparently no large-scale cross-sectional studies with this combined speed-and-attention task to allow comparisons of the training gain with the cross-sectional age trends. However, as has been found in most other cognitive intervention studies, there was little evidence of transfer in any of the groups to other types of cognitive tests, or to measures assumed to assess everyday functioning.

A unique feature of the ACTIVE project was that the participants were reassessed several times over a period of 2 years. Surprisingly, the decline in cognitive performance over this interval was somewhat greater for the training groups than for the control group. This apparently faster decline could be interpreted as indicating that the interventions accelerated the rate of age-related cognitive decline, but it is more likely attributable to gradual loss of the intervention benefit superimposed on effects of normal aging.

Although the ACTIVE project has many strengths, as with virtually every research study it also has several limitations. For example, the assessment of cognitive functioning was relatively narrow because it did not include the full range of cognitive abilities that have been found to exhibit age-related cognitive decline, and the outcomes of the interventions were fairly modest, with benefits primarily restricted to the types of tasks that were trained. Furthermore, although there has been some post-intervention monitoring, it has not yet been carried out long enough to determine whether the intervention had effects on the rate of age-related cognitive decline in the trained tasks or abilities.

Physical Exercise

Several meta-analyses have revealed that physical exercise interventions can lead to improvements of between 0.3 and 0.6 standard deviation units in measures of cognitive functioning.[23,24] However, it should be noted that negative findings have also been reported in a number of well-conducted studies, and the reasons for these discrepancies are not yet known. Nevertheless, physical exercise has been considered a promising mode of intervention because it has the potential to alter the neurobiological substrate responsible for a variety of different types of cognitive processes.

One of the most impressive interventions based on physical exercise was carried out by an interdisciplinary team of researchers at The University of

Illinois.[25] These researchers randomly assigned adults between 60 and 75 years of age to one of two groups who either did stretching and toning exercises ($n = 66$) or walking at an intensity corresponding to 65%–70% of their VO_2 max ($n = 58$). Both groups were scheduled for three 40-minute sessions per week over a period of 6 months. An interesting feature of this design is that both the experimental (walking) and control (stretching/ toning) groups had similar amounts of social interaction and physical activity, but presumably only the walking group had the critical ingredient of aerobic exercise.

Effect sizes for the physical fitness gains and cognitive functioning gains in the original study in this project, expressed in standard deviations of the initial (pre-intervention) assessment, are portrayed in Figure 6.5. These results clearly indicate that the walking group had greater improvements in measures of aerobic fitness over the treatment period than the group doing stretching and toning exercises. However, it should be noted that the average improvement in VO_2 max was only about 5%, which is much smaller than the value of 22.5% found in a meta-analysis of exercise interventions with older adults. (The VO_2 max improvement in this project was also much smaller than that reported in a later study by the same researchers, in which the

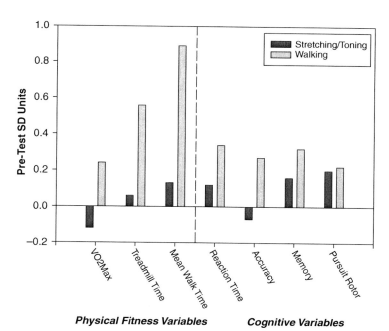

Figure 6.5. Effect sizes in terms of differences in standard deviation units for measures of fitness (left three sets of bars) and of cognitive performance (right four sets of bars) in the Kramer et al. (1999, 2002) physical exercise intervention study.

nonaerobic group improved about 5% and the aerobic group improved about 16%.) The relatively low fitness gains in this project may, at least in part, be related to the modest level of exercise, in the form of walking, compared to more vigorous running or stationary bicycle exercise used in many other exercise intervention studies. Regardless of the reason for the small change in VO_2 max in this study, however, it leads to questions about why the cognitive benefits in this study would be larger than those in other studies which found larger improvements in fitness. Another factor that complicates the interpretation of this study is that a later report based on the project revealed that the participants in the walking group had lower levels of physical activity than the stretching-and-toning group at the pre-intervention baseline, which raises the possibility that some of the greater fitness benefits in the walking group may have been attributable to the fact that they started at a lower level of physical activity than the stretching/toning control group.

Outcomes of the physical exercise intervention on different types of cognitive variables are portrayed in the right side of Figure 6.5. It can be seen that the walking group improved more than the stretching/toning group in three of the four categories of cognitive variables. Cognitive variables can be categorized in different ways, but it is noteworthy that the aerobic group had greater gains in several different types of cognitive variables, and not simply with one particular type. Later research by the same team of researchers also found that aerobic exercise was associated with increases in the gray matter density of several brain regions assumed to be involved in a variety of cognitive tasks.

This aerobic exercise project has generated considerable interest because in contrast to studies focusing on cognitive interventions, the effects on cognitive functioning appear to be relatively broad, and the exercise intervention has been linked to neurobiological changes in the brain. As with all projects, however, it has some limitations. Among these are that the cognitive variables were each analyzed separately as though they were independent of one another, and as a consequence it is difficult to determine the level (e.g., specific variable or broad ability) at which aerobic exercise affects cognitive functioning. Furthermore, the relation between the fitness gains and the cognitive gains was relatively modest, and therefore it is not clear how much of the exercise effects on cognition were directly mediated through improved fitness. Finally, although a recent report indicated that amount of self-reported physical activity decreased in the 5 years after the intervention, the absence of long-term monitoring of cognitive outcomes leaves unanswered the important question of whether the exercise intervention was effective in altering the rate of cognitive aging.

Summary of Interventions

The possibility that the trajectory of cognitive aging might be altered is enormously appealing, and thus it is not surprising that there has been a great deal of interest in this topic. However, many issues need to be considered when interpreting results of intervention studies, and unfortunately they are often neglected both in the popular media and in the scientific literature. Very few rigorous intervention studies have been published in scientific journals, most have found very limited generalizability beyond the trained activities, and none have followed the participants long enough to determine whether the interventions were effective in altering the course of age-related cognitive decline. However, one final point worth emphasizing is that merely because convincing evidence that the rate of cognitive aging has been altered with behavioral interventions is not yet available, this does not mean that effective interventions will not be discovered in the future. The truism that "absence of evidence is not the same as evidence of absence" is clearly applicable with respect to interventions designed to modify the rate of cognitive aging.

Conclusions

Age-related cognitive declines seem well established, but there are a number of factors that might explain why they do not have greater consequences in everyday life. Among these are that few situations require maximum levels of functioning, many activities have minimal cognitive demands, and in most situations there is a benefit of experience that is usually positively associated with age. Furthermore, one manifestation of increased experience may be accommodations in which activities are performed and in how they are performed.

Although there has been considerable interest in interventions that might prevent or reverse age-related cognitive decline, the currently available research findings are more intriguing than they are definitive. In the absence of conclusive evidence, only tentative recommendations can be offered regarding what an individual might do to minimize negative consequences of age-related cognitive declines. Perhaps the most important is to keep physically healthy and mentally active. Physical health is important because the brain is a physical organ that is dependent on the healthy functioning of other bodily systems. Causal linkages between physical exercise and rate of cognitive aging have not yet been definitively established, but at least some of the relations are highly plausible, and encouraging results have been reported from a few scientifically rigorous studies. And although mental activity has not yet been conclusively documented to be beneficial, it is very unlikely to do any harm, and future research may discover that it does have benefits in slowing the rate of age-related cognitive decline. A final recommendation is that engagement in the physical and mental activity should begin as early as possible. The reasons for the declines are still not understood, but it seems highly likely that they will be easier to alter, or prevent, when they are first beginning.

Notes

Chapter 1

1. The William James quote is from James (1890, Vol. 2, p. 402).
2. The 1927 quote is from Hollingworth (1927, p. 310). One of my favorite quotes on this topic is from the Austrian writer Marie von Ebner-Eschenbach, "In youth we learn; in age we understand."
3. The quote that no one is ever too old to learn is from Miles and Miles (1943, pp. 108–109).
4. Participants in studies conducted in my laboratory were recruited through newspaper advertisements, flyers, and referrals from other participants. This type of convenience sample is seldom representative of the general population, but the extent to which this is the case can be documented in this sample because all of the participants performed several standardized tests from commercial test batteries that have norms from nationally representative samples of the U.S. population. Comparison of the scores with the norms indicate that the participants in these studies perform quite a bit above the average expected for the general population (i.e., between 0.50 and 0.66 of a standard deviation above the mean of the normative sample.) However, it is noteworthy that this was true to nearly the same extent at all ages and thus there was no indication that the selectivity of the sample differed at different periods of adulthood.
5. The world track record data were retrieved on July 24, 2008, from http://www.iaaf.org/statistics/recbycat/index.html.
6. Early discussions of differential cognitive aging can be found in Beeson (1920), Bingham and Davis (1924), Foster and Taylor (1920), Gilbert (1935), Hollingworth (1927), Jones and Conrad (1933), Sorenson (1933;

1938), Thorndike et al. (1928), Weisenburg et al. (1936), and Willoughby (1927). Cattell (1943) introduced the terminology of fluid and crystallized abilities, and Welford (1958) used the labels Type A and Type B to refer to a similar distinction between the two types of cognition.

7. An extensive discussion of the advantages and disadvantages of extreme group designs is contained in Preacher et al. (2005).

8. Among the early researchers who discussed the issue of differential selection or representativeness are Jones and Conrad (1933), Sorenson (1938), and Yerkes (1921).

9. Other reports of late life decline in vocabulary are Alwin and McCammon (2001), Bowles et al. (2005), Bowles and Salthouse (2008), Mantyla and Nilsson (1997), Ronnlund et al. (2005), and Schaie (2005). Moreover, a meta-analysis revealed a negative correlation between age and vocabulary in samples over the age of 60 (Verhaeghen, 2003).

10. Additional discussions of how the idiosyncratic nature of knowledge makes comprehensive assessment of knowledge difficult can be found in Ackerman (1996), Cattell (1943, 1972), and Salthouse (2003). Nevertheless, it should be noted that several studies have reported high correlations between measures of culturally shared knowledge derived from traditional psychometric tests of vocabulary or general information and measures of more specialized knowledge. For example, 1,021 adults in our studies were administered a multiple-choice test of knowledge covering 10 different domains, including art, geography, history, literature, and sports. The total score on this general knowledge test had a correlation of .75 with a latent variable representing what was common across four measures of vocabulary word knowledge.

Ackerman and his colleagues have also conducted a number of studies comparing traditional psychometric measures of knowledge with measures of specialized knowledge. In Ackerman et al. (2000) the standardized partial correlation between a traditional psychometric knowledge measure and a composite measure of history, literature, biology, and technology knowledge was .97, in Beier and Ackerman (2001) the correlation with a measure of current events knowledge was .81, in Beier and Ackerman (2003) the standardized partial correlation with a measure of health knowledge was .90, and in Beier and Ackerman (2005) the correlation was .75 for a measure of health knowledge and .80 for a measure of technical (xerography) knowledge. Even though the items in these tests were selected to represent different domains, the tests may still predominantly reflect common or shared knowledge rather than the knowledge that is idiosyncratic to specific individuals, and hence they may not provide comprehensive assessments of any individual's total knowledge. Alternatively, as suggested by Beier and Ackerman (2005, p. 353), "scores on [psychometric knowledge] tests can be considered a general indicator of success acquiring knowledge throughout the lifespan," and therefore they may be a good proxy for many different types of knowledge.

11. Research has reported different age trends for vocabulary tests with difficult compared to easy items (Bowles et al., 2005; Bowles & Salthouse, 2008), and for measures of expressive than for measures of receptive vocabulary (Dunn & Dunn, 2007; Williams, 2007). Smaller positive age relations for measures obtained from production vocabulary tests than for

measures obtained from multiple choice vocabulary tests were also reported by Verhaeghen (2003).

12. Early discussions of large variability among people of the same age can be found in Thorndike et al. (1928), Weisenburg et al. (1936), Miles (1933), Miles and Miles (1943), and Sward (1945).

13. A meta-analysis of correlations of various cognitive variables with age was reported by Verhaeghen and Salthouse (1997).

14. One of the first studies to investigate relations of age to between-person variability was Jones and Conrad (1933).

15. A similar absence of a relation between age and between-person standard deviations has been reported in a large project conducted in Sweden. That is, Mantyla and Nilsson (1997; also see Ronnlund et al., 2005) reported nearly constant standard deviations from age 35 to 80 for block design and verbal fluency measures. Although the mean performance on 12 memory variables declined with increased age, there was little age difference in the standard deviations. To illustrate, the median ratio of the values for adults age 70 to 80 to the values for adults age 35 to 50 across the 12 variables was 0.70 for the means, and 1.02 for the standard deviations. A smaller-scale study by Li et al. (2004) also found nearly constant between-individual variance across six age groups.

    Means and standard deviations for six factor scores in nine different age groups ranging from 25 to 81 were reported by Schaie (2005, Table 4.4). The ratio of the standard deviations at age 81 to those at age 25 were Reasoning = 0.82, Space = 0.92, Number = 1.04, Speed = 1.10, Vocabulary = 1.17, and Verbal Memory = 1.21. It is noteworthy that for the two factors with large age-related declines (i.e., Reasoning and Space), the between-person variability was actually smaller in the older age group.

16. A recent article by Ardila (2008) claimed that individual differences in cognitive variables increased with advancing age. However, the analyses leading to this conclusion were based on the coefficient of variation (i.e., standard deviation/mean), which does not allow effects attributable to decreases in the mean to be distinguished from those attributable to increases in the standard deviation.

17. Tucker-Drob and Salthouse (2008) also found little evidence of weaker relations among the cognitive variables at older ages from the Salthouse projects with more complex analyses. A complicated pattern of correlations among variables at different ages was reported by Li et al. (2004), which is not easily interpreted.

18. Correlations among six factor scores in nine age groups ranging from 25 to 81 were also reported by Schaie (2005, Table A4.3). The median correlations ranged from a low of .37 at age 32 to a high of .47 at age 25. Furthermore, the correlation between age and the median correlation was only .10, indicating that there was little systematic relation between age and the average correlation.

19. More detailed discussion of the question of when age-related cognitive decline begins, along with relevant evidence, can be found in an article by Salthouse (2009).

20. Data for lifespan trends in cognition were obtained from the test manuals for the KBIT (Kaufman & Kaufman, 1990), WASI (Wechsler, 1999), and Woodcock-Johnson III (McGrew & Woodcock, 2001).

21. The report comparing effects in aging with those in childhood was by Jones and Conrad (1933).
22. The comparison of age relations in various organ systems was reported by Sehl and Yates (2001). Estimates of annual declines from standardized tests were obtained from the test manuals from the WAIS (Wechsler, 1997a), WASI (Wechsler, 1999), and KAIT (Kaufman & Kaufman, 1993).
23. The comparison of effect sizes for different types of relations was reported by Meyer et al. (2001).
24. Among the many reports of age and sex differences are Keith et al. (2008), Meinz and Salthouse (1998), Herlitz et al. (1997, 1999), and Herlitz and Rehnman (2008). Sex differences in the intercept parameter but not the slope parameter in analyses of longitudinal data have been reported by Aartsen et al. (2004), Finkel et al. (2003), Gerstorf et al. (2006), and Singer et al. (2003). Proust-Lima et al. (2008) found a slightly greater decline for women than for men in old age, but the effect was very small.
25. One of the first comparisons of age relations as a function of initial ability was reported by Thorndike et al. (1928, p. 17). Articles with the phrase "Is age kinder to the initially more able" were published by Christensen and Henderson (1991), Deary et al. (1999), Owens (1959), and Thompson (1954). Another study reporting the same basic result is Rabbitt et al. (2003).
26. Early speculations of the causes of age-related cognitive decline are contained in Foster and Taylor (1920), Jones and Conrad (1933), and Thorndike et al. (1928).
27. The interpretation of the results of the World War I testing is in Yerkes (1921, p. 815).
28. The APA Task Force conclusion is contained in Eisdorfer and Lawton (1973, p. ix).
29. Hebb's quotation is from Hebb (1978, p. 20), and the Skinner material is from Skinner and Vaughan (1983, pp. 66 and 71).
30. Among the authors who have mentioned the unpopularity of aging research are Welford (1958, p. 3) and Horn and Donaldson (1976, 1977). Nickerson (1980, pp. 355–356) also wrote that "Time is exceedingly unkind to human folk . . . Why anyone should want to do research that can only extend the list of ways in which we succumb to the ravages of time is difficult to understand."

Chapter 2

1. One of the earliest reports of a discrepancy in age trends in cross-sectional and longitudinal comparisons was in a book by Thorndike et al. (1928, p. 157). Although other researchers had reported cross-sectional declines from about 18 to 50 years of age on the Army Alpha test, these authors described a study in which the scores for people between 16 and 45 years of age increased over a 5-to-9 year interval. Two other early longitudinal studies also found age-related increases in longitudinal comparisons of cognitive functioning (Garrison, 1930; Miles, 1934).

2. The estimated annual differences in Figure 2.1 from cross-sectional comparisons were based on values reported in the Woodcock-Johnson III manual (McGrew & Woodcock, 2001), and the estimated annual changes from longitudinal comparisons were based on values reported in McArdle et al. (2002).

3. Data in Figure 2.2 are from Schaie (2005), upper left; Ronnlund et al. (2005), upper right; Alder et al. (1990), lower left; and Huppert and Whittington (1993), lower right. Figure 1 in Deary and Der (2005) is similar to the lower right panel of Figure 2.2, as they portray cross-sectional and longitudinal results for simple and choice reaction time data.
   This format for displaying cross-sectional and longitudinal data was
   . apparently first used by Horn and Donaldson (1976) in their Figure 3.

4. It can be noted that the discrepancies between the cross-sectional and longitudinal age relations in Figure 2.2 are smaller at older ages. Indeed, very similar cross-sectional and longitudinal age trends among older adults have been reported in several studies (e.g., Christensen et al., 2004; Colsher & Wallace, 1991; Finkel et al., 1998; Singer et al., 2003; Wilson et al., 2002a; Zelinski & Burnight, 1997). An intriguing exception is a report by Sliwinski and Buschke (1999) in which the age-related trends were actually more negative in the longitudinal comparisons than in the cross-sectional comparisons.

5. Classic discussions of developmental research designs are the monographs by Baltes, Reese, and Nesselroade (1977) and Campbell and Stanley (1963).

6. Evidence of short-term variation was reported in Salthouse (2007a), and this article also described a procedure to calibrate an individual's change in terms of units of his or her own short-term variability. A recent report by Salthouse and Nesselroade (unpublished manuscript) is apparently the only article in which short-term fluctuations were explicitly considered in analyses of longitudinal change.

7. Estimates of mobility from U.S. Census Bureau: Statistical Abstract of the United States: 2004–2005. Table 28. Morbidity Information from National Vital Statistics Reports, April 19, 2006, Vol. 54, no. 13, Table 3.

8. The total amount of magnitude of attrition in longitudinal studies can be very large. To illustrate, studies with adults age 55 and older have reported attrition rates of 33% over 6 years (Aartsen et al., 2002), 62% over 7.5 years (Christensen et al., 2004), 73% over 12 years (Dixon & deFrias, 2004), 74% over 6 years (Singer et al., 2003), 85% over 13 years (Backman et al., 2004), and about 50% over 20 years (Rabbitt et al., 2004b). Attrition rates have been variable in samples with broader age ranges, as it was only 27% over 5 years in the Betula project (Ronnlund et al., 2005), 73% over 5 years in a study of brain–behavior changes (Raz et al., 2007), and over 92% across a 42-year interval in the Seattle Longitudinal Study (Schaie, 2005). In one of the few studies reporting attrition at younger ages, Deary and Der (2005) reported attrition rates ranging from 22% to 32% over an 8-year interval for adults under the age of 60.

9. A few of the large number of studies reporting selectivity of the attrition in longitudinal studies are Brayne et al. (1999), Christensen et al. (2004), Deary and Der (2005), Hultsch et al. (1998), Kennison and Zelinski (2005), Owens (1953), Schaie et al. (1973), and Singer et al. (2003).

10. The Swedish research results summarized in Figure 2.3 were reported in Ronnlund et al. (2005). Similar results on selective attrition for adults with a mean age of 64 are described in Rabbitt et al. (2006a).
11. The meta-analysis of retest effects was reported by Hausknecht et al. (2007).
12. Analyses reported in Salthouse et al. (2004) suggest that reactive effects may last up to 12 years for adults under 60 years of age. The sample in that report was unique because different participants had different intervals between the assessments, and thus it was possible to determine the relation between the retest gain and the retest interval. Results from regression analyses suggested that between 7 and 12 years were needed for the retest gains to diminish to zero across different types of cognitive variables.
13. Estimates of retest effects with one versus two assessments are described in Salthouse (2009), Schaie (2005), Ronnlund et al. (2005, 2007), and Ronnlund and Nilsson (2006). These studies included adjustments for selective attrition, but there have apparently not been any studies in which the entire sample was identified at one point in time, and random assignment was used to determine which individuals would be tested immediately and after a delay and which would only be tested after a delay.

Several recent reports have revealed that the retest effects estimated when three or more assessments are available were quite large, and in some cases the adjusted longitudinal age trends were similar to the observed cross-sectional age differences (e.g., Ferrer et al., 2004; Ferrer et al., 2005; Finkel et al., 2005; Ghisletta & de Ribaupierre, 2005; Lovden et al., 2004; Rabbitt et al., 2001; Rabbitt et al., 2004a; Rodgers et al., 2003; Wilson et al., 2002a; Wilson et al., 2006).

Variable retest intervals have not been very common in longitudinal research, but two recent articles have analyzed this type of data. In the first report, McArdle and colleagues (2002) found that the effects associated with a retest on a measure of fluid intelligence were in the opposite direction and equal in magnitude to what would be expected across an interval of about 13.8 years, and for a measure of processing speed they were equivalent to about 4.4 years of the expected cross-sectional age difference. Additional analyses of the fluid intelligence variable in these data were reported in Salthouse et al. (2004). The cross-sectional age slope (in units referred to as W scores) for adults between 18 and 49 years of age was–0.36, the unadjusted longitudinal age slope was 2.0, and the retest-adjusted longitudinal age slope was–0.39. The estimated retest effect was 5.9 W units, which is in the opposite direction of, and nearly 15 times larger than, the estimated age effects.

Salthouse et al. (2004) also reported results from the same type of analytical model applied to a different data set with variable retest intervals. Two unusual features of this data set were that all of the participants in the project were under 60 years of age, and the interval between the first and the second test ranged from a few days to 35 years. As expected from previous research, negative cross-sectional and positive longitudinal age relations were apparent for all six variables. However, the estimated retest effects for each variable were quite large, and after adjusting for retest effects the longitudinal age relations were remarkably similar to the cross-sectional age relations in every cognitive variable. Salthouse (2009) also reported analyses of retest influences from a study with variable retest intervals.

The discovery that there is little or no discrepancy in cross-sectional and longitudinal age trends in measures of brain volume (e.g., Fotenos et al., 2005; Raz et al., 2005; Scahill et al., 2003) is also consistent with the interpretation that retest effects distort longitudinal comparisons of cognitive performance because it is unlikely that retest effects operate with measures of brain volume.

14. Not everyone agrees that it is necessarily desirable to try to distinguish retest influences from other components of change. For example, Thorvaldsson et al. (2006) stated: "One possibility is simply to reconsider retest effects as an intrinsic process associated with change in processes of interest, which as such cannot be disentangled from 'true change' associated with aging" (p. 353).

15. An interesting implication of the discovery of moderate to large retest effects is that it may be ill advised for research participants in a longitudinal study to participate in other projects during the interval between assessments because these other evaluations may function as additional retests that could distort the estimates of longitudinal change in the variables of primary interest. Unfortunately, it is not yet clear how similar the intervening tests must be to have effects. Any type of assessment might serve to reduce anxiety or increase test sophistication, and thus performance of a memory test, or even completion of a personality questionnaire, between the first and second assessment of tests of speed or reasoning might induce some reactive effects and affect the estimates of change. Although the analyses could become quite complicated, it may still be possible to estimate the influence of these other types of evaluations on the variable of primary interest if all of the intervening experiences are documented and can be incorporated into the analyses. Similar influences may also apply with cross-sectional comparisons if some of the participants have had prior testing experience, perhaps because they are members of a subject pool, and this previous experience affects the level of performance on the current test. At the present time, however, the issue of prior research experience is largely ignored in contemporary research, and it is typically assumed that there are little or no effects of previous research participation.

16. Owens (1953) expressed the concern about nonequivalent groups in cross-sectional designs eloquently in the following passage: "It is . . . true that cross-sectional studies demand an excessive number of somewhat unlikely assumptions and are therefore open to varying and ambiguous interpretations. Prominent among the problems involved is that it is extremely difficult to secure comparable samples of the population at successive ages, and to be assured that they are in fact *so* comparable that it is something more than gratuitous to attribute all differences between them to a single variable such as chronological age" (pp. 7–8). Among the characteristics mentioned by Owens that might differ across generations were number of years of education, test sophistication, and consequences of "innovations and improvements in the fields of transportation and communication" (p. 8).

17. Recent discussions of cohort effects in longitudinal research are contained in Au et al. (2004), Finkel et al. (2007), and Zelinski and Kennison (2007). An intriguing finding in the latter two studies was that there were cohort differences in the level of cognitive functioning, but weak and inconsistent effects on the rate of age-related change. In other words, people born in different periods had different average levels of performance but were similar in how performance changed as a function of increasing age.

18. The report comparing soldiers in WWI and WWII was by Tuddenham (1948), and comparisons of college freshman of different generations have been reported by Campbell (1965) and Owens (1953, 1966).

19. The original articles by Flynn were in 1984 and 1987. His recent book (Flynn, 2007) contains his latest speculations about the role of changes in amount of culturally supported scientific thinking as a primary cause of the effect. An interesting aspect of the Flynn effect is that several recent studies have suggested that the effect has either stabilized or reversed in recent years (e.g., Lynn & Harvey, 2008; Sundet et al., 2004; Teasdale & Owen, 2008).

20. The quote about the transient nature of cognitive aging is from Baltes and Schaie (1974).

21. Some of the earliest systematic studies containing relations between age and measures of cognitive functioning were by Foster and Taylor (1920), Jones and Conrad (1933), and Thorndike et al. (1928).

22. Similar age relations on the same tests in seven independent cross-sectional samples from 1956 to 1998 have also been reported by Schaie (2005, Figure 4.5). Ronnlund and Nilsson (2008) have also reported nearly identical cross-sectional age functions for assessments obtained between 1989 and 2004.

23. No standardized cognitive test batteries currently exist for nonhuman animals, although it is interesting that when a variety of different cognitive tests (e.g., associative fear conditioning, operant avoidance, discrimination, spatial navigation, delayed nonmatching to sample, reversal learning) have been administered to mice (Matzel et al., 2003), rats (Anderson, 1993), and monkeys (Herndon et al., 1997), moderate to large positive correlations among the variables have been found that are similar to those interpreted as evidence for a g-factor in humans.

24. Reports of cognitive aging in fruit flies are Brigui et al. (1990), Le Bourg (2004), and Tamura et al. (2003).

25. Solomon and Groccia-Ellison (1996) tested 96 rabbits ranging from 3.5 to 55 months of age and found a correlation of −.61 between age and the percentage of conditioned responses (i.e., eyeblinks to tone). It is noteworthy that two studies (i.e., Solomon et al., 1989; Woodruff-Pak & Thompson, 1988) in which a similar procedure was used in humans from 18 to 90 years of age both found correlations of −.58 between age and a measure of conditioning effectiveness. The upper left panel of Figure 2.7 portrays the average number of conditioned responses in rabbits at four different ages across delay, trace, and long-delay conditions in the Solomon and Groccia-Ellison (1996) study.

26. Some of the passive avoidance studies in rats are Kelly et al. (2003), McEchron et al. (2004), and Villarreal et al. (2004).

27. Studies comparing young and old rats in water mazes are as follows: Algeri et al. (1991), Burwell and Gallagher (1993), Dellu et al. (1997), Frick et al. (1995), Gage et al. (1989), Lukoyanov et al. (1999), Magnusson et al. (2003), Markowska (1999), Shukitt-Hale et al. (1998, 2004), Topic et al. (2005), Veng et al. (2003), and Wyss et al. (2000).

28. Cognitive aging research with dogs has been reported in Chan et al. (2002), Head et al. (1995), Milgram et al. (1994), Milgram et al. (2005), and Tapp et al. (2003). Milgram et al. (1994) reported that the correlation between age and the number of errors in different tasks ranged from .45 to .58, and Head et al. (1995) reported a correlation of .54 between age and trials to criterion in a learning task.

29. The study with squirrel monkeys was reported in Lyons et al. (2004).

30. The study with rhesus monkeys was reported in Herndon et al. (1997; also see Lacreuse et al., 2005).

31. Larger cross-sectional than longitudinal age declines in animals have been reported by Algeri et al. (1991), Caprioli et al. (1991), Dellu et al. (1997), and Markowska and Savonenko (2002).

32. There is some tension between certain advocates of longitudinal research and the large number of researchers who primarily rely on cross-sectional comparisons, as the former sometimes claim that cross-sectional data are merely a proxy for longitudinal data and that only within-person changes are relevant to theories of cognitive aging. The conflict is understandable because if this assertion were true it would suggest that cross-sectional research is of little value for understanding why people of different ages perform at different average levels in many cognitive tests. A more moderate view might be that both cross-sectional and longitudinal data have limitations, and that these limitations should be considered when using the results to interpret and understand cognitive aging phenomena.

33. Different results with different measures of change was reported in Reynolds et al. (2002). Among the many discussions of methodological complications associated with evaluating change are Arndt et al. (2000), Francis et al. (1991), Frerichs and Tuokko (2005), Hertzog et al. (2006), Hertzog and Nesselroade (2003), and Schaie (1988).

    Although seldom employed, one strategy that might facilitate progress in understanding strengths and weaknesses of different analytic procedures would be to report results from several different procedures with the same data. This strategy should not only yield stronger conclusions if the results were found to be robust across different sets of assumptions, but it might also prove informative with respect to the validity of the assumptions, and applicability, of different analytical methods. A report by Salthouse (2009) is an initial step in this direction as several different methods of estimating retest effects were reported for the same variables and the same samples of participants.

34. Another method of estimating reliability is based on the ratio of systematic, or nonerror, variance to total variance, as estimated from a particular statistical model.

    Although a systematic examination of the correspondence among the different types of reliability, and among the estimates derived from different types of statistical models, would likely be informative, there are apparently no published reports with this type of information.

35. A number of retest correlations as a function of retest interval were reported by Salthouse et al. (2004). The median retest correlation was .71 for a retest interval of less than 1 year, but it was .64 with an interval between 7 and 15 years. The Woodcock Johnson III Technical Manual (McGrew & Woodcock, 2001; Table 3.5) reports that with an interval less than 1 year the median retest correlation was .79 for adults age 19 to 44, and .84 for adults age 45 to 95, but with intervals of 3 to 10 years the retest correlations were .73 and .72, respectively. Larsen et al. (2008) reported 18-year retest correlations between age 20 and age 38 of .85 for a measure of general intelligence, and of .79 and .82 for two different tests.

    With latent constructs based on multiple indicators the retest correlations over a 5–7 year interval can be .85 or greater (Hultsch et al., 1999; Lovden et al., 2004, 2005; Ronnlund et al., 2005; Schaie, 2005, Table 8.10 and 8.11). Furthermore, Gold et al. (1995; also Schwartzman et al., 1987) reported that the 40-year stability for an intelligence measure was .78, and that the short-term retest reliability was .95.

36. Some of the recent studies reporting no significant individual differences in the change parameter from latent growth curve models in at least some cognitive variables or participant groups are Albert et al. (2007), Alley et al. (2007), Lovden et al. (2005), McArdle et al. (2005), Raz et al. (2008), and Small and Backman (2007). A likely reason why individual differences in change are often not detected is low statistical power (Hertzog et al., 2008).

37. The importance of individual differences in change for reliable assessment of change was clearly expressed by Hertzog and Nesselroade (2003), when they stated that "when the variance in true change is zero, one cannot reliably measure individual differences in change—because there aren't any" (p. 640).

38. One study in which reliability of change was estimated from changes in odd-numbered and even-numbered items was Salthouse (2007a).

39. Zelinski and Stewart (1998) is one of the few studies to have used a formula to estimate reliability of change from reliability at each occasion and the correlation across occasions.

40. A distinction between reliability in the sense of replicability, and reliability as related to the proportion of measurement error is potentially important because they are not necessarily equivalent. For example, Zhang et al. (2007) used latent growth models to estimate the level and slope of learning functions for a nearly identical task performed by the same participants in each of three sessions. Despite the fact that the growth curve parameters were theoretically free of measurement error, they were only weakly correlated with one another across sessions, which suggests that the short-term replicability was low.

41. The phrase "Does it all go together when it goes?" was used as the title of an article by Rabbitt (1993), but surprisingly there was no discussion of correlated change in the article.

42. Sliwinski and Buschke (2004) used the term "coupled change" to refer to association at the within-person level, and "correlated change" to associations at the between-person level.
43. Significant correlations among longitudinal changes have been reported in a number of studies, particularly when the analyses were based on factor scores or latent variables. Among these studies are Anstey et al. (2003), Christensen et al. (2004), Ferrer et al. (2005), Finkel et al. (2003), Ghisletta and Lindenberger (2003), Hertzog et al. (2003), Lindenberger & Ghisletta (2009), Lovden et al. (2004), MacDonald et al. (2003), Mackinnon et al. (2003), Reynolds et al. (2002), Sliwinski and Buschke (2004), Tucker-Drob (2009), Tucker-Drob et al. (2009), Wilson et al. (2002a, 2006), and Zimprich and Martin (2002).

    The moderate correlations among change scores for different cognitive variables are consistent with the idea that many cognitive variables change together, and as implied by cross-sectional analyses, that they do not age independently. In fact, on the basis of moderate correlations among the change slopes for different variables, Wilson et al. (2002a, p. 190) stated " . . . we think it is likely that change in cognition in old age is mostly global." Also see Christensen et al. (2004), Hultsch et al. (1998), Lindenberger and Ghisletta (2009), and Tucker-Drob (2009) for similar conclusions.
44. One attempt to distinguish maturation and retest components of correlated change was reported by Ferrer et al. (2005). In this project there was a reduction, after controlling for retest influences, in the correlations from .73 to .63 between speed and memory, and from .82 to .58 in another data set between speed and memory. Wilson et al. (2006) did not report the actual values, but they stated that correlations among age changes in different cognitive variables with and without control of retest effects were nearly identical. Finally, Tucker-Drob (2009) found strong correlations among measures of cognitive change after controlling for effects of retests.
45. The avalanche metaphor was first mentioned in Salthouse et al. (2004). Complications of attempting to identify causal influences based on observations in the middle of a pathologic process have also been discussed by Glymour (2007).

Chapter 3

1. The early quote about memory complaints is from Thorndike et al. (1928, p. 159).
2. The memory questionnaire was adapted from the Memory Functioning Questionnaire (Zelinski et al., 1990). The cognitive ability measures were based on composite scores created by averaging z-scores for the three to six variables representing each cognitive ability. Depression was measured with the CES-D (Radloff, 1977), anxiety with the Spielberger State-Trait Anxiety Inventory (Spielberger et al., 1983), and the "Big Five" personality traits with a scale developed by Goldberg (1999).

3. Among the numerous other studies that have reported weak relations between self-reported memory complaints and objective memory performance are Cargin et al. (2008), Jungwirth et al. (2004), and Zelinski et al. (2001).

4. Data in Figures 3.1 through 3.4 were obtained from the test manuals of the following tests: Wechsler Memory Scale (Wechsler, 1997b); Neuropsychological Assessment Battery (Stern & White, 2001), Kaplan Baycrest (Leach et al., 2000), Reynolds Intellectual Assessment Scales (Reynolds & Kamphaus, 1998), and Doors and People (Baddeley et al., 1994).

5. Among the recent studies with reports of age differences in multiple memory variables are Dixon et al. (2004), Dore et al. (2007), Nilsson et al. (1997), Nyberg et al. (2003a), Park et al. (2002), Ronnlund et al. (2005), Salthouse (2003), Siedlecki (2007), and Verhaeghen and Salthouse (1997).

6. The following are several of the meta-analyses of memory with their corresponding effect size estimates. Verhaeghen et al. (1993)—recall = 0.99, WM = 0.81; LaVoie and Light (1994)—recall = 0.97, recognition = 0.50; Spencer and Raz (1995)—recall = 1.01, recognition = 0.57, intentional = 0.62, incidental = 0.42; Henry et al. (2004)—recall = 1.22, and Old and Naveh-Benjamin (2008)—item memory = 0.73, associative memory = 0.92. A very impressive meta-analysis of age differences in prose memory was reported by Johnson (2003) based on 1,385 effect sizes from 194 studies. Some of the effect sizes from these analyses were as follows: overall age difference = 0.69, 9–12 years of education = 1.05, 16+ years of education = 0.60; lists of sentences = 0.89, text = 0.62, immediate = 0.70, longer than 10 min = 0.49, verbatim = 1.0, and gist = 0.71.

7. The quote about older adults having so much to forget is from Jones (1959, p. 731).

8. The anecdote about the ichythologist was described in James D. Watson's book (*Avoid boring [other] people,* 2007, p. 44), where he attributed the quote to David Starr Jordan who became President of Stanford University in 1891.

9. The distinctions among memory types based on the bicycle was described by D'Esposito and Weksler (2000).

10. The quote about the most recent information lost first was by Hollingworth (1927, p. 314).

11. Examples of studies based on probes of historical information are Botwinick and Storandt, 1974; Perlmutter, 1978; Squire, 1974 (see Salthouse, 1991, p. 227, for an early review). Among the studies of very long-term memory of information about high school classmates, campus landmarks, etc. are Bahrick (1984) and Bahrick et al. (2008).

12. Examples of studies using the procedure of reporting a memory associated with a specific word are Janssen et al. (2005) Janssen & Murre (2008), and Rubin and Schulkind (1997).

13. A small set of the many studies revealing larger age differences in measures of recollection than in measures of familiarity are Clarys et al. (2002), Clarys et al. (2009), Daselaar et al. (2006), Maylor (1995), Salthouse and Siedlecki (2007b), and Salthouse, Toth et al. (1997).

14. An article with the provocative title of "In defense of external invalidity" described the argument that the purest assessments may not be ecologically valid (Mook, 1983).

15. The following is a brief list of studies reporting age differences in tasks that can be presumed to be ecologically valid: golf shots (Backman & Molander, 1986; Molander & Backman, 1996); news stories in print, audio, and television (Frieske & Park, 1999; Stine et al., 1990); movie details (Conrad & Jones, 1929; Jones, Conrad, & Horn, 1928); eye witness identifications (Memon et al., 2002; Perfect & Harris, 2003; Searcy et al., 2001); recipes (Taub, 1975); musical tunes and lyrics (Maylor, 1991, 1995; Bartlett & Snelus, 1980); grocery prices (Castel, 2005), shopping lists (McCarthy et al., 1981); telephone numbers (Crook et al., 1980); museum exhibit locations (Loftus et al., 1992; Uttl & Graf, 1993); medical history (Cohen & Java, 1995); and product warning information (Hancock, Fisk, & Rogers, 2005).

16. Two early studies reporting no significant age differences in memory for activities were by Backman and Nilsson (1984, 1985). Later studies reporting significant age differences in memory for activities or performed actions are Earles (1996), Nyberg et al. (2002), Ronnlund et al. (2003, 2005), and Siedlecki et al (2005).

17. Age correlations for four prospective memory tasks were reported in Salthouse et al. (2004). The meta-analyses of prospective memory were reported by Henry et al. (2004) and Kliegel et al. (2008).

18. Carstensen and Charles (1994) reported age differences in the proportion of emotional material remembered, but a later study by Charles et al. (2003, Study 2) failed to replicate this finding. Furthermore, a number of studies failed to find significant interactions of age and emotion in various memory measures (e.g., Comblain et al., 2004; Denburg et al. 2003; Fernandes et al., 2008; Gruhn et al., 2005; Kensinger et al., 2002; Yoder & Elias, 1987). Additional results that complicate the interpretation of the role of emotion on age differences in memory are as follows: Knight et al. (2002) found that older adults recalled fewer negative (sad) words than young adults in some tasks but not in others; Gallo and Roediger (2003) found no age differences in ratings of degree of emotional response at study in a recognition memory task; and Kensinger (2008) found that older adults remembered more positive nonarousing words but not more arousing words. The confusing literature is reflected in two statements from recent reviews. In one, Kensinger (2009, p. 209) stated that " . . . although older adults' mnemonic benefit from emotion does not always exceed that derived by young adults, in some instances memories for emotional information seem to be less affected by ageing than memories for information without emotional content." However, a recent meta-analysis by Murphy and Isaacowitz (2008) concluded "that there were few age effects in emotion information processing" (p. 281).

19. The research results investigating the role of stereotype threat on memory aging are quite complex and not particularly consistent. For example, Levy and Langer (1994) found larger age differences in a composite memory score among Americans, who have less positive age stereotypes, than

among Chinese, but this finding was only partially replicated (in two of four variables) by Yoon et al. (2000). Levy (1996) found that subliminal primes of a negative stereotype (senile, forgetful) reduced memory performance of older adults in two of five measures, but Stein et al. (2002) only partially replicated these results with significant effects on different tasks than those reported by Levy.

Among the studies in which the pattern previously observed in young adults was not replicated in young adults or across multiple studies in the same project were Hess et al. (2003, 2004) and Hess and Hinson (2006). No interaction of age and instructions or conditions designed to investigate the role of stereotype threat were reported by Andreoletti and Lachman (2004) and Chasteen et al. (2005).

A study by Rahhal et al. (2001) investigated the effects of instructions that mentioned memory and remembering. In one experiment the older adults were better when memory was not mentioned, but inexplicably, the young adults were worse by 0.37 standard deviation units. In the second experiment, the magnitude of negative age differences was nearly the same with (~7%) and without (~5%) memory instructions, and there was no mention of an interaction.

20. Andreoletti et al. (2006) also found no age differences in two measures of anxiety, although one of the measures was related to memory in middle-aged adults and older adults, but not in young adults.

21. The different emphases on task variance and person variance in micro and macro approaches were discussed in Salthouse (2005a).

22. It is sometimes assumed that micro and macro approaches differ in the types of variables examined, but that is not necessarily the case because the same variables considered in micro approaches could be incorporated in studies using a macro approach. A possible reason why this is seldom done is that few of the variables that have been the focus in micro studies have had their reliabilities established.

23. One of the major analytical tools in the micro approach is a test of an age-by-condition interaction in an analysis of variance because it is considered a test of differential aging based on the assumption that different magnitudes of age effects correspond to qualitatively different influences. However, there is no necessary correspondence between the magnitude of the age relation and the nature, or number of causes, of the age relations because, as described by Salthouse (2000), there are at least three reasons why an interaction could occur when there is only a single age-related influence.

24. An unsuccessful attempt to demonstrate construct validity for hypothesized components in two reasoning tasks was reported by Salthouse (2001).

25. Advantages of the macro approach are that theoretical constructs can be assessed more broadly without assuming a one-to-one correspondence between variable and construct, construct validity and measurement invariance can be investigated, and independence of age-related influences can be examined.

26. Recent examples of the variance control method, sometimes in the form of a mediational model, are Chen and Li (2007), Fritsch et al. (2007), Kennedy et al. (2008), de Ribaupierre and Lecerf (2006), Schretlen et al. (2001), and Singh-Manoux et al. (2003).

Caution must be used when interpreting these types of models because it can be difficult to distinguish among alternative models, particularly concerning the direction of the influence, when most or all of the variables are at the same level of analysis and are obtained at the same point in time. See Christenfeld et al. (2004) for other cautions about statistical control techniques.

27. It is important to emphasize that proportions of age-related variance estimated in analyses of cross-sectional data should not be interpreted as necessarily implying anything about relations among age-related changes in longitudinal data. Nevertheless, these types of variance-partitioning procedures can be informative in attempting to identify factors involved in the observed differences. That is, the age variable in these analyses can be considered to be a static variable, somewhat analogous to sex or ethnicity, with the goal of trying to estimate the contribution of specific factors on the individual difference relations.

28. Discussions of hierarchical structures in cognitive abilities can be found in Carroll (1993), Deary (2000), Gustafsson (1988, 2002), and Jensen (1998).

29. Examples of hierarchical structural models with age-related influences are Jopp and Hertzog (2007), Salthouse (1998), Salthouse and Czaja (2000), Salthouse and Ferrer-Caja (2003), and Schroeder and Salthouse (2004). Although not framed as a hierarchical analysis, Rabbitt and colleagues have reported an analogous result in that statistical control of a measure of fluid ability known to correlate highly with the highest order factor in a hierarchical structure reduced the age-related variance in several different cognitive variables (e.g., Rabbitt, 2005; Rabbitt & Lowe, 2000).

30. References to the literature on correlations among the cognitive changes in different cognitive variables and factors are provided in the notes to Chapter 2. The distinction between evaluating change in already established factors and determining whether different estimates of change can be organized into factors is analogous to a contrast between what McArdle (1988) referred to as a "curves of factors" versus "factors of curves." One example of the factor of curves approach is Christensen et al. (2004). A recent dissertation by Tucker-Drob (2009) directly examined the dimensionality of change in longitudinal data from our project and found that the structure of short-term change was very similar to the structure of cognitive variables at a single occasion.

31. Almost any variable could be used as a reference variable in contextual analyses, but the variables are most meaningful when they are reliable, when there is evidence of both convergent and discriminant validity of the relevant constructs, and when there is evidence of measurement invariance across the relevant age range. Analyses based on variables of low or unknown reliability, weak convergent validity, and unknown measurement equivalence are difficult to interpret.

32. Examples of contextual analyses are Salthouse (2005b), Salthouse and Siedlecki (2007a, 2007b), Salthouse et al. (2004, 2006, 2008), and Siedlecki et al. (2005).

Chapter 4

1. The now classical discussion of mediation methods is Baron and Kenny (1986), and a recent review is in MacKinnon et al. (2007). Longitudinal mediation has been discussed in Cole and Maxwell (2003) and MacKinnon (2008).

2. There have been several attempts to investigate the temporal sequence of mediation by examining the relation between the initial level of one variable and the subsequent change in another variable. However, because the initial level reflects all determinants on the level prior to any change in the variable, it is a weak approximation of the relation of early change in one variable to later change in another variable. See the section "Identification of Risk Factors for Cognitive Decline and Dementia" in Chapter 5 for further discussion of temporal sequencing of causes and effects.

3. Gollub and Reichardt (1987, 1991) discussed the importance of considering time lags between possible causes and consequences in longitudinal research.

4. Causal relations are often postulated among variables or constructs, but it is difficult to establish causal priority when all of the variables are assessed at the same time. Causal hypotheses might be more convincing if lead–lag relations were clearly established in longitudinal comparisons, or by appeal to a compelling reductionist argument in which the hypothesized cause is closer to a presumed neurobiological substrate. However, for most mediational models one can only be confident that at least some of the age-related influences are shared, and the causal direction among the variables is ambiguous.

5. The logical status of mediation inferences was also discussed in Salthouse (2006a).

6. The influence of the relations of age on the variables in these types of variance partitioning procedures have been discussed in Salthouse (1985), Salthouse and Ferrer-Caja (2003), and Salthouse and Nesselroade (2002).

7. Another complication with mediation analyses is that suppressor relations may exist. That is, there may be no relation between age and variable X unless variable Z is included in the analysis because it could be related in opposite directions to age and X, such that the age–X relation is suppressed when Z is not considered.

8. One concern about moderation is that the power to detect interactions is often rather low (McClelland & Judd, 1993). However, this is less of an issue in the current analyses because the sample sizes were frequently greater than 2,000 and thus power was moderately high.

9. The early speculations about possible causes of cognitive aging, and reasons why the potential causes were not considered plausible, were discussed by Jones and Conrad (1933).

10. Correlations of about .63 and .66 between IQ at age 11 and IQ at age 77 and at age 79 were reported in Deary et al. (2000, 2004). Richards et al. (2004) reported significant correlations of cognitive ability at age 15 and an estimate of decline in memory and speed from age 43 to age 53, and Plassman et al. (1995) reported a correlation of .46 between score on a

cognitive ability test taken when entering the military and score on a different cognitive test at age 67. Significant relations between IQ in high school and cognitive performance at age 75 were reported by Fritsch et al. (2007).

    Relations between measures of adult cognitive ability have also been reported with paternal occupation (e.g., Richards & Sacker, 2003; Kaplan et al., 2001), early childhood environment (Everson-Rose et al., 2003), and birth weight (e.g., Richards et al., 2002; Shenkin et al., 2001; Sorensen et al., 1997).

11. Reduced age effects after controlling for education were reported by Ronnlund and colleagues (e.g., 2005), but the range of education in their sample was quite large, with some age groups averaging less than 8 years of education. This raises the possibility that years of education may not have had the same meaning in all age groups.

    Other studies have found little evidence of a moderating influence of education on cross-sectional age trends, as there were nearly parallel age trends at different amounts of education (e.g., Birren & Morrison, 1961; Christensen et al., 2001; Droege et al., 1963; Smits et al., 1997).

    The results regarding an influence of education on longitudinal change have also been inconsistent. Several studies reviewed in Anstey and Christensen (2000) and in Valenzuela and Sachdev (2006a, 2006b) found greater decline in individuals with lower levels of education, but a number of recent studies found no effects of education on the slope or rate of change in one or more cognitive variables (e.g., Albert et al., 2007; Christensen et al., 2001; Gerstorf et al., 2006; Tucker-Drob et al., 2009; Van Dijk et al., 2008). In fact, the lack of consistency is evident in a single study, as Alley et al. (2007) found that higher education was associated with slower decline on two variables, faster decline on one variable, and no effect on another variable.

12. It may seem strange to combine self-ratings of health with measures of medication usage that presumably alleviate certain health problems. Nevertheless, these measures were moderately correlated with one another, which suggests that it is meaningful to consider them as all reflecting a common health construct.

13. Early speculations of the role of sensory factors can be found in Foster and Taylor (1920) and Jones and Conrad (1933). Lovden and Wahlin (2005) and Wahlin et al. (2006) also found that statistical control of a measure of visual acuity attenuated the cross-sectional relations of age with several cognitive variables. In contrast to the weak or nonexistent relations in our project, the Wahlin et al. (2006) study found evidence for both moderating and mediating effects of self-rated health and sensory acuity on a number of cognitive variables. The older age of their sample (i.e., age 61 to 95) may be responsible for the different results.

    In a sample of adults 55 years and older, Valentijn et al. (2005) found that change in visual acuity was correlated with change in measures of cognitive functioning.

14. Among the studies reporting significant correlations between measures of cognition and measures of olfaction, balance, lower limb strength, lung function, or blood pressure are Anstey et al. (2001), Baltes and

Lindenberger (1997), Christensen et al. (2004), Lindenberger and Baltes (1994), Salthouse et al. (1996), Swan and Carmelli (2002), Tabert et al. (2005), and Westervelt et al. (2005). A recent study even found a significant correlation between number of teeth and score on the Digit Symbol test (Wu et al., 2008). Some of this literature was reviewed in Li and Lindenberger (2002).

15. A few of the studies investigating relations between age and measures of cognitive functioning after adjusting for sensory deficits are Gilmore et al. (2006), Lindenberger et al. (2001), McCoy et al. (2005), and Murphy et al. (2000).

16. In contrast to the weak relations of physical exercise to cognition in our project, Singh-Manoux et al. (2005) found higher levels of cognitive functioning among adults with greater levels of physical activity. The different outcomes could be attributable to the much larger sample size and more detailed assessment of physical activity in the Singh-Manoux et al. (2005) study. An intriguing study by Richards et al. (2003) found that after controlling for IQ at age 15, physical exercise at age 36 was associated with a slower decline in memory from age 43 to 53. Additional research with physical exercise as a potential mediator or moderator of cognitive aging is discussed in Chapter 5.

17. Among the early publications with discussions of mental exercise are Foster and Taylor (1920), Thorndike et al. (1928), Jones and Conrad (1933), Miles (1935), Sorenson (1938), and Sward (1945).

18. The review of research on mental exercise and mental aging is in Salthouse (2006b), and a critique was published by Schooler (2007) followed by a reply by Salthouse (2007b). A study by Mackinnon et al. (2003) found significant correlations between change in activity and change in cognition, but nearly the same amount of cognitive decline in people without activity decline as in people with activity decline. Other longitudinal studies reporting evidence for reciprocal relations of activity and cognition are Aartsen et al. (2002), Bosma et al. (2002), Hultsch et al. (1999), and Schooler and Mulatu (2001). Ghisletta et al. (2006) discussed some methodological and analytical issues that may have contributed to some of the inconsistent results in the past.

19. The sources of the psychosocial measures were CES-D (Radloff, 1977); Satisfaction with Life (Diener et al., 1985); trait anxiety (Spielberger et al., 1983); Need for Cognition (Cacioppo & Petty, 1982); Positive and Negative Affect (Watson et al., 1988), and the "Big Five" Personality Traits (Goldberg, 1999).

20. Although little cross-sectional age relations on measures of personality were reported in early studies (e.g., Costa & McCrae, 1994), more recent studies have reported modest but significant age differences in some traits in both cross-sectional (e.g., Allemand et al., 2007; Allemand et al., 2008; Donnellan & Lucas, 2008; Srivastava et al., 2003; Terracciano et al., 2005), and longitudinal studies (e.g., Allemand et al., 2008; Roberts & Mroczek, 2008; Roberts et al., 2006; Small et al., 2003; Terracciano et al., 2005).

21. Relations between age and negative affect in a subset of the participants in our project were reported by Teachman (2006).

22. A number of studies have reported mediational analyses with neurobiological measures hypothesized to be involved in age–cognition relations. Among those with measures of brain volume as the mediator are Brickman et al. (2006), Cook et al. (2002), Gunning-Dixon and Raz (2003), Head et al. (2002, 2008, 2009), Rabbitt et al. (2006b), Schretlen et al. (2000), and Walhovd et al. (2005). Backman et al. (2000) and Erixon-Lindroth et al. (2005) used measures of dopamine binding as the mediator, and a number of studies used measures of white matter integrity as the mediator (e.g., Bucur et al., 2007; Charlton et al., 2008; Deary et al., 2006; Gootjes et al., 2007; Rabbitt et al., 2007a, 2007b).

A few studies have also reported relations between the level or change in a neurobiological variable and the change in a cognitive variable (e.g., Kramer et al., 2007; Persson et al., 2006; Prins et al., 2005; Raz et al., 2007; Schmidt et al., 2005; van den Heuvel et al., 2006).

23. Many correlations have been reported among various neurobiological variables, one or more measures of cognitive functioning, and age. However, only a few studies have examined the relation between two of the variables after controlling for the other variable. Some researchers have been interested in whether the X–cognition relation was due to the influence of age on both variables, and consequently have examined the relation after controlling the influence of age. If the neurobiological variable is a mediator of the age–cognition relations, then the X–cognition relation should still be significant after controlling age, and this has been found in a number of studies (e.g., Charlton et al., 2006, 2007; Gong et al., 2005; Kovari et al., 2004; O'Sullivan et al., 2001; Salat et al., 2002; Volkow et al., 1998; but not Tisserand et al., 2000).

Chapter 5

1. The citation to fear of dementia is in Gatz (2007).
2. Prevalence estimates for dementias have been reported in Hebert et al. (2003), Lobo et al. (2000), McDowell et al. (2004), Plassman et al. (2007), and Qiu et al. (2007). Incidence estimates have been reported in Jorm and Jolley (1998) and Petersen et al. (2001).
3. Miscellaneous information about Alzheimer disease, including estimates of annual expenses can be found in AD Facts (Alzheimer's Association, 2008). Useful overviews of dementia, including some historical information, are in Breitner (2006), Keller (2006), Kelley and Petersen (2007), Reisberg (2006), and Salmon and Bondi (2009).
4. A review of the CERAD project is in Fillenbaum et al. (2008).
5. Statistics on the accuracy of diagnosis confirmed by autopsy have been reported in Massoud et al. (1999) and Salmon et al. (2002).
6. The quote about the effects of currently available medications on AD is from AD Facts (Alzheimer's Association, 2008).
7. The view that early intervention is critical in the treatment of AD is discussed in DeKosky (2003).

8. Other studies reporting little or no relation of age to MMSE score (Folstein, Folstein & McHugh, 1975) among healthy adults up to about age 75 are Crum et al. (1993), Grigoletto et al. (1999), and Ronnlund et al. (2005). However, declines at older ages are more common, as reported in Chatfield et al. (2007) and Lyketsos et al. (1999).

9. Actual data closely resembling the patterns schematically illustrated in Figure 5.3 have been reported by Amieva et al. (2005), Chen et al. (2001), and Small and Backman (2007). However, it should be noted that there are also reports of stable levels of cognitive performance prior to dementia diagnosis (e.g., Albert et al., 2007; Galvin et al., 2005), and the reasons for these discrepancies are not yet well understood.

10. A meta-analysis of preclinical cognitive impairment in AD was published by Backman et al. (2005), where effect sizes of approximately 1.0 were found for measures of episodic memory, executive functioning, and perceptual speed. Among the studies reporting lower levels of cognitive functioning several years prior to diagnosis are Amieva et al. (2005), Backman et al. (2001), Cerhan et al. (2007), Chen et al. (2001), DeSanti et al. (2008), Elias et al. (2000), Jacobs et al. (1995), Jorm et al. (2005), Lange et al. (2002), Laukka et al. (2006), Saxton et al. (2004), Sliwinski et al. (1996), and Small et al. (2000).

11. Discussions of the various proposals for characterizing the preclinical stage of dementia can be found in Chertkow et al. (2007), Davis and Rockwood (2004), Dierckx et al. (2007), Panza et al. (2005), Reisberg et al. (2008), Ritchie and Touchon (2000), Rivas-Vazquez et al. (2004), and Stephan et al. (2007).

12. The consensus report on MCI was published in Winblad et al. (2004). An earlier report by a subcommittee of the American Academy of Neurology was published by Petersen et al. (2001).

13. The SOUND acronym for MCI was proposed by Rivas-Vasquez et al. (2004).

14. Distinctions among MCI subtypes are discussed in Aggarwal et al. (2005), Busse et al. (2006), and Lopez et al. (2003).

15. Studies reporting conversion and reversion rates for MCI are Boyle et al. (2006), Fischer et al. (2007), Larrieu et al. (2002), Lopez et al. (2007), Petersen et al. (2001), and Ritchie et al. (2001).

16. The status of a distinct preclinical category is controversial as Petersen and O'Brien (2006) argued that MCI should be a separate diagnostic category in the next *Diagnostic and Statistical Manual,* but Morris et al. (2001) and Storandt et al. (2006) claim that it may represent an early stage of AD, and Backman et al. (2005, p. 527) stated that " . . . labels such as 'normal aging,' 'pre-clinical AD,' 'MCI,' and 'early AD' may best be viewed as instances on a dimension of brain and cognitive functioning rather than as discrete categories."

17. Advantages of the predictive approach to investigating preclinical dementia were discussed in Amieva et al. (2005).

18. Among the publications describing results of the Nun study are Riley et al. (2005), Snowdon et al. (1996), and Tyas et al. (2007).

19. The reports of relations of childhood IQ to incidence of AD in late life are Whalley et al. (2000) and Starr et al. (2000). Borenstein et al. (2006)

reviewed risk factors associated with the first 25 years of life and concluded that " . . . risk of Alzheimer disease is probably not determined in any single time period but results from the complex interplay between genetic and environmental exposures throughout the life course" (p. 63).

20. The meta-analysis on preclinical cognitive deficits was published by Backman et al. (2005).

21. One of the first articles to describe the complications of including preclinical dementia patients in studies intended to investigate normal aging was Sliwinski et al. (1996). These researchers also introduced the concept of robust norms, and recent discussions of this concept are in De Santi et al. (2008), Holtzer et al. (2008), and Ritchie et al. (2007).

22. Although the mere existence of a risk factor can be informative for some purposes, information about mechanism is needed before the risk factor results can be used as the basis for intervention or prevention. Christenfeld et al. (2004) made this point in the following statement: "It would be one thing to find that *B'nai B'rith Magazine* readers were more likely to be carriers of Tay-Sachs; it would be another to suggest that canceling their subscriptions would help" (p. 868).

23. General discussions of epidemiological research and identification of risk factors can be found in Christenfeld et al. (2004), Gatz (2005), Glymour (2007), Hill (1965), and Kraemer et al. (2001). Hill (1965) proposed risk factor criteria of strength, consistency, specificity of association, temporality, dose dependency, and biological plausibility. Methodological and analytical issues associated with determining relations with late-life cognitive change were also discussed in Ghisletta et al. (2006).

24. The quotes about relations between cognitive activity and cognitive decline and risk of dementia are in Rundek and Bennett (2006). Discussions of risk factors frequently imply causal relations among changes even when they do not use explicitly causal language. As an example, Schooler (2007) stated that " . . . doing . . . mental exercise increases the likelihood that a given individual's level of cognitive functioning will be better than if he or she had not done such exercise and will continue to be better for a consequential period of time" (p. 24). This statement has a clear causal implication because it claims that if there is a change in X (mental exercise), then there will likely be a change Y (better cognitive functioning . . . for a consequential period of time).

25. The taxonomy in Table 5.1 is incomplete in many respects. For example, a cross-panel design involves measurement of both X and Y at two points in time (i and j), with the interest in whether the lagged relations are asymmetric (i.e., X_i—$Y_j > X_j$—Y_i). Two recent examples of this type of cross-lagged analysis are Deary et al. (2009) and Perrino et al. (2008).

26. Another possibility not represented in Figure 5.4 is that people who start at a higher level have a faster rate of decline in the second segment of the function, and there are some reports with this type of outcome (e.g., Andel et al. 2006; Hall et al. 2007). The faster declines may be attributable to the individuals being farther along the disease process when they are diagnosed and in the region of the function where declines are accelerating.

27. The consensus report on risk factors for cognitive decline appeared in Hendrie et al. (2006), and another review of epidemiological risk factors

was published by Fratiglioni et al. (2004). Interestingly, a recent study by Bielak et al. (2007) found that although there were many significant correlations between level of activity and level of cognition (Type 1 research in the taxonomy of Table 5.1), very few correlations between change in activity and change in cognition (Type 3 research) were significant.

28. The estimates of genetic influences were reported by Whalley et al. (2000), who stated that 7% of early-onset AD, and less than 1% of late-onset AD cases, were caused by known inherited factors. The twin study of AD was published by Gatz et al. (2006).

29. An informative discussion of the role of ApoE on AD can be found in Deary, Wright et al. (2004).

30. The consensus committee statement on genetic testing for AD was published by the National Institute on Aging, Alzheimer's Association Working Group (1996). A similar recommendation was made by a committee of the American Academy of Neurology in 2001 (Knopman et al., 2001).

31. A meta-analysis on ApoE effects on cognition was published by Small et al. (2004). At least two studies reported no association of ApoE4 with cognition in children (Deary et al., 2003; Turic et al., 2001). Mixed results have been found in middle age as some studies found differences (e.g., Flory et al., 2000; Greenwood et al., 2005), but others did not (e.g., Alexander et al., 2007; Jorm et al., 2007).

32. A recent meta-analysis of education as a risk factor for dementia revealed that individuals with low education were associated with an increased risk of 30% to 80% for developing dementia relative to individuals with higher education (Caamano-Isorna et al., 2006).

33. Albert et al. (1995) found that higher physical activity associated with less decline over a 2–3 year period. The study reporting a small difference in annual decline among women who walked was Yaffe et al. (2001). The replication study in 2004 was Weuve et al. (2004). The study finding the relation only in women was Laurin et al. (2001), and the study finding a relation with dementia incidence only in men was Simons et al. (2006). The study reporting only a relation with cardiovascular fitness and cognitive decline was Barnes et al. (2003). The two studies in 2004 with no relation between initial physical activity and subsequent cognitive decline were Abbott et al. (2004), and Van Gelder et al. (2004), with the former finding a relation with incidence of dementia and the latter finding a relation between decrease in activity and decrease in cognition. The study with a relation only among e4 noncarriers was reported by Podewils et al. (2005), and the study with a relation only among carriers of the e4 allele was Schuitt et al. (2001). Larsen et al. (2006) found that physical exercise at baseline was related to the risk of developing dementia, but the high and low exercise groups also differed significantly in amount of education, amount of physical activity, and level of depression at baseline, and one or more of these factors could have contributed to the dementia risk.

Studies finding no relation of physical activity to decline in cognitive functioning or probability of dementia are Hultsch et al. (1999),

Verghese et al. (2003), Wang et al. (2006), and Wilson et al. (2002b). Interestingly, Rundek and Bennett (2006) suggested that one possible reason for the inconsistency in the physical activity risk factor results was difficulty of uniform assessment, particularly compared to assessment of cognitive activity. As noted above, an alternative view is that assessment of cognitive activity has been very crude and subjective, and possibly more so than physical activity.

34. Reviews of studies reporting lower incidence or later onset of dementia among individuals with higher levels of cognitive stimulation have been published by Fratiglioni et al. (2004) and Valenzuela and Sachdev (2006a, 2006b). A recent study reporting a relation between cognitive engagement and rate of decline and incidence of dementia is Wilson et al. (2007). At least one study has reported that nondemented older adults reported greater increases in engagement in intellectual activities from young to middle adulthood than demented older adults (Friedland et al., 2001).

35. A relatively large number of studies have investigated the relation between smoking and cognitive function. Anstey et al. (2007) reported a meta-analysis of smoking effects and concluded that smokers were at a higher risk for AD and had greater cognitive declines than nonsmokers. Based on comparisons of carefully matched participants from a large database, Paul et al. (2006) concluded that "Cigarette smoking is associated with isolated and subtle cognitive difficulties among very healthy individuals" (p. 457).

36. Some of the reports describing post-operative cognitive disorder are Abildstrom et al. (2000), Dodds and Allison (1998), Moller et al. (1998), Newman et al. (2001), Ritchie et al. (1997), and Selnes et al. (2001).

37. The participants in our project reported whether they had ever had general anesthesia. This is a very crude question because we have no information about how many times they received general anesthesia, for what purpose, or the duration of the anesthesia. Nevertheless, a very high proportion (76.7%) of the participants reported that they had undergone general anesthesia, and the frequency was higher at older ages. However, the correlations of this variable with the composite cognitive scores after controlling for influences of age were all less than .03, and thus there is no evidence of a detrimental effect of general anesthesia on the measures of cognitive functioning in our project.

38. Fratiglioni et al. (2004) reviewed longitudinal studies investigating the relations between social support and cognition, and they concluded that there were small but positive effects. However, two recent studies reported discrepant results, as Bennett et al. (2006) found a positive effect of social support, and Wang et al. (2006) found no relation between social activity and cognitive decline.

39. Reviews of research investigating relations of estrogen to level of cognitive functioning and incidence of AD are Bagger et al. (2005) and Sherwin (2005).

40. The review of dietary supplements and cognition was published by McDaniel et al. (2002) and the quotation is from page 35, and the review of the role of gingko biloba on cognition was published by Gold et al. (2002), and the quotation is from page 9. Burns et al. (2006) found little or no effects on cognitive functioning in a clinical trial involving young and

older adults, and no evidence for a protective effect on gingko biloba for the development of dementia was reported in DeKosky et al. (2008).

41. The concept of cognitive or brain reserve has been the focus of many publications. A succinct statement of the concept is in Scarmeas and Stern (2003, p. 625)—"Something must account for the disjunction between the degree of brain damage and its outcome, and the concept of reserve has been proposed to serve this purpose.... Innate intelligence or aspects of life experience like educational, or occupational attainment may supply reserve, in the form of a set of skills or repertoires that allows some people to cope with pathology better than others."

Recent reviews of the cognitive reserve concept are in Christensen et al. (2008), Fritsch et al. (2007), Rundek and Bennett (2006), and Stern (2006). Very similar ideas have been discussed by Greenwood (2007) and Park and Reuter-Lorenz (2009).

Chapter 6

1. It is clearly possible that some individuals experience little or no cognitive decline even into very late adulthood. Identifying those individuals and determining what might be responsible for their preserved levels of functioning should obviously be an important priority for future research.

2. Among those who have distinguished between typical and maximum performance are Ackerman (1994) and Cronbach (1949).

3. Gottfredson (2002) used the terms "can do," "will do," and "have done" as determinants of work performance.

4. An insightful discussion of the benefits of experience was provided by Birren (1964), which includes the following quotation, "It seems plausible that the adult enlarges his repertory of ready-made solutions over a lifetime and becomes effective by virtue of them. The mode of address to a problem thus tends with age to be one of searching within the existing repertory of responses rather than of looking to the generation of novel approaches" (p. 194).

5. The research on typing has been published in Salthouse (1984) and Salthouse and Saults (1987).

6. The research on crossword puzzles was described in Hambrick et al. (1999).

7. Skinner's book is *Enjoy Old Age* (Skinner & Vaughan, 1983).

8. The linkage of fewer medication adherence errors with increased age is likely due to greater use of timers, reminder notes, and links to ritual; this has been discussed by Hertzog et al. (2000), Maylor (1990), and Park et al. (1999).

9. The distinction between strategic and tactical decisions in driving was discussed by De Raedt and Ponjaert-Krisotfferson (2000) and Withaar et al. (2000).

10. The age differences in fatal crashes with a passenger was described in Bedard and Meyers (2004).

11. It should be noted that opinions differ with respect to issues relevant to the design of intervention studies. For example, in the introduction of a special

section of a journal devoted to cognitive interventions, it was stated that "... most researchers can agree on what the ideal training study should look like ..." (Mayr, 2008, p. 682).

12. Another issue that should be considered when evaluating interventions concerns the number of variables that could be used as measures of intervention effectiveness and how they are reported. Because intervention studies are often very expensive and time consuming, researchers often administer many different tasks before and after the intervention. This is not necessarily a problem if results from all of the variables are reported and appropriate adjustments are made for capitalization on chance. However, interpretations can become very complicated when only some of the variables are reported or many independent statistical tests are carried out without considering the possibility that some would be significant by chance.

13. Among the studies reporting smaller training or intervention benefits at older ages are Baltes and Kliegl (1992), Brehmer et al. (2007, 2008), Gothe et al. (2007), Kliegl et al. (1989, 1990), Kray and Epplinger (2006), and Nyberg et al. (2003b). Reports of greater benefit in older individuals have been reported with dogs in which only older dogs exhibited effects of scopolamine on performance (Araujo et al., 2005), and Cotman et al. (2002) in which a dietary supplement only affected performance of older dogs. A study with monkeys found that only older monkeys had a benefit of dopamine d1 agonist on performance (Castner & Goldman-Rakic, 2004).

14. The meta-analysis examining effect sizes for fitness effects and for cognition effects was reported by Etnier et al. (2006). Colcombe and Kramer (2003) also found no significant differences in cognitive effect size across differences in VO_2 max gain. It is noteworthy that a recent study by Cassilhas et al. (2007) found benefits of resistance training exercise on several measures of cognitive functioning, which suggests that aerobic exercise may not be the critical determinant of exercise-related improvements in cognitive functioning.

15. Verhaeghen et al. (1993) conducted a meta-analysis of memory training in older adults and found an effect size of .73 on trained tasks compared to .38 for no-contact control groups. Among the intervention studies reporting significant improvements in trained tasks but little or no transfer to other cognitive abilities are Baltes et al. (1988), Belleville et al. (2006), Bherer et al. (2005), Craik et al. (2007), Dahlin et al. (2008), Edwards et al. (2005), Jennings et al. (2005), Kliegl et al. (1989, 1990), Kramer et al. (1995); Mahncke et al. (2006), Rasmusson et al. (1999), Stigsdotter Neely and Backman (1995), and Wood and Pratt (1987). Li et al. (2008) reported that both young and old adults exhibited improvements after working memory training but that neither group revealed transfer to a different type of working memory task. However, the participants in the training group in this study apparently also completed several self-report evaluations and performed additional tests of postural control, vigilance, and perceptual speed in every session, and therefore the basis for the training gains is not clear.

16. In addition to the question of the relation between the immediate target of training and the primary outcome variable is the question of the relation between near transfer and far transfer (cf. McArdle & Prindle, 2008).

17. Possible benefits of broad-based interventions have been discussed in Carlson et al. (2008), Noice et al. (2004), McDaniel et al. (2008), Park et al. (2007), and Stine-Morrow et al. (2007, 2008). McKhann and Albert (2002, p. 19) even made an argument that shopping might be a useful intervention as they state: "We can't prove this, but it may be that women not only live longer but possibly maintain their brain functions better than most men, in part because they shop. While shopping, they are physically active, wandering through stores carrying parcels. They are mentally active, comparing process and making choices. And, after completing their shopping, they feel they have accomplished something."

18. The nature of training transfer is a complicated issue (see Barnett & Ceci, 2002). Transfer could be defined in terms of abstract entities such as elements or cognitive processes, but this may not be particularly meaningful in the absence of accepted operational definitions of elements or processes. Potentially more objective candidates for evaluating transfer are across cognitive abilities, defined in terms of individual differences in cognitive functioning (e.g., Carroll, 1993), or across neurobiological substrates, such as regions or circuits of coactivation.

    An illustration of the confusing nature of transfer is evident in a study by Edwards et al. (2005). Older adults receiving attention-speed training did not show any greater gains in several commonly used measures of speed, but they did exhibit greater reductions than a control group in the time to perform activities such as finding a telephone number or counting out correct change. In this case, there was apparently far transfer without any near transfer, which seems paradoxical.

19. It is interesting that some researchers have justified interventions only in older adults because of a claim that there is no cognitive decline until old age. For example, Willis and Schaie (1994, p. 95) stated: "Since most adults do not experience reliably detectable decline in psychometric mental abilities until old age, interventions begun in middle age would need to treat those rare individuals suffering unusually early decline."

20. The term *plasticity* is used in many different ways in the research literature. A thoughtful discussion of the concept from both neurobiological and behavioral perspectives is in Pascual-Leone et al. (2005).

21. The distinction between plasticity and modifiability of age relations is frequently blurred, which can lead to some confusion. For example, in an introduction to a special section of a journal devoted to cognitive plasticity, the author (Mayr, 2008, p. 682) implied that the research would alter the rate of decline (i.e., slow down or stop the decline). Furthermore, one of the articles in that section used the phrase "attenuate cognitive decline" in the title despite no long-term monitoring of age-related changes.

22. The ACTIVE project has been described in Ball et al. (2002) and Willis et al. (2006). The 2006 article found that over the 5 years of the project the control group reported more difficulty completing tasks such as meal preparation, housework, and shopping than the groups receiving cognitive training. However, as the authors note, these results could be related to effects on self-efficacy instead of "real" benefits of the interventions. Furthermore, there were no significant effects of cognitive training on

objective, performance-based, measures of everyday problem solving or everyday speed of processing.

23. Meta-analyses of the effects of exercise on cognition, with estimated effect sizes are Colcombe and Kramer (2003), $d = 0.48$; Etnier et al. (1997), $d = 0.25$; Etnier et al. (2006), $d = 0.25$, and Heyn et al. (2004), $d = 0.57$.

24. Meta-analyses of the effect sizes for fitness improvement with exercise, with estimated effect sizes, are Green and Crouse (1995), $d = 0.65$; Etnier et al. (2006), $d = 0.55$, and Heyn et al. (2004), $d = 0.69$ and 0.65. The average improvement in VO_2 max from the Green and Crouse (1995) meta-analysis was 22.5%. General reviews of research on exercise and cognition are in Kramer et al. (2005) and Kramer and Erikson (2007). Among the studies finding little effects of physical exercise training on cognition are Blumenthal et al. (1991), Blumenthal and Madden (1988), Emery and Gatz (1990), Hill et al. (1993), and Madden et al. (1989).

25. Reports of the aerobic exercise intervention conducted at the University of Illinois have been reported in Kramer et al. (1999, 2002) and Colcombe et al. (2006). In a recent report, McAuley et al. (2007) noted that the walking group had much lower self-reported physical activity at baseline and immediately after the intervention than the control group.

References

Aartsen, M.J., Martin, M., & Zimprich, D. (2004). Gender differences in level and change in cognitive functioning. *Gerontology, 50*, 35–38.

Aartsen, M.L, Smits, C.H.M., van Tilburg, T., Knipscheer, KC.P.M., & Deeg, D.J.H. (2002). Activity in older adults: Cause or consequence of cognitive functioning? A longitudinal study of everyday activities and cognitive performance in older adults. *Journal of Gerontology: Psychological Sciences, 57B*, P153–P162.

Abbott, R.D., White, L.R., Ross, G.W., Masaki, K.H., Curb, J.D., & Petrovitch, H. (2004). Walking and dementia in physically capable elderly men. *Journal of American Medical Association, 292*, 1447–1453.

Abildstrom, H., Rasmussen, L.S., Rentowl, P., Hanning, C.D., Rasmussen, H., Kristensen, P.A., & Moller, J.T. (2000). Cognitive dysfunction 1–2 years after non-cardiac surgery in the elderly. *Acta Anaesthesiologica Scandinavica, 44*, 1246–1251.

Ackerman, P.L. (1994). Intelligence, attention, and learning: Maximal and typical performance. In D.K. Detterman (Ed.), *Current topics in human intelligence: Vol. 4: Theories.* Norwood, NJ: Ablex.

Ackerman, P.L. (1996). A theory of adult intellectual development: Process, personality, interests, and knowledge. *Intelligence, 22*, 227–257.

Ackerman, P.L., Beier, M.E., & Bowen, K.R. (2000). Explorations of crystallized intelligence: Completion tests, cloze tests, and knowledge. *Learning and Individual Differences, 12*, 105–121.

Aggarwal, N.T., Wilson, R.S., Beck, T.L., Bienias, J.L., & Bennett, D.A. (2005). Mild cognitive impairment in different functional domains and incident Alzheimer's disease. *Journal of Neurology Neurosurgery and Psychiatry, 76*, 1479–1484.

Albert, M.S., Jones, K., & Savage, C.R. (1995). Predictors of cognitive change in older persons: MacArthur studies of successful aging. *Psychology and Aging, 10*, 578–589.

Albert, M.S., Blacker, D., Moss, M.B., Tanzi, R., & McArdle, J.J. (2007). Longitudinal change in cognitive performance among individuals with mild cognitive impairment. *Neuropsychology, 21*, 158–169.

Alder, A.G., Adam, J., & Arenberg, D. (1990). Individual differences assessment of the relationship between change in and initial level of adult cognitive functioning. *Psychology and Aging, 5*, 560–568.

Alexander, D.M., Williams, L.M., Gatt, J.M., Dobson-Stone, C., Kuan, S.A., Todd, E.G., Schofield, P.R., Cooper, N.J., & Gordon, E. (2007). The contribution of apolipoprotein E alleles on cognitive performance and dynamic neural activity over six decades. *Biological Psychology, 75*, 229–238.

Algeri, S., Biagini, L., Manfridi, A., & Pitsikas, N. (1991). Age-related ability of rats kept on a life-long hypocaloric diet in a spatial memory test: Longitudinal observations. *Neurobiology of Aging, 12*, 277–282.

Allemand, M., Zimprich, D., & Hendriks, A.A.J. (2008). Age differences in five personality domains across the life span. *Developmental Psychology, 44*, 758–770.

Allemand, M., Zimprich, D., & Hertzog, C. (2007). Cross-sectional age differences and longitudinal age changes of personality in middle adulthood and old age. *Journal of Personality, 75*, 323–358.

Allemand, M., Zimprich, D., & Martin, M. (2008). Long-term correlated change in personality traits in old age. *Psychology and Aging, 23*, 545–557.

Alley, D., Suthers, K., & Crimmins, E. (2007). Education and cognitive decline in older Americans: Results from the AHEAD sample. *Research on Aging, 29*, 73–94.

Alwin, D.F., & McCammon, R.J. (2001). Aging, cohorts, and verbal ability. *Journal of Gerontology: Social Sciences, 56(B)*, S151–S161.

Alzheimer's Association. (2008). 2008 Alzheimer's disease facts and figures. *Alzheimer's & Dementia, 4*, 110–133.

Amieva, H., Jacqmin-Gadda, H., Orgogozo, J-M., Le Carret, N., Helmer, C., Letenneur, L., Barberger-Gateau, P., Fabrigoule, C., & Dartigues, J-F. (2005). The 9-year cognitive decline before dementia of the Alzheimer type: A prospective population-based study. *Brain, 128*, 1093–1101.

Andel, R., Vigen, C., Mack, W.J., Clark, L.J., & Gatz, M. (2006). The effect of education and occupational complexity on rate of cognitive decline in Alzheimer's patients. *Journal of the International Neuropsychological Society, 12*, 147–152.

Anderson, B. (1993). Evidence from the rat for a general factor that underlies cognitive performance and relates to brain size: Intelligence? *Neuroscience Letters, 153*, 98–102.

Andreloetti, C., & Lachman, M. E. (2004). Susceptibility and resilience to memory aging stereotypes: Education matters more than age. *Experimental Aging Research, 30*, 129–148.

Andreoletti, C., Veratti, B.W., & Lachman, M.E. (2006). Age differences in the relationship between anxiety and recall. *Aging & Mental Health, 10*, 265–271.

Anstey, K., & Christensen, H. (2000). Education, activity, health, blood pressure and apolipoprotein E as predictors of cognitive change in old age: A review. *Gerontology, 48*, 163–177.

Anstey, K.J., Hofer, S.M., & Luszcz, M.A. (2003). Cross-sectional and ongitudinal patterns of dedifferentiation in later-life cognitive and sensory function: The effects of age, ability, attrition, and occasion of measurement. *Journal of Experimental Psychology: General, 132*, 470–487.

Anstey, K.J., Luszcz, M.A., & Sanchez, L. (2001). A reevaluation of the common factor theory of shared variance among age, sensory function, and cognitive function in older adults. *Journal of Gerontology: Psychological Sciences, 56B*, P3–P11.

Anstey, K.J., von Sanden, C., Salim, A., & O'Kearney, R. (2007). Smoking as a risk factor for dementia and cognitive decline: A meta-analysis of prospective studies. *American Journal of Epidemiology, 166,* 367–378.

Araujo, J.A., Studzinski, C.M., & Milgram, N.W. (2005). Further evidence for the cholinergic hypothesis of aging and dementia from the canine model of aging. *Progress in Neuro-Psychopharmacology, & Biological Psychiatry, 29,* 411–422.

Ardila, A. (2008). Normal aging increases cognitive heterogeneity: Analysis of dispersion in WAIS-III scores across age. *Archives of Clinical Neuropsychology, 22,* 1003–1011.

Arndt, S., Turvey, C., Coryell, W.H., Dawson, J.D., Leon, A.C., & Akiskal, H.S. (2000). Charting patients' course: A comparison of statistics used to summarize patient course in longitudinal and repeated measures studies. *Journal of Psychiatric Research, 34,* 105–113.

Au, R., Seshadri, S., Wolf, P.A., Elias, M.F., Elias, P.K., Sullivan, L., Beiser, A., & D'Agostino, R.B. (2004). New norms for a new generation: Cognitive performance in the Framingham offspring cohort. *Experimental Aging Research, 30,* 333–358.

Backman, L., Ginovart, N., Dixon, R.A., Robins Whalin, T.B., Wahlin, A., Halldin, C., & Farde, L. (2000). Age-related cognitive deficits mediated by changes in the striatal dopamine system. *American Journal of Psychiatry, 157,* 635–637.

Backman, L., Jones, S., Berger, A.K., Laukka, E.J., & Small, B.J. (2005). Cognitive impairment in preclinical Alzheimer's disease: A meta-analysis. *Neuropsychology, 19,* 520–531.

Backman, L., & Molander, B. (1986). Effects of adult age and level of skill on the ability to cope with high stress conditions in a precision sport. *Psychology and Aging, 1,* 334–336.

Backman, L., & Nilsson, L.-G. (1984). Aging effects in free recall: An exception to the rule. *Human Learning, 3,* 53–69.

Backman, L., & Nilsson, L.-G. (1985). Prerequisites for lack of age differences in memory performance. *Experimental Aging Research, 11,* 67–73.

Backman, L., Small, B.J., & Fratiglioni, L. (2001). Stability of the preclinical episodic memory deficit in Alzheimer's disease. *Brain, 124,* 96–102.

Backman, L., Wahlin, A., Small, B. J., Herlitz, A., Winblad, B., & Fratiglioni, L. (2004). Cognitive functioning in aging and dementia: The Kungsholmen Project. *Aging, Neuropsychology and Cognition, 11,* 212–244.

Baddeley, A., Emslie, H., & Nimmo-Smith, I. (1994). *Doors and People: A test of visual and verbal recall and recognition.* Bury St. Edmonds, England: Thames Valley Test Company.

Bagger, Y.Z., Tanko, L.B., Alexandersen, P., Qin, G., & Christiansen, C. (2005). Early postmenopausal hormone therapy may prevent cognitive impairment later in life. *Menopause, 12,* 12–17.

Bahrick, H.P., (1984). Semantic memory content in permastore: 50 years of memory for Spanish learned in school. *Journal of Experimental Psychology: General, 113,* 1–29.

Bahrick, H.P., Hall, L.K., & Da Costa, L.A. (2008). Fifty years of memory of college grades: Accuracy and distortions. *Emotion, 8,* 13–22.

Ball, K., Berch, D.B., Helmers, K.F., Jobe, J.B., Leveck, M.D., Marsiske, M., Morris, J.N., Rebok, G.W., Smith, D.M., Tennstedt, S.L., Unverzagt, F.W., & Willis, S.L. (2002). Effects of cognitive training interventions with older adults: A randomized controlled trial. *Journal of the American Medical Association, 288,* 2271–2281.

Baltes, P.B., & Kliegl, R. (1992). Further testing of limits of cognitive plasticity: Negative age differences in a mnemonic skill are robust. *Developmental Psychology, 28,* 121–125.

Baltes, P.B., Kliegl, R., & Dittmann-Kohli, F. (1988). On the locus of training gains in research on the plasticity of fluid intelligence in old age. *Journal of Educational Psychology, 80,* 392–400.

Baltes, P.B., & Lindenberger, U. (1997). Emergence of a powerful connection between sensory and cognitive functions across the adult life span: A new window to the study of cognitive aging? *Psychology and Aging, 12,* 12–21.

Baltes, P.B., Reese, H.W., & Nesselroade, J.R. (1977). *Life-span developmental psychology: Introduction to research methods.* Belmont, CA: Wadsworth.

Baltes, P.B., & Schaie, K.W. (March 1974). The myth of the twilight years. *Psychology Today,* 35–40.

Barnes, D.E., Yaffe, K., Satariano, W.A., & Tager, I.B. (2003). A longitudinal study of cardiorespiratory fitness and cognitive function in healthy older adults. *Journal of American Geriatrics Society, 51,* 459–465.

Barnett, S.M., & Ceci, S.J. (2002). When and where do we apply what we learn? A taxonomy for far transfer. *Psychological Bulletin, 128,* 612–637.

Baron, R.M., & Kenny, D.A. (1986). The moderator-mediator variable distinction in social psychological research: Conceptual, strategic, and statistical considerations. *Journal of Personality and Social Psychology, 51,* 1173–1182.

Bartlett, J.C., & Snelus, P. (1980). Lifespan memory for popular songs. *American Journal of Psychology, 93,* 551–560.

Bedard, M., & Meyers, J. (2004). The influence of passengers on older drivers involved in crashes. *Experimental Aging Research, 30,* 205–215.

Beeson, M.F. (1920). Intelligence at senescence. *Journal of Applied Psychology, 4,* 219–234.

Beier, M.E., & Ackerman, P.L. (2001). Current-events knowledge in adults: An investigation of age, intelligence, and nonability determinants. *Psychology and Aging, 16,* 615–628.

Beier, M.E., & Ackerman, P.L. (2003). Determinants of health knowledge: An investigation of age, gender, abilities, personality, and interests. *Journal of Personality and Social Psychology, 84,* 439–448.

Beier, M.E., & Ackerman, P.L. (2005). Age, ability, and the role of prior knowledge on the acquisition of new domain knowledge: Promising results in a real-world learning environment. *Psychology and Aging, 20,* 341–355.

Belleville, S., Gilbert, B., Fontaine, F., Gagnon, L., Menard, E., & Gauthier, S. (2006). Improvement of episodic memory in persons with mild cognitive impairment and healthy older adults: Evidence from a cognitive intervention program. *Dementia and Geriatric Cognitive Disorders, 22,* 486–299.

Bennett, D.A., Schneider, J.A., Arvanitakis, Z., Kelly, J.F., Aggarwal, N.T., Shah, R.C., & Wilson, R.S. (2006). Neuropathology of older persons without cognitive impairment from two community-based studies. *Neurology, 66,* 1837–1844.

Bennett, D.A., Schneider, J.A., Tang, Y., Arnold, S.E., Wilson, R.S. (2006). The effect of social networks on the relation between Alzheimer's disease pathology and level of cognitive function in old people: A longitudinal cohort study. *Lancet Neurology, 5,* 406–412.

Bherer, L., Kramer, A.F., Peteson, M.S., Colcombe, S., Erickson, K., & Becic, E. (2005). Training effects on dual-task performance: Are there age-related differences in the plasticity of attentional control? *Psychology and Aging, 20,* 695–709.

Bielak, A.A.M., Hughes, T.F., Small, B.J., & Dixon, R.A. (2007). It's never too late to engage in lifestyle activities: Significant concurrent but not change relationships between lifestyle activities and cognitive speed. *Journal of Gerontology: Psychological Sciences, 62B*, P331–P339.

Bingham, W.V., & Davis, W.T. (1924). Intelligence test scores and business success. *Journal of Applied Psychology, 8*, 1–22.

Birren, J.E. (1964). *The psychology of aging.* Englewood Cliffs, NJ: Prentice-Hall.

Birren, J.E., & Morrison, D.F. (1961). Analysis of the WAIS subtests in relation to age and education. *Journal of Gerontology, 16*, 363–369.

Blumenthal, J.A., Emery, C.F., Madden, D.J., Schniebolk, S., Walsh-Riddle, M., & George, L.K. (1991). Long-term effects of exercise on psychological functioning in older men and women. *Journal of Gerontology, 46*, P352–P361.

Blumenthal, J.A., & Madden, D.J. (1988). Effects of aerobic exercise training, age, and physical fitness on memory-search performance. *Psychology and Aging, 3*, 280–285.

Borenstein, A.R., Copenhaven, C.I., & Mortimer, J.A. (2006). Early-life risk factors for Alzheimer Disease. *Alzheimer's Disease and Associated Disorders, 20*, 63–72.

Bosma, H., van Boxtel, M.P.J., Ponds, R.W.H.M., Jelicic, M., Houx, P., Metsemakers, J., & Jolles, J. (2002). Engaged lifestyle and cognitive function in middle and old-aged, non-demented persons: A reciprocal association? *Zeitschrift fur Gerontologie und Geriatrics, 35*, 575–581.

Botwinick, J., & Storandt, M. (1974). *Memory, related functions and age.* Springfield, IL: Charles C. Thomas.

Bowles, R.P., Grimm, K.J., & McArdle, J.J. (2005). A structural factor analysis of vocabulary knowledge and relations to age. *Journal of Gerontology: Psychological Sciences, 60*, P234–P241.

Bowles, R.P., & Salthouse, T.A. (2008). Vocabulary test format and differential relations to age. *Psychology and Aging, 23*, 366–376.

Boyle, P.A., Wilson, R.S., Aggarwal, N.T., Tang, Y., & Bennett, D.A. (2006). Mild cognitive impairment: Risk of Alzheimer disease and rate of cognitive decline. *Neurology, 67*, 441–445.

Brayne, C., Spiegelhalter, D.J., Dufouil, C., Chi, L.Y., Dening, T.R., Paykel, E.S., O'Connor, D.W., Ahmed, A., McGee, M.A., & Huppert, F.A. (1999). Estimating the true extent of cognitive decline in the old. *Journal of the American Geriatrics Society, 47*, 1283–1289.

Brehmer, Y., Li, S-C., Muller, V., von Oertzen, T., & Lindenberger, U. (2007). Memory plasticity across the life span: Uncovering children's latent potential. *Developmental Psychology, 43*, 465–478.

Brehmer, Y., Li, S-C., Straube, B., Stoll, G., von Oertzen, T., Muller, V., & Lindenberger, U. (2008). Comparing memory skill maintenance across the life span: Preservation in adults, increase in children. *Psychology and Aging, 23*, 227–238.

Breitner, J.C.S. (2006). Dementia—epidemiological considerations, nomenclature, and a tacit consensus definition. *Journal of Geriatrics, Psychiatry and Neurology, 19*, 129–136.

Brickman, A.M., Zimmerman, M.E., Paul, R.H., Grieve, S.M., Tate, D.F., Cohen, R.A., Williams, L.M., Clark, C.R., & Gordon, E. (2006). Regional white matter and neuropsychological functioning across the adult lifespan. *Biological Psychiatry, 60*, 444–453.

Brigui, N., Le Bourg, E., & Medioni, J. (1990). Conditioned suppression of the Proboscis-Extension response in young, middle-aged, and old *Drosophila melanogaster* flies: Acquisition and extinction. *Journal of Comparative Psychology, 104,* 289–296.

Bucur, B., Madden, D.J., Spaniol, J., Provenzale, J.M., Cabeza, R., White, L.E., & Huettel, S.A. (2007). Age-related slowing of memory retrieval: Contributions of perceptual speed and cerebral white matter integrity. *Neurobiology of Aging, 29,* 1070–1079.

Burns, N.R., Bryan, J., & Nettelbeck, T. (2006). *Ginkgo biloba:* No robust effect on cognitive abilities or mood in healthy young or older adults. *Human Psychopharmacology, 21,* 27–37.

Burwell, R.D., & Gallagher, M. (1993). A longitudinal study of reaction time performance in Long-Evans rats. *Neurobiology of Aging, 14,* 57–64.

Busse, A., Hensel, A., Guhne, U., Angermeyer, M.C., & Riedel-Heller, S.G. (2006). Mild cognitive impairment: Long-term course of four clinical subtypes. *Neurology, 67,* 2176–2185.

Caamano-Isorna, F., Corral, M., Montes-Martinez, A., & Takkouche, B. (2006). Education and dementia: A meta-analytic study. *Neuroepidemiology, 26,* 226–232.

Cacioppo, J.T., & Petty, R.E. (1982). The need for cognition. *Journal of Personality and Social Psychology, 42,* 116–131.

Campbell, D.P. (1965). A cross-sectional and longitudinal study of scholastic abilities over twenty-five years. *Journal of Counseling Psychology, 12,* 55–61.

Campbell, D.T., & Stanley, J.C. (1963). *Experimental and quasi-experimental designs for research.* Chicago: Rand McNally & Co.

Caprioli, A., Ghirardi, O., Giuliani, A., Ramacci, M.T., & Angelucci, L. (1991). Spatial learning and memory in the radial maze: A longitudinal study in rats from 4 to 25 months of age. *Neurobiology of Aging, 12,* 650–607.

Cargin, J.W., Collie, A., Masters, C., & Maruff, P. (2008). The nature of cognitive complaints in healthy older adults with and without objective memory decline. *Journal of Clinical and Experimental Neuropsychology, 30,* 245–257.

Carlson, M.C., Saczynski, J.S., Rebok, G.W., Seeman, T., Glass, T.A., McGill, S., Tielsch, J., Frick, K.D., Hill, J., & Fried, L.P. (2008). Exploring the effects of an "everyday" activity program on executive function and memory in old adults: Experience Corps®. *The Gerontologist, 48,* 793–801.

Carroll, J.B. (1993). *Human cognitive abilities.* Cambridge, England: Cambridge University Press.

Carstensen, L.L., & Turk-Charles, S. (1994). The salience of emotion across the adult life course. *Psychology and Aging, 9,* 259–264.

Cassilhas, R.C., Viana, V.A.R., Grassmann, V., Santos, R.T., Santos, R.F., Tufik, S., & Mello, M.T. (2007). The impact of resistance exercise on the cognitive function of the elderly. *Medicine & Science in Sports & Exercise, 39,* 1401–1407.

Castel, A.D. (2005). Memory for grocery prices in younger and older adults: The role of schematic support. *Psychology and Aging, 20,* 718–721.

Castner, S.A., & Goldman-Rakic, P.S. (2004). Enhancement of working memory in aged monkeys by a sensitizing regimen of dopamine D1 receptor stimulation. *Journal of Neuroscience, 24,* 1446–1450.

Cattell, R.B. (1943). The measurement of adult intelligence. *Psychological Bulletin, 40,* 153–193.

Cattell, R.B. (1972). *Abilities: Their structure, growth, and action.* Boston: Houghton-Mifflin.

Cerhan, J.H., Ivnik, R.J., Smith, G.E., Machulda, M.M., Boeve, B.F., Knopman, D.S., Petersen, R.C., & Tangalos, E.G. (2007). Alzheimer's disease patients' cognitive status and course years prior to symptom recognition. *Aging, Neuropsychology and Cognition, 14*, 227–235.

Chan, A.D.F., Nippak, P.M.D., Murphey, H., Ikeda-Douglas, C.J., Muggenburg, B., Head, E., Cotman, C.W., & Milgram, N.W. (2002). Visuospatial impairments in aged canines (*Canis familiaris*): The role of cognitive-behavioral flexibility. *Behavioral Neuroscience, 116*, 443–454.

Charles, S.T., Mather, M., & Carstensen, L.L. (2003). Aging and emotional memory: The forgettable nature of negative images for older adults. *Journal of Experimental Psychology: General, 132*, 310–324.

Charlton, R.A., Barrick, T.R., McIntyre, D.J., Shen, Y., O'Sullivan, M., Howe, F.A., Clark, C.A., Morris, R.G., & Markus, H.S. (2006). White matter damage on diffusion tensor imaging correlates with age-related cognitive decline. *Neurology, 66*, 217–222.

Charlton, R.A., Landau, S., Schiavone, F., Barrick, T.R., Clark, C.A., Markus, H.S., & Morris, R.G. (2008). A structural equation modeling investigation of age-related variance in executive function and DTI measured white matter damage. *Neurobiology of Aging, 29*, 1547–1555.

Charlton, R.A., McIntyre, D.J.O., Howe, F.A., Morris, R.G., & Markus, H.S. (2007). The relationship between white matter brain metabolites and cognition in normal aging: The GENIE study. *Brain Research, 1164*, 108–116.

Chasteen, A.L., Bhattacharyya, S., Horhota, M., Tam, R., & Hasher, L. (2005). How feelings of stereotype threat influence older adults' memory performance. *Experimental Aging Research, 31*, 235–260.

Chatfield, M., Matthews, F.E., & Brayne, C. (2007). Using the Mini-Mental State Examination for tracking cognition in the older population based on longitudinal data. *Journal of the American Geriatrics Society, 55*, 1066–1071.

Chen, P., Ratcliff, G., Belle, S.H., Cauley, J.A., DeKosky, S.T., & Ganguli, M. (2001). Patterns of cognitive decline in presymptomatic Alzheimer disease. *Archives of General Psychiatry, 58*, 853–858.

Chen, T., & Li, D. (2007). The roles of working memory updating and processing speed in mediating age-related differences in fluid intelligence. *Aging, Neuropsychology and Cognition, 14*, 631–646.

Chertkow, H., Nasreddine, Z., Joanette, Y., Drolet, V., Kirk, J., Massoud, F., Belleville, S., & Bergman, H. (2007). Mild cognitive impairment and cognitive impairment, no dementia: Part A, concept and diagnosis. *Alzheimer's & Dementia, 3*, 266–282.

Christenfeld, N.J.S., Sloan, R.P., Carroll, D., & Greenland, S. (2004). Risk factors, confounding, and the illusion of statistical control. *Psychosomatic Medicine, 66*, 868–875.

Christensen, H., Anstey, K.J., Leach, L.S., & Mackinnon, A.J. (2008). Intelligence, education, and the brain reserve hypothesis. In F.I.M. Craik & T.A. Salthouse (Eds.), *Handbook of aging and cognition* (3rd ed.) (pp. 133–188). New York: Psychology Press.

Christensen, H., & Henderson, A.S. (1991). Is age kinder to the initially more able? A study of eminent scientists and academics. *Psychological Medicine, 221*, 935–946.

Christensen, H., Hofer, S.M., Mackinnon, A., Korten, A., Jorm, A.F., & Henderson, A.S. (2001). Age is no kinder to the better educated: Absence of an association investigated using latent growth techniques in a community sample. *Psychological Medicine, 31*, 15–28.

Christensen, H., Mackinnon, A., Jorm, A.F., Korten, A., Jacomb, P., Hofer, S.M., & Henderson, S. (2004). The Canberra Longitudinal Study: Design, aims, methodology, outcomes and recent empirical investigations. *Aging, Neuropsychology and Cognition, 11,* 169–195.

Clarys, D., Bugaiska, A., Tapia, G., & Baudouin, A. (2009). Ageing, remembering, and executive function. *Memory, 17,* 158–168.

Clarys, D., Isingrini, M., & Gana, K. (2002). Mediators of age-related differences in recollective experience in recognition memory. *Acta Psychologica, 109,* 315–329.

Cohen, G., & Java, R. (1995). Memory for medical history: Accuracy of recall. *Applied Cognitive Psychology, 9,* 273–288.

Colcombe, S.J., Erickson, K.I., Scalf, P.E., Kim, J.S., Prakash, R., McAuley, E., Elavsky, S., Marquez, D.X., Hu, L., & Kramer, A.F. (2006). Aerobic exercise training increases brain volume in aging humans. *Journal of Gerontology: Medical Sciences, 61A,* 1166–1170.

Colcombe, S.J., & Kramer, A.F. (2003). Fitness effects on the cognitive function of older adults: A meta-analytic study. *Psychological Science, 14,* 125–130.

Cole, D.A., & Maxwell, S.E. (2003). Testing mediational models with longitudinal data: Questions and tips in the use of structural equation modeling. *Journal of Abnormal Psychology, 112,* 558–577.

Colsher, P.L., & Wallace, R.B. (1991). Longitudinal application of cognitive function measures in a defined population of community-dwelling elders. *Annals of Epidemiology, 1,* 215–230.

Comblain, C., D'Argembeau, A., van der Linden, M., & Aldenhoff, L. (2004). The effect of ageing on the recollection of emotional and neutral pictures. *Memory, 12,* 673–684.

Conrad, H.S., & Jones, H.E. (1929). Psychological studies of motion pictures: III. Fidelity of report as a measure of adult intelligence. *University of California Publications in Psychology, 3,* 245–276.

Cook, I.A., Leuchter, A.F., Morgan, M.L., Conlee, E.W., David, S., Lufkin, R., Babaie, A., Dunkin, J.J., O'Hara, R., Simon, S., Lighner, A., Thomas, S., Broumandi, D., Badjatia, N., Mickes, L., Mody, R.K., Arora, S., Zheng, Z., Abrams, M., & Rosenberg-Thompson, S. (2002). Cognitive and physiologic correlates of subclinical structural brain disease in elderly healthy control subjects. *Archives of Neurology, 59,* 1612–1620.

Costa, P.T., Jr., & McCrae, R.R. (1994). Set like plaster? Evidence for the stability of the adult personality. In T.F. Heatherton & J.L. Weinberger (Eds.), *Can personality change?* (pp. 21–40). Washington, D.C.: American Psychological Association.

Cotman, C.W., Head, E., Muggenburg, B.A., Zicker, S., & Milgram, N.W. (2002). Brain aging in the canine: A diet enriched in antioxidants reduces cognitive dysfunction. *Neurobiology of Aging, 23,* 809–818.

Craik, F.I.M., Winocur, G., Palmer, H., Binns, M.A., Edwards, M., Bridges, K., Glazer, P., Chavannes, R., & Stuss, D.T. (2007). Cognitive rehabilitation in the elderly: Effects on memory. *Journal of the International Neuropsychological Society, 13,* 132–142.

Cronbach, L.J. (1949). *Essentials of psychological testing.* New York: Harper.

Crook, T.H., Ferris, S., McCarthy, M., & Rae, D. (1980). Utility of digit recall tasks for assessing memory in the aged. *Journal of Consulting and Clinical Psychology, 48,* 228–233.

Crum, R.M., Anthony, J.C., Bassett, S.S., & Folstein, M.F. (1993). Population-based norms for the Mini-Mental State Examination by age and education level. *Journal of American Medical Association, 269,* 2386–2391.

Dahlin, E., Nyberg, L., Backman, L., & Neely, A.S. (2008). Plasticity of executive functioning in young and older adults: Immediate training grains, transfer, and long-term maintenance. *Psychology and Aging, 23*, 720–730.

Daselaar, S.M., Fleck, M.S., Dobbins, I.G., Madden, D.J., & Cabeza, R. (2006). Effects of healthy aging on hippocampal and rhinal memory functions: An event-related fMRI study. *Cerebral Cortex, 16*, 1771–1782.

Davis, H.S., & Rockwood, K. (2004). Conceptualization of mild cognitive impairment: A review. *International Journal of Geriatric Psychiatry, 19*, 313–319.

Deary, I.J. (2000). *Looking down on human intelligence: From psychometrics to the brain.* Oxford, England: Oxford University Press.

Deary, I.J., Allerhand, M., & Der, G. (2009). Smarter in middle age, faster in old age: A cross-lagged panel analysis of reaction time and cognitive ability over 13 years in the West of Scotland Twenty-07 Study. *Psychology and Aging, 24*, 40–47.

Deary, I.J., Bastin, M.E., Pattie, A., Clayden, J.D., Whalley, L.J., Starr, J.M., & Wardlaw, .M. (2006). White matter integrity and cognition in childhood and old age. *Neurology, 66*, 505–512.

Deary, I.J., & Der, G. (2005). Reaction time, age, and cognitive ability: Longitudinal findings from age 16 to 63 years in representative population samples. *Aging, Neuropsychology and Cognition, 12*, 187–215.

Deary, I.J., MacLennan, W.J., & Starr, J.M. (1999). Is age kinder to the initially more able? Differential ageing of a verbal ability in the healthy old people in Edinburgh study. *Intelligence, 26*, 357–375.

Deary, I.J., Whalley, L.J., Lemmon, H., Crawford, J.R., & Starr, J.M. (2000). The stability of individual differences in mental ability from childhood to old age: Follow-up of the 1932 Scottish Mental Survey. *Intelligence, 28*, 49–55.

Deary, I.J., Whalley, L.J., St. Clair, D., Breen, G., Leaper, S., Lemmon, H., Hayward, C., & Starr, J.M. (2003). The influence of the e4 allele of the apolipoprotein E gene on childhood IQ, nonverbal reasoning in old age, and lifetime cognitive change. *Intelligence, 31*, 85–92.

Deary, I.J., Whiteman, M.C., Starr, J.M., Whalley, L.J., & Fox, H.C. (2004). The impact of childhood intelligence on later life: Following up the Scottish Mental Surveys of 1932 and 1947. *Journal of Personality and Social Psychology, 86*, 130–147.

Deary, I.J., Wright, A.F., Harris, S.E., Whalley, L.J., & Starr, J.M. (2004). Searching for genetic influences on normal cognitive aging. *Trends in Cognitive Sciences, 8*, 178–184.

DeKosky, S. (2003). Early intervention is key to successful management of Alzheimer's disease. *Alzheimer's Disease and Associated Disorders, 17*, S99–S104.

DeKosky, S., Williamson, J.D., Fitzpatrick, A.L., Kronmal, R.A., Ives, D.G., Saxton, J.A., Lopez, O.L., Burke, G., Carlson, M.C., Fried, L.P., Kuller, L.H., Robbins, J.A., Tracy, R.P., Woolard, N.F., Dunn, L., Snitz, B.E., Nahin, R.L., & Furberg, C.D. (2008). *Gingko biloba* for prevention of dementia: A randomized controlled trial. *Journal of the American Medical Association, 300*, 2253–2262.

Dellu, F., Mayo, W., Vallee, M., Le Moal, M., & Simon, H. (1997). Facilitation of cognitive performance in aged rats by past experience depends on the type of information processing involved: A combined cross-sectional and longitudinal study. *Neurobiology of Learning and Memory, 67*, 121–128.

Denburg, N.L., Buchanan, T.W., Tranel, D., & Adolphs, R. (2003). Evidence for preserved emotional memory in normal older persons. *Emotion, 3*, 239–253.

De Raedt, R., & Ponjaert-Kristoffersen, I. (2000). Can strategic and tactical compensation reduce crash risk in older drivers? *Age and Ageing, 29*, 517–521.

De Ribaupierre, A., & Lecerf, T. (2006). Relationships between working memory and intelligence from a developmental perspective: Convergent evidence from a neo-Piagetian and a psychometric approach. *European Journal of Cognitive Psychology*, *18*, 109–137.

De Santi, S., Pirraglia, E., Barr, W., Babb, J., Williams, S., Rogers, K., Glodzik, L., Brus, M., Mosconi, L., Reisberg, B., Ferris, S., & de Leon, M.J. (2008). Robust and conventional neuropsychological norms: Diagnosis and prediction of age-related cognitive decline. *Neuropsychology, 22*, 469–484.

D'Esposito, M., & Weksler, M.E. (2000). Brain aging and memory: New findings may help differentiate forgetfulness and dementia. *Geriatrics, 55*, 55–58, 61–62.

Diener, E., Emmons, R.A., Larsen, R.J., & Griffin, S. (1985). The satisfaction with life scale. *Journal of Personality Assessment, 49*, 71–75.

Dierckx, E., Engelborghs, S., De Raedt, R., De Deyn, P.P., & Ponjaert-Kristoffersen, I. (2007). Mild cognitive impairment: What's in a name? *Gerontology, 53*, 28–35.

Dixon, R.A., & de Frias, C.M. (2004). The Victoria Longitudinal Study: From characterizing cognitive aging to illustrating changes in memory compensation. *Aging, Neuropsychology and Cognition, 11*, 346–376.

Dixon, R.A., Wahlin, A., Maitland, S.B., Hertzog, C., & Backman, L. (2004). Episodic memory change in late adulthood: Generalizability across samples and performance indices. *Memory & Cognition, 32*, 768–778.

Dodds, C., & Allison, J. (1998). Postoperative cognitive deficit in the elderly surgery patient. *British Journal of Anaesthesia, 81*, 449–462.

Donnellan, M.B., & Lucas, R.E. (2008). Age differences in the Big Five across the life span: Evidence from two national samples. *Psychology and Aging, 23*, 558–566.

Dore, G.A., Elias, M.F., Robbins, M.A., Elias, P.K., & Brennan, S.L. (2007). Cognitive performance and age: Norms from the Maine-Syracuse study. *Experimental Aging Research, 33*, 205–271.

Driscoll, I., Resnick, S.M., Troncoso, J.C., An, Y., O'Brien, R., & Zonderman, A.B. (2006). Impact of Alzheimer's pathology on cognitive trajectories in nondemented elderly. *Annals of Neurology, 60*, 688–695.

Droege, R.C., Crambert, A.C., & Henkin, J.B. (1963). Relationship between G.A.T.B. aptitude scores and age for adults. *Personnel and Guidance Journal, 41*, 502–508.

Dunn, L.M., & Dunn, D.M. (2007). *Peabody Picture Vocabulary Test* (4th ed.). Bloomington, MN: Pearson Assessments.

Earles, J.L. (1996). Adult age differences in recall of performed and nonperformed items. *Psychology and Aging, 11*, 638–648.

Edwards, J.D., Wadley, V.G., Vance, D.E., Wood, K., Roenker, D.L., & Ball, K.K. (2005). The impact of speed of processing training on cognitive and everyday performance. *Aging & Mental Health, 9*, 262–271.

Eisdorfer, C., & Lawton, M.P. (1973). Introduction. In C. Eisdorfer & M.P. Lawton (Eds.), *Psychology of adult development and aging* (pp. vii—xiv). Washington, D.C.: American Psychological Association.

Elias, M.F., Beiser, A., Wolf, P.A., Au, R., White, R.F., & D'Agostino, R.B. (2000). The preclinical phase of Alzheimer Disease: A 22-year prospective study of the Framingham cohort. *Archives of Neurology, 57*, 808–813.

Emery, C.F., & Gatz, M. (1990). Psychological and cognitive effects of an exercise program for community-residing older adults. *Gerontologist, 30*, 184–188.

Erixon-Lindroth, N., Farde, L., Whalin, T-B.R., Sovago, J., Halldin, C., & Backman, L. (2005). The role of the striatal dopamine transporter in cognitive aging. *Psychiatry Research: Neuroimaging, 138,* 1–12.

Etnier, J.L., Nowell, P.M., Landers, D.M., & Sibley, B.A. (2006). A meta-regression to examine the relationship between aerobic fitness and cognitive performance. *Brain Research Reviews, 52,* 119–130.

Etnier, J.L., Salazar, W., Landers, D.M., Petruzzello, S.J., Han, M., & Nowell, P. (1997). The influence of physical fitness and exercise upon cognitive functioning: A meta-analysis. *Journal of Sport & Exercise Psychology, 19,* 249–277.

Everson-Rose, S.A., Mendes de Leon, C.F., Bienias, J.L., Wilson, R.S., & Evans, D.A. (2003). Early life conditions and cognitive functioning in later life. *American Journal of Epidemiology, 158,* 1083–1089.

Fernandes, M., Ross, M., Wiegand, M., & Schryer, E. (2008). Are the memories of older adults positively biased? *Psychology and Aging, 23,* 297–306.

Ferrer, E., Salthouse, T.A., McArdle, J.J., Stewart, W.F., & Schwartz, B.S. (2005). Multivariate modeling of age and retest in longitudinal studies of cognitive abilities. *Psychology and Aging, 20,* 412–422.

Ferrer, E., Salthouse, T.A., Stewart, W.F., & Schwartz, B.S. (2004). Modeling age and retest processes in longitudinal studies of cognitive abilities. *Psychology and Aging, 19,* 243–259.

Fillenbaum, G.G., van Belle, G., Morris, J.C., Mohs, R.C., Mirra, S.S., Davis, P.C., Tariot, P.N., Silverman, J.M., Clark, C.M., Welsh-Bohmer, K.A., & Heyman, A. (2008). Consortium to establish a registry for Alzheimer's disease (CERAD): The first twenty years. *Alzheimer's & Dementia, 4,* 96–109.

Finkel, D., Pedersen, N.L., Plomin, R., & McClearn, G. (1998). Longitudinal and cross-sectional twin data on cognitive abilities in adulthood: The Swedish Adoption/Twin Study of Aging. *Developmental Psychology, 34,* 1400–1413.

Finkel, D., Reynolds, C.A., McArdle, J.J., Gatz, M., & Pedersen, N.L. (2003). Latent growth curve analyses of accelerating decline in cognitive abilities in late adulthood. *Developmental Psychology, 39,* 535–550.

Finkel, D., Reynolds, C.A., McArdle, J.J., & Pedersen, N.L. (2005). The longitudinal relationship between processing speed and cognitive ability: Genetic and environmental influences. *Behavior Genetics, 35,* 535–549.

Finkel, D., Reynolds, C.A., McArdle, J.J., & Pedersen, N.L. (2007). Cohort differences in trajectories of cognitive aging. *Journal of Gerontology: Psychological Sciences, 62B,* P286–P294.

Fischer, P., Jungwirth, S., Zehetmayer, S., Weissgram, S., Hoenigschnabl, S., Gelpi, E., Krampla, W., & Tragl, K.H. (2007). Conversion from subtypes of mild cognitive impairment to Alzheimer dementia. *Neurology, 68,* 288–291.

Flory, J.D., Manuck, S.B., Ferrerll, R.E., Ryan, C.M., & Muldoon, M.F., (2000). Memory performance and the Apolipoprotein E polymorphism in a community sample of middle-aged adults. *American Journal of Medical Genetics (Neuropsychiatric Genetics), 96,* 707–711.

Flynn, J.R. (1984). The mean IQ of Americans: Massive gains 1932 to 1978. *Psychological Bulletin, 95,* 29–51.

Flynn, J.R. (1987). Massive IQ gains in 14 nations: What IQ tests really measure. *Psychological Bulletin, 101,* 171–191

Flynn, J.R. (2007). *What is intelligence?* New York: Cambridge University Press.

Folstein, M.F., Folstein, S.E., & McHugh, P.R. (1975). Mini-mental state: A practical method for grading the cognitive state of patients for the clinician. *Journal of Psychiatric Research, 12,* 189–198.

Foster, J.C., & Taylor, G.A. (1920). The applicability of mental tests to persons over 50. *Journal of Applied Psychology, 4,* 39–58.

Fotenos, A.F., Snyder, A.Z., Girton, L.E., Morris, J.C., & Buckner, R.L. (2005). Normative estimates of cross-sectional and longitudinal brain volume decline in aging and AD. *Neurology, 64,* 1032–1039.

Francis, D.J., Fletcher, J.M., Stuebing, K.K., Davidson, K.C., & Thompson, N.M. (1991). Analysis of change: Modeling individual growth. *Journal of Consulting and Clinical Psychology, 59,* 27–37.

Fratiglioni, L., Paillard-Borg, S., & Winblad, B. (2004). An active and socially integrated lifestyle in late life might protect against dementia. *Lancet Neurology, 3,* 343–353.

Frerichs, R.J., & Tuokko, H.A. (2005). A comparison of methods for measuring change in older adults. *Archives of Clinical Neuropsychology, 20,* 321–333.

Frick, K.M., Baxter, M.G., Markowska, A.L., Olton, D.S., & Price, D.L. (1995). Age-related spatial reference and working memory deficits assessed in the water maze. *Neurobiology of Aging, 16,* 149–160.

Friedland, R.P., Fritsch, T., Smyth, K.A., Koss, E., Lerner, A.J., Chen, C.H., Petot, G.J., & Debanne, S.M. (2001). Patients with Alzheimer's disease have reduced activities in midlife compared with healthy control-group members. *Proceedings of the National Academy of Sciences, 98,* 3440–3445.

Frieske, D.A., & Park, D.C. (1999). Memory for news in young and old adults. *Psychology and Aging, 14,* 90–98.

Fritsch, T., McClendon, M.J., Smyth, K.A., Lerner, A.J., Friedland, R.P., & Larsen, J.D. (2007). Cognitive functioning in healthy aging: The role of reserve and lifestyle factors early in life. *The Gerontologist, 47,* 307–322.

Gage, F.H., Dunnett, S.B., & Bjorklund, A. (1989). Age-related impairments in spatial memory are independent of those in sensorimotor skills. *Neurobiology of Aging, 10,* 347–352.

Gallo, D.A., & Roediger, H.L. (2003). The effects of associations and aging on illusory recollection. *Memory & Cognition, 31,* 1036–1044.

Galvin, J.E., Powlishta, K.K., Wilkins, K., McKeel, D.W., Xiong, C., Grant, E., Storandt, M., & Morris, J.C. (2005). Predictors of preclinical Alzheimer's disease and dementia. *Archives of Neurology, 62,* 758–765.

Garrison, S.C. (1930). Retests on adults at an interval of ten years. *School and Society, 32,* 326–328.

Gatz, M. (2005). Educating the brain to avoid dementia: Can mental exercise prevent Alzheimer Disease? *PLoS Medicine, 2,* 38–40.

Gatz, M. (2007). Genetics, dementia, and the elderly. *Current Directions in Psychological Science, 16,* 123–127.

Gatz, M., Reynolds, C.A., Fratiglioni, L., Johansson, B., Mortimer, J.A., Berg, S., Fiske, A., & Pedersen, N.L. (2006). Role of genes and environments for explaining Alzheimer disease. *Archives of General Psychiatry, 63,* 168–174.

Gerstorf, D., Herlitz, A., & Smith, J. (2006). Stability of sex differences in cognition in advanced old age: The role of education and attrition. *Journals of Gerontology: Series B: Psychological Sciences and Social Sciences, 61,* P245–P249.

Ghisletta, P., Bickel, J-F., & Lovden, M. (2006). Does activity engagement protect against cognitive decline in old age? Methodological and analytical considerations. *Journal of Gerontology: Psychological Sciences, 61B*, P253–P261.

Ghisletta, P., & de Ribaupierre, A. (2005). A dynamic investigation of cognitive dedifferentiation with control for retest: Evidence from the Swiss interdisciplinary longitudinal study on the oldest old. *Psychology and Aging, 20*, 671–682.

Ghisletta, P., & Lindenberger, U. (2004). Static and dynamic longitudinal structural analyses of cognitive changes in old age. *Gerontology, 50*, 12–16.

Gilbert, J.G. (1935). Memory efficiency in senescence. *Archives of Psychology, 27* (188), entire issue.

Gilmore, G.C., Spinks, R.A., & Thomas, C.W. (2006). Age effects in coding tasks: Componential analysis and test of the sensory deficit hypothesis. *Psychology and Aging, 21*, 7–18.

Glymour, M.M. (2007). Invited commentary: When bad genes look good—APOE*E4, cognitive decline, and diagnostic thresholds. *American Journal of Epidemiology, 165*, 1239–1246.

Gold, D.P., Andres, D., Etezadi, J., Arbuckle, T., Schwartzman, A., & Chaikelson, J. (1995). Structural equation model of intellectual change and continuity and predictors of intelligence in older men. *Psychology and Aging, 10*, 294–303.

Gold, P.E., Cahill, L., & Wenk, G.L. (2002). *Ginkgo biloba:* A cognitive enhancer? *Psychological Science in the Public Interest, 3*, 2–11.

Goldberg, L.R. (1999). A broad-bandwidth, public domain, personality inventory measuring the lower-level facets of several five-factor models. In I. Mervielde, I. Deary, F. De Fruyt, & F. Ostendorf (Eds.), *Personality psychology in Europe*, Vol. 7 (pp. 7–28). Tilburg, The Netherlands: Tilburg University Press.

Gollob, H.F., & Reichardt, C.S. (1987). Taking account of time lags in causal models. *Child Development, 58*, 80–92.

Gollub, H.F., & Reichardt, C.S., (1991). Interpreting and estimating indirect effects assuming time lags really matter. In L.M. Collins & J.L. Horn (Eds.), *Best methods for the analysis of change: Recent advances, unanswered questions, future directions* (pp. 243–259). Washington, D.C.: American Psychological Association.

Gong, Q-Y., Sluming, V., Mayes, A., Keller, S., Barrick, T., Cezayirli, E., & Roberts, N. (2005). Voxel-based morphometry and stereology provide convergent evidence of the importance of medial prefrontal cortex for fluid intelligence in healthy adults. *Neuroimage, 25*, 1175–1186.

Gootjes, L., Scheltens, P., van Strien, J.W., & Bouma, A. (2007). Subcortical white matter pathology as a mediating factor for age-related decreased performance in dichotic listening. *Neuropsychologia, 45*, 2322–2332.

Gothe, K., Oberauer, K., & Kliegl, R. (2007). Age differences in dual-task performance after practice. *Psychology and Aging, 22*, 596–606.

Gottfredson, L.S. (2002). Where and why *g* matters: Not a mystery. *Human Performance, 15*, 25–46.

Green, J.S., & Crouse, S.F. (1995). The effects of endurance training on functional capacity in the elderly: a meta-analysis. *Medicine and Science in Sports and Exercise, 27*, 920–926.

Greenwood, P.M. (2007). Functional plasticity in cognitive aging: Review and hypothesis. *Neuropsychology, 21*, 657–673.

Greenwood, P.M., Sunderland, T., Putnam, K., Levy, J., & Parasuraman, R. (2005). Scaling of visuospatial attention undergoes differential longitudinal change as a function of APOE genotype prior to old age: Results from the NIMH BIOCARD study. *Neuropsychology*, *19*, 830–840.

Grigoletto, F., Zappala, G., Anderson, D.W., & Lebowitz, B.D. (1999). Norms for the Mini-Mental State Examination in a healthy population. *Neurology*, *53*, 315–320.

Gruhn, D., Smith, J., & Baltes, P.B. (2005). No aging bias favoring memory for positive material: Evidence from a heterogeneity-homogeneity list paradigm using emotionally toned words. *Psychology and Aging*, *20*, 579–588

Gunning-Dixon, F.M., & Raz, N. (2003). Neuroanatomical correlates of selected executive functions in middle-aged and older adults: A prospective MRI study. *Neuropsychologia*, *41*, 1929–1941.

Gustafsson, J.E. (1988). Hierarchical models of individual differences in cognitive abilities. In R. J. Sternberg (Eds.), *Advances in the psychology of human intelligence*, Vol. 4 (pp. 35–71). Hillsdale, NJ: Lawrence Erlbaum Associates.

Gustafsson, J.E. (2002). Measurement from a hierarchic point of view. In H.I. Braun, D.N. Jackson, & D.E. Wiley (Eds.), *The role of constructs in psychological and educational measurement* (pp. 73–95). Mahwah, NJ: Lawrence Erlbaum Associates.

Hall, C.B., Derby, C., LeValley, A., Katz, M.J., Verghese, J., & Lipton, R.B. (2007). Education delays accelerated decline on a memory test in persons who develop dementia. *Neurology*, *69*, 1657–1664.

Hambrick, D.Z., Salthouse, T.A., & Meinz, E.J. (1999). Predictors of crossword puzzle proficiency and moderators of age-cognition relations. *Journal of Experimental Psychology: General*, *128*, 131–164.

Hancock, H.E., Fisk, A.D., & Rogers, W.A. (2005). Comprehending product warning information: Age-related effects and the roles of memory, inferencing, and knowledge. *Human Factors*, *47*, 219–234.

Hausknecht, J.P., Halpert, J.A., Di Paolo, N.T., & Gerrard, M.O.M. (2007). Retesting in selection: A meta-analysis of coaching and practice effects for tests of cognitive ability. *Journal of Applied Psychology*, *92*, 373–385.

Head, D., Kennedy, K.M., Rodrigue, K.M., & Raz, N. (2009). Age differences in perseveration: Cognitive and neuroanatomical mediators of performance on the Wisconsin Card Sorting Test. *Neuropsychologia*, *47*, 1200–1203.

Head, D., Raz, N., Gunning-Dixon, F., Williamson, A., & Acker, J.D. (2002). Age-related differences in the course of cognitive skill acquisition: The role of regional cortical shrinkage and cognitive resources. *Psychology and Aging*, *17*, 72–84.

Head, D., Rodrigue, K.M., Kennedy, K.M., & Raz, N. (2008). Neuroanatomical and cognitive mediators of age-related differences in episodic memory. *Neuropsychology*, *22*, 491–507.

Head, E., Mehta, R., Hartley, J., Kameka, M., Cummings, B.J., Cotman, C.W., Ruehl, W.W., & Milgram, N.W. (1995). Spatial learning and memory as a function of age in the dog. *Behavioral Neuroscience*, *109*, 851–858.

Hebb, D.E. (1978, November). Watching myself grow old. *Psychology Today*, 15–23.

Hebert, L.E., Scherr, P.A., Bienias, J.L., Bennett, D.A., & Evans, D.A. (2003). Alzheimer Disease in the US Population: Prevalence estimates using the 2000 census. *Archives of Neurology*, *60*, 1119–1122.

Hendrie, H.C., Albert, M.S., Butters, M.A., Gao, S., Knopman, D.S., Launer, L.J., Yaffe, K., Cuthbert, B.N., Edwards, E., & Wagster, M.V. (2006). The NIH cognitive and emotional health project: Report of the critical evaluation study committee. *Alzheimer's & Dementia*, *2*, 12–32.

Henry, J.D., MacLeod, M.S., Phillips, L.H., & Crawford, J.R. (2004). A meta-analytic review of prospective memory and aging. *Psychology and Aging, 19*, 27–39.

Herlitz, A., Airaksinen, E., & Nordstrom, E. (1999). Sex differences in episodic memory: The impact of verbal and visuospatial ability. *Neuropsychology, 13*, 590–597.

Herlitz, A., Nilsson, L-G., & Backman, L. (1997). Gender differences in episodic memory. *Memory, & Cognition, 25*, 801–811.

Herlitz, A., & Rehnman, J. (2008). Sex differences in episodic memory. *Current Directions in Psychological Science, 17*, 52–56.

Herndon, J.G., Moss, M.B., Rosene, D.L., & Killiany, R.J. (1997). Patterns of cognitive decline in aged rhesus monkeys. *Behavioural Brain Research, 87*, 25–34.

Hertzog, C., Dixon, R.A., Hultsch, D.F., & MacDonald, S.W. S. (2003). Latent change models of adult cognition: Are changes in processing speed and working memory associated with changes in episodic memory? *Psychology and Aging, 18*, 755–769.

Hertzog, C., Lindenberger, U., Ghisletta, P., & von Oertzen, T. (2006). On the power of multivariate latent growth curve models to detect correlated change. *Psychological Methods, 11*, 244–252.

Hertzog, C., & Nesselroade, J.R. (2003). Assessing psychological change in adulthood: An overview of methodological issues. *Psychology and Aging, 18*, 639–657.

Hertzog, C., Park, D.C., Morrell, R.W., & Martin, M. (2000). Ask and ye shall receive: Behavioral specificity in the accuracy of subjective memory complaints. *Applied Cognitive Psychology, 14*, 257–275.

Hertzog, C., von Oertzen, T., Ghisletta, P., & Lindenberger, U. (2008). Evaluating the power of latent growth curve models to detect individual differences in change. *Structural Equation Modeling, 15*, 541–563.

Hess, T.M., Auman, C., Colcombe, S.J., & Rahhal, T.A. (2003). The impact of stereotype threat on age differences in memory performance. *Journal of Gerontology: Psychological Sciences, 58B*, P3–P11.

Hess, T.M., & Hinson, J.T. (2006). Age-related variation in the influences of aging stereotypes on memory in adulthood. *Psychology and Aging, 21*, 621–625.

Hess, T.M., Hinson, J.T., & Statham, J.A. (2004). Implicit and explicit stereotype activation effects on memory: Do age and awareness moderate the impact of priming? *Psychology and Aging, 19*, 495–505.

Heyn, P., Abreu, b.c., & Ottenbacher, K.J. (2004). The effects of exercise training on elderly persons with cognitive impairment and dementia: A meta-analysis. *Archives of Physical Medicine and Rehabilitation, 85*, 1694–1704.

Hill, A.B. (1965). The environment and disease: Association or causation? *Proceedings of the Royal Society of Medicine, 58*, 295–300.

Hill, R.D., Storandt, M., & Malley, M. (1993). The impact of long-term exercise training on psychological function in older adults. *Journal of Gerontology, 48*, P12–P17.

Hollingworth, H.L. (1927). *Mental growth and decline.* New York: Appleton.

Holtzer, R., Goldin, Y., Zimmerman, M., Katz, M., Buschke, H., & Lipton, R.B. (2008). Robust norms for selected neuropsychological tests in older adults. *Archives of Clinical Neuropsychology, 23*, 531–541.

Horn, J.L., & Donaldson, G. (1976). On the myth of intellectual decline. *American Psychologist, 31*, 701–719.

Horn, J.L., & Donaldson, G. (1977). Faith is not enough: A response to the Baltes-Schaie claim that intelligence does not wane. *American Psychologist, 32*, 369–373.

Hultsch, D.F., Hertzog, C., Dixon, R.A., & Small, B.J. (1998). *Memory change in the aged.* New York: Cambridge University Press.

Hultsch, D.F., Small, B.J., Hertzog, C., & Dixon, R.A. (1999). Use it or lose it: Engaged lifestyle as a buffer of cognitive decline in aging? *Psychology and Aging, 14,* 245–263.

Huppert, F.A., & Whittington, J.E. (1993). Changes in cognitive function in a population sample. In B.D. Cox, F.A. Huppert, & M.J. Whichelow (Eds.), *The Health and Lifestyle Survey: Seven years on* (pp. 155–172). Dartmouth, England: Aldershot.

Jacobs, D.M., Sano, M., Dooneief, G., Marder, K., Bell, K.L., & Stern, Y. (1995). Neuropsychological detection and characterization of preclinical Alzheimer's disease. Neurology, *45,* 957–962.

James, W. (1890). *The principles of psychology: Volume two.* New York: Holt.

Janssen, S.M.J., Chessa, A.G., & Murre, J.M.J. (2005). The reminiscence bump in autobiographical memory: Effects of age, gender, education, and culture. *Memory, 13,* 658–668.

Janssen, S.M.J., & Murre, J.M.J. (2008). Reminiscence bump in autobiographical memory: Unexplained by novelty, emotionality, valence, or importance of personal events. *Quarterly Journal of Experimental Psychology, 61,* 1847–1860.

Jennings, J.M., Webster, L.M., Kleykamp, B.A., & Dagenbach, D. (2005). Recollection training and transfer effects in older adults: Successful use of a repetition-lag procedure. *Aging, Neuropsychology and Cognition, 12,* 278–298.

Jensen, A.R. (1998). *The g factor: The science of mental ability.* Westport, CT: Prager.

Johnson, R.E. (2003). Aging and the remembering of text. *Developmental Review, 23,* 261–346.

Jones, H.E. (1959). Intelligence and problem solving. In J.E. Birren (Ed.), *Handbook of aging and the individual: Psychological and biological aspects* (pp. 700–738). Chicago: University of Chicago Press.

Jones, H. E., & Conrad, H. (1933). The growth and decline of intelligence: A study of a homogeneous group between the ages of ten and sixty. *Genetic Psychological Monographs, 13,* 223–298.

Jones, H.E., Conrad, H., & Horn, A. (1928). Psychological studies of motion pictures: II. Observation and recall as a function of age. *University of California Publications in Psychology, 3,* 225–243.

Jopp, D., & Hertzog, C. (2007). Activities, self-referent beliefs, and cognitive performance: Evidence for direct and mediated relations. *Psychology and Aging, 22,* 811–825.

Jorm, A.F., & Jolley, D. (1998). The incidence of dementia: A meta-analysis. *Neurology, 51,* 728–733.

Jorm, A.F., Masaki, K.H., Petrovitch, H., Ross, G.W., & White, L.R. (2005). Cognitive deficits 3 to 6 years before dementia onset in a population sample: The Honolulu-Asia aging study. *Journal of American Geriatrics Society, 53,* 452–455.

Jorm, A.F., Mather, K.A., Butterworth, P., Anstey, K.J., Christensen, H., & Easteal, S. (2007). APOE genotype and cognitive functioning in a large age-stratified population sample. *Neuropsychology, 21,* 1–8.

Jungwirth, S., Fischer, P., Weissgram, S., Kirchmey, W., Bauer, P., & Tragl, K.-H. (2004). Subjective memory complaints and objective memory impairment in the Vienna-Transdanube aging community. *Journal of American Geriatrics Society, 52,* 263–268.

Kaplan, G.A., Turrell, G., Lynch, J.W., Everson, S.A., Helkala, E-L., & Salonen, J.T. (2001). Childhood socioeconomic position and cognitive function in adulthood. *International Journal of Epidemiology, 30,* 256–263.

Kaufman, A.S., & Kaufman, N.L. (1990). *Kaufman Brief Intelligence Test (KBIT) Manual*. Circle Pines, MN: American Guidance Service.

Kaufman, A.S., & Kaufman, N.L. (1993). *Kaufman Adolescent and Adult Intelligence Test (KAIT)*. Bloomington, MN: Pearson Assessments.

Keith, T.Z., Reynolds, M.R., Patel, P.G., & Ridley, K.P. (2008). Sex differences in latent cognitive abilities ages 6 to 59: Evidence from the Woodcock-Johnson II tests of cognitive abilities. *Intelligence, 36*, 502–525.

Keller, J.N. (2006). Age-related neuropathology, cognitive decline, and Alzheimer's disease. *Ageing Research Reviews, 5*, 1–13.

Kelley, B.J., & Petersen, R.C. (2007). Alzheimer's disease and mild cognitive impairment. *Neurologic Clinics, 25*, 577–609.

Kelly, P.H., Bondolfi,L., Hunziker, D., Schlecht, H.P., Carver, K., Maguire, E., Abramowski, D., Wiederhold, K.H., Sturchler-Pierrat, C., Jucker, M., Bergmann, R., Staufenbiel, M., & Sommer, B. (2003). Progressive age-related impairment of cognitive behavior in APP23 transgenic mice. *Neurobiology of Aging, 24*, 365–378.

Kennedy, K.M., Partridge, T., & Raz, N. (2008). Age-related differences in acquisition of perceptual-motor skills: Working memory as a mediator. *Aging, Neuropsychology, and Cognition, 15*, 165–183.

Kennison, R.F., & Zelinski, E.M. (2005). Estimating age change in list recall in asset and health dynamics of the oldest-old: The effects of attrition bias and missing data treatment. *Psychology and Aging, 20*, 460–475.

Kensinger, E.A. (2008). Age differences in memory for arousing and nonarousing emotional words. *Journal of Gerontology: Psychological Sciences, 63B*, P13–P18.

Kensinger, E.A. (2009). How emotion affects older adults' memories for event details. *Memory, 17*, 208–219.

Kensinger, E.A., Brierley, B., Medford, N., Growdon, J.H., & Corkin, S. (2002). Effects of normal aging and Alzheimer's disease on emotional memory. *Emotion, 2*, 118–134.

Kliegel, M., Jager, T., & Phillips, L.H. (2008). Adult age differences in event-based prospective memory: A meta-analysis on the role of focal versus nonfocal cues. *Psychology and Aging, 23*, 203–208.

Kliegl, R., Smith, J., & Baltes, P.B. (1989). Testing-the-limits and the study of adult age differences in cognitive plasticity of a mnemonic skill. *Developmental Psychology, 25*, 247–256.

Kliegl, R., Smith, J., & Baltes, P.B. (1990). On the locus and process of magnification of adult age differences during mnemonic training. *Developmental Psychology, 26*, 894–904.

Knight, B.G., Maines, M.L., & Robinson, G.S. (2002). The effects of sad mood on memory in older adults: A test of the mood congruence effect. *Psychology and Aging, 17*, 653–661.

Knopman, D.S., DeKosky, S.T., & Cummings, J.L. (2001). Practice parameter: Diagnosis of dementia (an evidence-based review). Report of the Quality Standards Subcommittee of the American Academy of Neurology. *Neurology, 56*, 1143–1153.

Kovari, E., Gold, G., Herrmann, F.R., Canuto, A., Hof, P.R., Michel, J-P., Bouras, C., & Giannakopoulos, P. (2004). Cerebral microinfarcts and demyelination significantly affect cognition in brain aging. *Stroke, 35*, 410–414.

Kraemer, H.C., Stice, E., Kazdin, A., Offord, D., & Kupfer, D. (2001). How do risk factors work together? Mediators, moderators, and independent, overlapping, and proxy risk factors. *American Journal of Psychiatry, 158*, 848–856.

Kramer, A.F., Colcombe, S.J., McAuley, E., Scalf, P.E., & Erikson, K.I. (2005). Fitness, aging and neurocognitive function. *Neurobiology of Aging, 26S*, S124–S127.

Kramer, A.F., & Erickson, K.I. (2007). Capitalizing on cortical plasticity: Influence of physical activity on cognition and brain function. *Trends in Cognitive Sciences, 11*, 342–348.

Kramer, A.F., Hahn, S., Cohen, N.J., Banich, M.T., McAuley, E., Harrison, C.R., Chason, J., Vakil, E., Bardell, L., & Colcombe, A. (1999). Aging, fitness, and neurocognitive function. *Nature, 400*, 418–419.

Kramer, A.F., Hahn, S., McAuley, E., Cohen, N.J., Banich, M.T., Harrison, C., Chason, J., Boiluea, R.A., Bardell, L., Colcombe, A., & Vakil, E. (2002). Exercise, aging, and cognition: Healthy body, healthy mind? In W.A. Rogers & A.D. Fisk (Eds.), *Human factors interventions for the health care of older adults* (pp. 91–120). Mahwah, NJ: Lawrence Erlbaum Associates.

Kramer, A.F., Larish, J.F., & Strayer, D.L. (1995). Training for attentional control in dual task settings: A comparison of young and old adults. *Journal of Experimental Psychology: Applied, 1*, 50–76.

Kramer, J.H., Mungas, D., Reed, B.R., Wetzel, M.E., Burnett, M.M., Miller, B.L., Weinder, M.W., & Chui, H.C. (2007). Longitudinal MRI and cognitive change in healthy elderly. *Neuropsychology, 21*, 412–418.

Kray, J., & Epplinger, B. (2006). Effects of associative learning on age differences in task-set switching. *Acta Psychologica, 123*, 187–203.

Lacreuse, A., Kim, C.B., Rosene, D.L., Killiany, R.J., Moss, M.B., Moore, T.L., Chennareddi, L., & Herndon, J.G. (2005). Sex, age, and training modulate spatial memory in the Rhesus monkey (*Macaca mulatta*). *Behavioral Neuroscience, 119*, 118–126.

Lange, K.L., Bondi, M.W., Salmon, D.P., Galasko, D., Delis, D.C., Thomas, R.G., & Thal, L.J. (2002). Decline in verbal memory during preclinical Alzheimer's disease: Examination of the effect of APOE genotype. *Journal of the International Neuropsychological Society, 8*, 943–955.

Larrieu, S., Letenneur, L., Orgogozo, J.M., Fabriguole, C., Amieva, H., Le Carret, N., Barberger-Gateau, P., & Dartigues, J.F. (2002). Incidence and outcome of mild cognitive impairment in a population-based prospective cohort. *Neurology, 59*, 1594–1599.

Larsen, E.B., Wang, L., Bowen, J.D., McCormick, W.C., Teri, L., Crane, P., & Kukull, W. (2006). Exercise is associated with reduced risk for incident dementia among persons 65 years of age and older. *Annals of Internal Medicine, 144*, 73–81.

Larsen, L., Hartmann, P., & Nyborg, H. (2008). The stability of general intelligence from early adulthood to middle age. *Intelligence, 36*, 29–34.

Laukka, E.J., MacDonald, S.W.S., & Backman, L. (2006). Contrasting cognitive trajectories of impending death and preclinical dementia in the very old. *Neurology, 66*, 833–838.

Laurin, D., Verreault, R., Lindsay, J., MacPherson, K., & Rockwood, K. (2001). Physical activity and risk of cognitive impairment and dementia in elderly persons. *Archives of Neurology, 58*, 498–504.

LaVoie, D., & Light, L.L. (1994). Adult age differences in repetition priming: A meta-analysis. *Psychology and Aging, 9*, 539–553.

Leach, L., Kaplan, E., Rewilak, D., Richards, B, & Proulx, G.-B. (2000). *Kaplan Baycrest Neurocognitive Assessment.* San Antonio, TX: The Psychological Corporation.

Le Bourg, E. (2004). Effects of aging on learned suppression of photopositive tendencies in *Drosophila melanogaster*. *Neurobiology of Aging, 25*, 1241–1252.

Levy, B. (1996). Improving memory in old age through implicit self-stereotyping. *Journal of Personality and Social Psychology, 71,* 1092–1107.

Levy, B., & Langer, E. (1994). Aging free from negative stereotypes: Successful memory in China and among the American Deaf. *Journal of Personality and Social Psychology, 66,* 989–997.

Li, K.Z.H., & Lindenberger, U. (2002). Relations between aging sensory/sensorimotor and cognitive functions. *Neuroscience and Behavior Reviews, 26,* 777–783.

Li, S-C., Lindenberger, U., Hommel, B., Aschersleben, G., Prinz, W., & Baltes, P.B. (2004). Transformations in the couplings among intellectual abilities and constituent cognitive processes across the life span. *Psychological Science, 15,* 155–163.

Li, S-C., Schmiedek, F., Huxhold, O., Rocke, C., Smith, J., & Lindenberger, U. (2008). Working memory plasticity in old age: Practice gain, transfer, and maintenance. *Psychology and Aging, 23,* 731–742.

Lindenberger, U., & Baltes, P.B. (1994). Sensory functioning and intelligence in old age: A strong connection. *Psychology and Aging, 2,* 339–355.

Lindenberger, U., & Ghisletta, P. (2009). Cognitive and sensory declines in old age: Gauging the evidence for a common cause. *Psychology and Aging, 24,* 1–16.

Lindenberger, U., Scherer, H., & Baltes, P.B. (2001). The strong connection between sensory and cognitive performance in old age: Not due to sensory acuity reductions operating during cognitive assessment. *Psychology and Aging, 16,* 196–205.

Lobo, A., Launer, L.J., Fratiglioni, L., Andersen, K., Di Carlo, A., Breteler, M.M.B., Copeland, J.R.M., Dartigues, J.F., Jagger, C., Martinez-Lage, J., Soninen, H., & Hofman, A. (2000). Prevalence of dementia and major subtypes in Europe: A collaborative study of population-based cohorts. *Neurology, 54,* S4–S9.

Loftus, E.F., Levidow, B., & Duensing, S. (1992). Who remembers best? Individual differences in memory for events that occurred in a science museum. *Applied Cognitive Psychology, 6,* 93–107.

Lopez, O.L., Jagust, W.J., DeKosky, S.T., Becker, J.T., Fitzpatrick, A., Dulberg, C., Britner, J., Lyketsos, C., Jones, B., Kawas, C., Carlson, C., & Kuller, L.H. (2003). Prevalence and classification of mild cognitive impairment in the Cardiovascular Health Study Cognition Study. *Archives of Neurology, 60,* 1385–1389.

Lopez, O.L., Kuller, L.H., Becker, J.T., Dulberg, C., Sweet, R.A., Gach, H.M., & DeKosky, S.T. (2007). Incidence of dementia in mild cognitive impairment in the Cardiovascular Health Study Cognition Study. *Archives of Neurology, 64,* 416–420.

Lovden, M., Ghisletta, P., & Lindenberger, U. (2004). Cognition in the Berlin Aging Study (BASE): The first 10 years. *Aging, Neuropsychology and Cognition, 11,* 104–133.

Lovden, M., Ghisletta, P., & Lindenberger, U. (2005). Social participation attenuates decline in perceptual speed in old and very old age. *Psychology and Aging, 20,* 423–434.

Lovden, M., & Wahlin, A. (2005). The sensory-cognition association in adulthood: Different magnitudes for processing speed, inhibition, episodic memory, and false memory? *Scandinavian Journal of Psychology, 46,* 253–262.

Lukoyanov, N.V., Andrade, J.P., Madeira, M.D., & Paula-Barbosa, M.M. (1999). Effects of age and sex on the water maze performance and hippocampal fibers in rats. *Neuroscience Letters, 269,* 141–144.

Lyketsos, C.G., Chen, L-S., & Anthony, J.C. (1999). Cognitive decline in adulthood: An 11.5 year follow-up of the Baltimore Epidemiological Catchment Area Study. *American Journal of Psychiatry, 156,* 58–65.

Lynn, R., & Harvey, J. (2008). The decline of the world's IQ. *Intelligence*, *36*, 112–120.

Lyons, D.M., Yang, C., Eliez, S. Reiss, A.L., & Schatzberg, A.F. (2004). Cognitive correlates of white matter growth and stress hormones in female squirrel monkey adults. *Journal of Neuroscience*, *24*, 3655–3662.

MacDonald, S.W.S., Hultsch, D.F., Strauss, E., & Dixon, R.A. (2003). Age-related slowing of digit symbol substitution revisited: What do longitudinal age changes reflect? *Journal of Gerontology: Psychological Science*, *58B*, P187–P194.

Mackinnon, A., Christensen, H., Hofer, S.M., Korten, A.E., & Jorm, A.F. (2003). Use it and still lose it? The association between activity and cognitive performance established using latent growth techniques in a community sample. *Aging, Neuropsychology and Cognition*, *10*, 215–229.

MacKinnon, D.P. (2008). *Introduction to statistical mediation analysis*. New York: Lawrence Erlbaum Associates.

MacKinnon, D.P., Fairchild, A.J., & Fritz, M.S. (2007). Mediation analysis. *Annual Review of Psychology*, *58*, 593–614.

Madden, D.J., Blumenthal, J.A., Allen, P.A., & Emery, C.F. (1989). Improving aerobic capacity in healthy older adults does not necessarily lead to improved cognitive performance. *Psychology and Aging*, *4*, 307–320.

Magnusson, K.R., Scruggs, B., Aniya, J., Wright, K.C., Ontl, T., Xing, Y., & Bai, L. (2003). Age-related deficits in mice performing working memory tasks in a water maze. *Behavioral Neuroscience*, *117*, 485–495.

Mahncke, H.W., Connor, B.B., Appelman, J., Ahsanuddin, O.N., Hardy, J.L., Wood, R.A., Joyce, N.M., Boniske, T., Atkins, S.M., & Merzenich, M.M. (2006). Memory enhancement in healthy older adults using a brain plasticity-based training program: A randomized controlled study. *Proceedings of the National Academy of Sciences*, *103*, 12523–12528.

Mantyla, T., & Nilsson, L.-G. (1997). Remembering to remember in adulthood: A population-based study on aging and prospective memory. *Aging, Neuropsychology, and Cognition*, *4*, 81–92.

Markowska, A.L. (1999). Sex dimorphisms in the rate of age-related decline in spatial memory: Relevance to alterations in the estrous cycle. *Journal of Neuroscience*, *19*, 8122–8133.

Markowska, A.L., & Savonenko, A.V. (2002). Protective effect of practice on cognition during aging: Implications for predictive characteristics of performance and efficacy of practice. *Neurobiology of Learning and Memory*, *78*, 294–320.

Massoud, F., Devi, G., Stern, Y., Lawton, A., Goldman, J.E., Liu, Y., Chin, S.S., & Mayeux, R.1. (1999). A clinicopathological comparison of community-based and clinic-based cohorts of patients with dementia. *Archives of Neurology*, *56*, 1368–1373.

Matzel, L.D., Han, Y.R., Grossman, H., Karnik, M.S., Patel, D., Scott, N., Specht, S.M., & Gandhi, C.C. (2003). Individual differences in the expression of a "general" learning ability in mice. *Journal of Neuroscience*, *23*, 6423–6433.

Maylor, E.A. (1990). Age and prospective memory. *Quarterly Journal of Experimental Psychology*, *42A*, 471–493.

Maylor, E.A. (1991). Recognizing and naming tunes: Memory impairment in the elderly. *Journal of Gerontology: Psychological Sciences*, *46*, P207–P217.

Maylor, E.A. (1995). Remembering versus knowing television theme tunes in middle-aged and elderly adults. *British Journal of Psychology*, *86*, 21–25.

Mayr, U. (2008). Introduction to the special section on cognitive plasticity in the aging mind. *Psychology and Aging*, *23*, 681–683.

McArdle, J.J. (1988). Dynamic but structural equation modeling of repeated measures data. In J.R. Nesselroade, & R.B. Cattell (Eds.), *The handbook of multivariate experimental psychology, Volume 2* (pp. 561–614). New York: Plenum Press.

McArdle, J.J., Ferrer-Caja, E., Hamagami, F., & Woodcock, R.W. (2002). Comparative longitudinal structural analyses of growth and decline of multiple intellectual abilities over the life span. *Developmental Psychology, 38,* 115–142.

McArdle, J.J., & Prindle, J.J. (2008). A latent change score analysis of a randomized clinical trial in reasoning training. *Psychology and Aging, 23,* 702–719.

McArdle, J.J., Small, B.J., Backman, L., & Fratiglioni, L. (2005). Longitudinal models of growth and survival applied to the early detection of Alzheimer's disease. *Journal of Geriatric Psychiatry and Neurology, 18,* 234–241.

McAuley, E., Morris, K.S., Motl, R.W., Hu, L., Konopack, J.F., & Elavsky, S. (2007). Long-term follow-up of physical activity behavior in older adults. *Health Psychology, 26,* 375–380.

McCarthy, M., Ferris, S.H., Clark, E., & Crook, T. (1981). Acquisition and retention of categorized material in normal aging and senile dementia. *Experimental Aging Research, 7,* 127–135.

McClelland, G.H., & Judd, C.M. (1993). Statistical difficulties of detecting interactions and moderator effects. *Psychological Bulletin, 114,* 376–390.

McCoy, S.L., Tun, P.A., Cox, L.C., Colangelo, M., Steward, R.A., & Wingfield, A. (2005). Hearing loss and perceptual effort: Downstream effects on older adults' memory for speech. *Quarterly Journal of Experimental Psychology, 58A,* 22–33.

McDaniel, M.A., Einstein, G.O., & Jacoby, L.L. (2008). New considerations in aging and memory: The glass may be half full. In F.I.M. Craik & T.A. Salthouse (Eds.), *The handbook of aging and cognition* (3rd ed.) (pp. 251–310). New York: Psychology Press.

McDaniel, M.A., Maier, S.F., & Einstein, G.O. (2002). "Brain-specific" nutrients: A memory cure? *Psychological Science in the Public Interest, 3,* 12–38.

McDowell, I., Xi, G., Lindsay, J., & Tuokko, H. (2004). Canadian Study of Health and Aging: Study description and patterns of early cognitive decline. *Aging, Neuropsychology and Cognition, 11,* 149–168.

McEchron, M.D., Cheng, A.Y., & Gilmartin, M.R. (2004). Trace fear conditioning is reduced in the aging rat. *Neurobiology of Learning and Memory, 82,* 71–76.

McGrew, K.S., & Woodcock, R.W. (2001). *Technical manual. Woodcock-Johnson III.* Itasca, IL: Riverside Publishing.

McKhann, G., & Albert, M. (2002). *Keep your brain young.* New York: Wiley.

Meinz, E.J., & Salthouse, T.A. (1998). Is age kinder to females than to males? *Psychonomic Bulletin & Review, 5,* 56–70.

Memon, A., Hope, L., Bartlett, J., & Bull, R. (2002). Eyewitness recognition errors: The effects of mugshot viewing and choosing in young and old adults. *Memory & Cognition, 30,* 1219–1227.

Meyer, G.J., Finn, S.E., Eyde, L.D., Kay, G.G., Moreland, K.L., Dies, R.R., Eisman, E.J., Kubiszyn, T.W., & Reed, G.M. (2001). Psychological testing and psychological assessment: A review of evidence and issues. *American Psychologist, 56,* 128–165.

Miles, C.C. (1934). Influence of speed and age on intelligence scores of adults. *Journal of Genetic Psychology, 10,* 208–210.

Miles, W.R. (1933). Age and human ability. *Psychological Review, 40,* 99–123.

Miles, W.R. (1935). Age and human society. In C. Murchison (Ed.), *A handbook of social psychology* (pp. 596–682). Worcester, MA: Clark University Press.

Miles, W.R., & Miles, C.C. (1943). Principal mental changes with normal aging. In E.J. Steglitz (Ed.), *Geriatric medicine* (pp. 99–117). Philadelphia: W.B. Saunders.

Milgram, N. W., Head, E., Weiner, E., & Thomas, E. (1994). Cognitive functions and aging in the dog: Acquisition of nonspatial visual tasks. *Behavioral Neuroscience, 108*, 57–68.

Milgram, N.W., Head, E., Zicker, S.C., Ikeda-Douglas, C.J., Murphey, H., Muggenburg, B., Siwak, C., Tapp, D., & Cotman, C.W. (2005). Learning ability in aged beagle dogs is preserved by behavioral enrichment and dietary fortification: A two-year longitudinal study. *Neurobiology of Aging, 26*, 77–90.

Molander, B., & Backman, L. (1996). Cognitive aging in a precision sport context. *European Psychologist, 1*, 166–179.

Moller, J.T., Cluitmans, P., Rasmussen, L.S., Houx, P., Rasmussen, H., Canet, J., Rabbitt, P., Jolles, J., Larsen, K., Hanning, C.D., Langeron, O., Johnson, T., Lauven, P.M., Kristensen, P.A., Biedler, A., van Beem, H., Fraidakis, O., Silverstein, J.H., Beneken, J.E.W., & Gravenstein, J.S. (1998). Long-term postoperative cognitive dysfunction in the elderly: ISPOCD1 study. *Lancet, 351*, 857–861.

Mook, D.G. (1983). In defense of external invalidity. *American Psychologist, 38*, 379–387.

Morris, J.C., Storandt, M., Miller, J.P., McKeel, D.W., Price, J.L., Rubin, E.H., & Berg, L. (2001). Mild cognitive impairment represents early-stage Alzheimer disease. *Archives of Neurology, 58*, 397–405.

Murphy, D.R., Craik, F.I.M., Li, K.Z.H., & Schneider, B.A. (2000). Comparing the effects of aging and background noise on short-term memory performance. *Psychology and Aging, 15*, 323–334.

Murphy, N.A., & Isaacowitz, D.M. (2008). Preferences for emotional information in older and younger adults: A meta-analysis of memory and attention tasks. *Psychology and Aging, 23*, 263–286.

National Institute on Aging, Alzheimer's Association Working Group. (1996). Apolipoprotein E genotyping in Alzheimer's disease. *Lancet, 347*, 1091–1095.

Newman, M.F., Kirchner, J.L., Phillips-Bute, B., Gaver, V., Grocott, H., Jones, R.H., Mark, D.B., Reves, J.G., & Blumenthal, J. A. (2001). Longitudinal assessment of neurocognitive function after coronary artery bypass surgery. *The New England Journal of Medicine, 344*, 395–402.

Nickerson, R.S. (1980). Retrieval efficiency, knowledge assessment and age: Comments on some welcome findings. In L.W. Poon, J.L. Fozard, L.S. Cermak, D. Arenberg, & L.W. Thompson (Eds.), *New directions in memory and aging: Proceedings of the George A. Talland Memorial Conference* (pp. 355–366). Hillsdale, NJ: Lawrence Erlbaum Associates.

Nilsson, L-G., Backman, L., Erngrund, K., Nyberg, L., Adolfsson, R., Bucht, G., Karlsson, S., Widing, M., & Winblad, B. (1997). The Betula prospective cohort study: Memory, health, and aging. *Aging, Neuropsychology and Cognition, 4*, 1–32.

Noice, H., Noice, T., & Staines, G. (2004). A short-term intervention to enhance cognitive and affective functioning in older adults. *Journal of Aging and Health, 16*, 562–585.

Nyberg, L., Maitland, S. B., Ronnlund, M., Backman, L., Dixon, R. A., Wahlin, A., & Nilsson, L.-G. (2003a). Selective adult age differences in an age-invariant multifactor model of declarative memory. *Psychology and Aging, 18*, 149–160.

Nyberg, L., Persson, J., & Nilsson, L-G. (2002). Individual differences in memory enhancement by encoding enactment: Relationships to adult age and biological factors. *Neuroscience and Biobehavioral Reviews, 26,* 835–839.

Nyberg, L., Sandblom, J., Jones, S., Stigsdotter Neely, A., Petersson, K.M., Ingvar, M., & Backman, L. (2003b). Neural correlates of training-related memory improvement in adulthood and aging. *Proceedings of the National Academy of Sciences, 100,* 13728–13733.

Old, S.R., & Naveh-Benjamin, M. (2008). Differential effects of age on item and associative measures of memory: A meta-analysis. *Psychology and Aging, 23,* 104–118.

O'Sullivan, M., Jones, D.K., Summers, P.E., Morris, R.G., Williams, S.C.R., & Markus, H.S. (2001). Evidence for cortical "disconnection" as a mechanism of age-related cognitive decline. *Neurology, 57,* 632–638.

Owens, W.A. (1953). Age and mental abilities: A longitudinal study. *Genetic Psychology Monographs, 48,* 3–54.

Owens, W.A. (1959). Is age kinder to the initially more able? *Journal of Gerontology, 14,* 334–337.

Owens, W.A. (1966). Age and mental abilities: A second adult follow-up. *Journal of Educational Psychology, 57,* 311–325

Panza, F., D'Introno, A., Colacicco, A.M., Capurso, C., Del Parigi, A., Caselli, R.J., Pilotto, A., Argentieri, G., Scapicchio, P.L., Scafato, E., Capurso, A., & Solfrizzi, V. (2005). Current epidemiology of mild cognitive impairment and other predementia syndromes. *American Journal of Geriatric Psychiatry, 13,* 633–644.

Park, D.C., Gutchess, A.H., Meade, M.L., & Stine-Morrow, E.A.L. (2007). Improving cognitive function in older adults: Nontraditional approaches. *Journals of Gerontology: Series B, 62B (Special Issue),* 45–52.

Park, D.C., Hertzog, C., Leventhal, H., Morrell, R.W., Leventhal, E., Birchmore, D., Martin, M., & Bennett, J. (1999). Medication adherence in rheumatoid arthritis patients: Older is wiser. *Journal of American Geriatrics Society, 47,* 172–183.

Park, D.C., Lautenschlager, G., Hedden, T., Davidson, N.S., Smith, A.D., & Smith, P.K. (2002). Models of visuospatial and verbal memory across the adult life span. *Psychology and Aging, 17,* 299–320.

Park, D.C., & Reuter-Lorenz, P. (2009). The adaptive brain: Aging and neurocognitive scaffolding. *Annual Review of Psychology, 60,* 173–196.

Pascual-Leone, A., Amedi, A., Fregni, F., & Merabet, L.B. (2005). The plastic human brain cortex. *Annual Review of Neuroscience, 28,* 377–401.

Paul, R.H., Birckman, A.M., Cohen, R.A., Williams, L.M., Niaura, R., Pogun, S., Clark, C.R., Gunstad, J., & Gordon, E. (2006). Cognitive status of young and older cigarette smokers: Data from the international brain database. *Journal of Clinical Neuroscience, 13,* 457–465.

Perfect, T.J., & Harris, L.J. (2003). Adult age differences in unconscious transference: Source confusion or identity blending? *Memory & Cognition, 31,* 570–580.

Perlmutter, M. (1978). What is memory aging the aging of? *Developmental Psychology, 14,* 330–345.

Perrino, T., Mason, C.A., Brown, S.C., Spokane, A., & Szapocznik, J. (2008). Longitudinal relationships between cognitive functioning and depressive symptoms among Hispanic older adults. *Journal of Gerontology: Psychological Sciences, 63B,* P309–P317.

Persson, J., Nyberg, L., Lind, J., Larsson, A., Nilsson, L-G., Ingvar, M., & Buckner, R.L. (2006). Structure-function correlates of cognitive decline in aging. *Cerebral Cortex*, *16*, 907–915,

Petersen, R.C., & O'Brien, J. (2006). Mild cognitive impairment should be considered for DSM-V. *Journal of Geriatric Psychiatry and Neurology*, *19*, 147–154.

Petersen, R.C., Stevens, J.C., Ganguli, M., Tangalos, E.G., Cummings, J.L., & DeKosky, S.T. (2001). Practice parameter: Early detection of dementia: Mild cognitive impairment (an evidence-based review). *Neurology*, *56*, 1133–1142.

Plassman, B.L., Langa, K.M., Fisher, G.G., Heeringa, S.G., Weir, D.R., Ofstedal, M.B., Burke, J.R., Hurd, M.D., Potter, G.G., Rodgers, W.L., Steffens, D.C., Willis, R.J., & Wallace, R.B. (2007). Prevalence of dementia in the United States: The Aging, Demographics, and Memory Study. *Neuroepidemiology*, *29*, 125–132.

Plassman, B.L., Welsh, K.A., Helms, M., Brandt, J., Page, W.F., & Breitner, J.C.S. (1995). Intelligence and education as predictors of cognitive state in late life: A 50-year follow-up. *Neurology*, *45*, 1446–1450.

Plato. (360 BC). *Phaedrus—dialogue with Socrates.* Retrieved June 23, 2009, from http://books.mirror.org/plato/phaedrus/.

Podewils, L.J., Guallar, E., Kuller, L.H., Fried, L.P., Lopez, O.L., Carlson, M., & Lyketsos, C.G. (2005). Physical activity, APOE genotype, and dementia risk: Findings from the Cardiovascular Health Cognition Study. *American Journal of Epidemiology*, *161*, 639–651.

Preacher, K.J., Rucker, D.D., MacCallum, R.C., & Nicewander, W.A. (2005). Use of the extreme groups approach: A critical reexamination and new recommendations. *Psychological Methods*, *10*, 178–192.

Prins, N.D., van Dijk, E.J., den Heijer, T., Vermeer, S.E., Jolles, J., Koudstaal, P.J., Hofman, A., & Breteler, M.M.B. (2005). Cerebral small-vessel disease and decline in information processing speed, executive function and memory. *Brain*, *128*, 2034–2041.

Proust-Lima, C., Amieva, H., Letenneur, L., Orgogozo, J-M., Jacqmin-Gadda, H., & Dartigues, J-F. (2008). Gender and education impact on brain aging: A general cognitive factor approach. *Psychology and Aging*, *23*, 608–620.

Qiu, C., De Ronchi, D., & Fratiglioni, L. (2007). The epidemiology of dementias: An update. *Current Opinion in Psychiatry*, *20*, 380–385.

Rabbitt, P. (1993). Does it all go together when it goes? The Nineteenth Bartlett Memorial Lecture. *Quarterly Journal of Experimental Psychology*, *46A*, 385–434.

Rabbitt, P. (2005). Frontal brain changes and cognitive performance in old age. *Cortex*, *41*, 238–240.

Rabbitt, P., Chetwynd, A., & McInnes, L. (2003). Do clever brains age more slowly? Further exploration of a nun result. *British Journal of Psychology*, *94*, 63–71.

Rabbitt, P., Diggle, P., Holland, F., & McInnes, L. (2004a). Practice and drop-out effects during a 17-year longitudinal study of cognitive aging. *Journal of Gerontology: Psychological Science*, *59B*, P84–P97

Rabbitt, P., Diggle, P., Smith, D., Holland, F., & McInnes, L. (2001). Identifying and separating the effects of practice and of cognitive ageing during a large longitudinal study of elderly community residents. *Neuropsychologia*, *39*, 532–543.

Rabbitt, P., & Lowe, C. (2000). Patterns of cognitive ageing. *Psychological Research*, *63*, 308–316.

Rabbitt, P., Lunn, M., & Wong, D. (2006a). Understanding terminal decline in cognition and risk of death: Methodological and theoretical implications of practice and dropout effects. *European Psychologist*, *11*, 164–171.

Rabbitt, P., McInnes, L., Diggle, P., Holland, F., Bent, N., Abson, V., Pendleton, N., & Horan, M. (2004b). The University of Manchester Longitudinal Study of Cognition in Normal Healthy Old Age, 1983 through 2003. *Aging, Neuropsychology and Cognition*, *11*, 245–279.

Rabbitt, P., Mogapi, O., Scott, M., Thacker, N., Lowe, C., Horan, M., Pendleton, N., Jackson, A., & Lunn, D. (2007a). Effects of global atrophy, white matter lesions, and cerebral blood flow on age-related changes in speed, memory, intelligence, vocabulary, and frontal function. *Neuropsychology*, *21*, 684–695.

Rabbitt, P., Scott, M., Lunn, M., Thacker, N., Lowe, C., Pendleton, N. Horan, M., & Jackson, A. (2007b). White matter lesions account for all age-related declines in speed but not in intelligence. *Neuropsychology*, *21*, 363–370.

Rabbitt, P., Scott, M., Thacker, N., Lowe, C., Jackson, A., Horan, M., & Pendleton, N. (2006b). Losses in gross brain volume and cerebral blood flow account for age-related differences in speed but not in fluid intelligence. *Neuropsychology*, *20*, 549–557.

Radloff, L.S. (1977). The CES-D Scale: A self-report depression scale for research in the general population. *Applied Psychological Measurement*, *1*, 385–401.

Rahhal, T.A., Hasher, L., & Colcombe, S. J. (2001). Instructional manipulations and age differences in memory: Now you see them, now you don't. *Psychology and Aging*, *16*, 697–706.

Rasmusson, D.X., Rebok, G.W., Bylsma, F.W., & Brandt, J. (1999). Effects of three types of memory training in normal elderly. *Aging, Neuropsychology, and Cognition*, *6*, 56–66.

Raz, N., Lindenberger, U., Ghisletta, P., Rodrigue, K.M., & Acker, J.D. (2008). Neuroanatomical correlates of fluid intelligence in healthy adults and persons with vascular risk factors. *Cerebral Cortex*, *18*, 718–726.

Raz, N., Lindenberger, U., Rodrigue, K.M., Kennedy, K.M., Head, D., Williamson, A., Dahle, C., Gerstorf, D., & Acker, J.D. (2005). Regional brain changes in aging healthy adults; General trends, individual differences, and modifiers. *Cerebral Cortex*, *15*, 1676–1689.

Raz, N., Rodrigue, K.M., Kennedy, K.M., & Acker, J.D. (2007). Vascular health and longitudinal changes in brain and cognition in middle-aged and older adults. *Neuropsychology*, *21*, 149–157.

Reisberg, B. (2006). Diagnostic criteria in dementia: A comparison of current criteria, research challenges, and implications for DSM-V. *Journal of Geriatric Psychiatry and Neurology*, *19*, 137–146.

Reisberg, B., Prichep, L., Mosconi, L., John, E.R., Glodzik-Sobanska, L., Boksay, I., Monteiro, I., Torossian, C., Vedvyas, A., Ashraf, N., Jamil, I.A., & de Leon, M.J. (2008). The pre-mild cognitive impairment, subjective cognitive impairment stage of Alzheimer's disease. *Alzheimer's & Dementia*, *4*, S98–S108.

Reynolds, C.A., Gatz, M., & Pedersen, N.L. (2002). Individual variation for cognitive decline: Quantitative methods for describing patterns of change. *Psychology and Aging*, *17*, 271–287.

Reynolds, C.R., & Kamphaus, R.W. (1998). *RIAS: Reynolds Intellectual Assessment Scales and the RIST Reynolds Intellectual Screening Test: Professional Manual.* Lutz, FL: Psychological Assessment Resources, Inc.

Richards, M., Hardy, R., Kuh, D., & Wadsworth, M.E.J. (2002). Birthweight, postnatal growth and cognitive function in a national UK birth cohort. *International Journal of Epidemiology, 31*, 342–348.

Richards, M., Hardy, R., & Wadsworth, M.E.J. (2003). Does active leisure protect cognition? Evidence from a national birth cohort. *Social Science & Medicine, 56*, 785–792.

Richards, M., & Sacker, A. (2003). Lifetime antecedents of cognitive reserve. *Journal of Clinical and Experimental Neuropsychology, 25*, 614–624.

Richards, M., Shipley, B., Fuhrer, R., & Wadsworth, M.E.J. (2004). Cognitive ability in childhood and cognitive decline in mid-life: Longitudinal birth cohort study. *BMJ*, doi: 10.1136/bmj.37392.513819.EE (published 3 February 2004).

Riley, K.P., Snowdon, D.A., Desroiers, M.F., & Markesbery, W.R. (2005). Early life linguistic ability, late life cognitive function, and neuropathology: Findings from the Nun study. *Neurobiology of Aging, 26*, 341–347.

Ritchie, K., Artero, S., & Touchon, J. (2001). Classification criteria for mild cognitive impairment: A population-based validation study. *Neurology, 56*, 37–42.

Ritchie, K., Polge, C., de Roquefeuil, G., Djakovic, M., & Ledesert, B. (1997). Risk factors for dementia: Impact of anesthesia on the cognitive functioning of the elderly. *International Psychogeriatrics, 9*, 309–326.

Ritchie, K., & Touchon, J. (2000). Mild cognitive impairment: Conceptual basis and current nosological status. *Lancet, 355*, 225–228.

Ritchie, L.J., Frerichs, R.J., & Tuokko, H. (2007). Effective normative samples for the detection of cognitive impairment in older adults. *The Clinical Neuropsychologist, 21*, 863–874.

Rivas-Vazquez, R.A., Mendez, C., Rey, G.J., & Carrazana, E.J. (2004). Mild cognitive impairment: New neuropsychological and pharmacological target. *Archives of Clinical Neuropsychology, 19*, 11–27.

Roberts, B.W., & Mroczek, D. (2008). Personality trait change in adulthood. *Current Directions in Psychology, 17*, 31–35.

Roberts, B.W., Walton, K.E., & Viechtbauer, W. (2006). Patterns of mean-level change in personality traits across the life course: A meta-analysis of longitudinal studies. *Psychological Bulletin, 132*, 1–25.

Rodgers, W.L., Ofstedal, M.B., & Herzog, A.R. (2003). Trends in scores on tests of cognitive ability in the elderly U.S. population, 1993–2000. *Journal of Gerontology: Social Science, 58B*, S338–S346.

Ronnlund, M., Lovden, M., & Nilsson, L.-G. (2007). Cross-sectional versus longitudinal age gradients of Tower of Hanoi performance: The role of practice effects and cohort differences in education. *Aging, Neuropsychology, and Cognition, 15*, 1–28.

Ronnlund, M., & Nilsson, L-G., (2006). Adult life-span patterns in WAIS-R Block Design performance; Cross-sectional versus longitudinal age gradients and relations to demographic factors. *Intelligence, 34*, 63–78.

Ronnlund, M., & Nilsson, L.-G. (2008). The magnitude, generality, and determinants of Flynn effects on forms of declarative memory and visuospatial ability: Time-sequential analyses of data from a Swedish cohort study. *Intelligence, 36*, 192–209.

Ronnlund, M., Nyberg, L., Backman, L., & Nilsson, L.-G. (2003). Recall of subject-performed tasks, verbal tasks, and cognitive activities across the adult life span: Parallel age-related deficits. *Aging, Neuropsychology, and Cognition, 10*, 182–201.

Ronnlund, M., Nyberg, L., Backman, L., & Nilsson, L.-G. (2005). Stability, growth, and decline in adult life span development of declarative memory: Cross-sectional and longitudinal data from a population-based study. *Psychology and Aging, 20,* 3–18.

Rubin, D.C., & Schulkind, M.D. (1997). The distribution of autobiographical memories across the lifespan. *Memory & Cognition, 25,* 859–866.

Rundek, T., & Bennett, D.A. (2006). Cognitive leisure activities, but not watching TV, for future brain benefits. *Neurology, 66,* 794–795.

Salat, D.H., Kaye, J.A., & Janowsky, J.S. (2002). Greater orbital prefrontal volume selectively predicts worse working memory performance in older adults. *Cerebral Cortex, 12,* 494–505.

Salmon, D.P., & Bondi, M. (2009). Neuropsychological assessment of dementia. *Annual Review of Psychology, 60,* 257–282.

Salmon, D.P., Thomas, R.G., Pay, M.M., Booth, A., Hofstetter, C.R., Thal, L., & Katzman, R. (2002). Alzheimer's disease can be accurately diagnosed in very mildly impaired individuals. *Neurology, 49,* 1022–1028.

Salthouse, T.A. (1984). Effects of age and skill in typing. *Journal of Experimental Psychology: General, 113,* 345–371.

Salthouse, T.A. (1985). *A theory of cognitive aging.* Amsterdam: North-Holland.

Salthouse, T.A. (1991). *Theoretical perspectives on cognitive aging.* Hillsdale, NJ: Lawrence Erlbaum Associates.

Salthouse, T.A. (1998). Independence of age-related influences on cognitive abilities across the life span. *Developmental Psychology, 34,* 851–864.

Salthouse, T.A. (2000). Methodological assumptions in cognitive aging research. In Craik, F.I.M., & Salthouse, T.A. (Eds.). *Handbook of aging and cognition* (2nd ed.) (pp. 467–498). Hillsdale, NJ: Lawrence Erlbaum Associates.

Salthouse, T.A. (2001). Attempted decomposition of age-related influences on two tests of reasoning. *Psychology and Aging, 16,* 251–263.

Salthouse, T.A. (2003). Interrelations of aging, knowledge, and cognitive performance. In U. Staudinger & U. Lindenberger (Eds.), *Understanding human development: Lifespan psychology in exchange with other disciplines* (pp. 265–287). Berlin: Kluwer Academic Publishers.

Salthouse, T.A. (2005a). From description to explanation in cognitive aging. In R. Sternberg, J. Davidson, & J. Pretz (Eds.), *Cognition and intelligence: Identifying the mechanisms of the mind* (pp. 288–305). New York: Cambridge University Press.

Salthouse, T.A. (2005b). Relations between cognitive abilities and measures of executive functioning. *Neuropsychology, 19,* 532–545.

Salthouse, T.A. (2006a). Theoretical issues in the psychology of aging. In J.E. Birren & K.W. Schaie (Eds.), *Handbook of the psychology of aging* (6th ed.) (pp. 3–13). San Diego, CA: Academic Press.

Salthouse, T.A. (2006b). Mental exercise and mental aging: Evaluating the validity of the use it or lose it hypothesis. *Perspectives on Psychological Science, 1,* 68–87.

Salthouse, T.A. (2007a). Implications of within-person variability in cognitive and neuropsychological functioning on the interpretation of change. *Neuropsychology, 21,* 401–411.

Salthouse, T.A. (2007b). Reply to Schooler: Consistent is not conclusive. *Perspectives on Psychological Science, 2,* 30–32.

Salthouse, T.A. (2009). When does age-related cognitive decline begin? *Neurobiology of Aging, 30,* 507–514.

Salthouse, T.A., Berish, D.E., & Siedlecki, K.L. (2004). Construct validity and age sensitivity of prospective memory. *Memory & Cognition, 32,* 1133–1148.

Salthouse, T.A., & Czaja, S. (2000). Structural constraints on process explanations in cognitive aging. *Psychology and Aging, 15*, 44–55.

Salthouse, T.A., & Ferrer-Caja, E. (2003). What needs to be explained to account for age-related effects on multiple cognitive variables? *Psychology and Aging, 18*, 91–110.

Salthouse, T.A., Hancock, H.E., Meinz, E.J., & Hambrick, D.Z. (1996). Interrelations of age, visual acuity, and cognitive functioning. *Journal of Gerontology: Psychological Sciences, 51B*, P317–P330.

Salthouse, T.A., & Nesselroade, J.R. (2002). An examination of the Hofer and Sliwinski (2001) evaluation. *Gerontology, 48*, 18–21.

Salthouse, T.A., & Nesselroade, J.R. (unpublished manuscript). *Dealing with short-term fluctuation in longitudinal research.*

Salthouse, T.A., Pink, J.E., & Tucker-Drob, E.M. (2008). Contextual analysis of fluid intelligence. *Intelligence, 36*, 464–486.

Salthouse, T.A., & Saults, J.S. (1987). Multiple spans in transcription typing. *Journal of Applied Psychology, 22*, 187–196.

Salthouse, T.A., Schroeder, D.H., & Ferrer, E. (2004). Estimating retest effects in longitudinal assessments of cognitive functioning in adults between 18 and 60 years of age. *Developmental Psychology, 40*, 813–822.

Salthouse, T.A., & Siedlecki, K.L. (2007a). Efficiency of route selection as a function of adult age. *Brain and Cognition, 63*, 279–287.

Salthouse, T.A., & Siedlecki, K.L. (2007b). An individual differences analysis of false recognition. *American Journal of Psychology, 120*, 429–458.

Salthouse, T.A., Siedlecki, K.L., & Krueger, L.E. (2006). An individual differences analysis of memory control. *Journal of Memory and Language, 55*, 102–125.

Salthouse, T.A., Toth, J.P., Hancock, H.E., & Woodard, J.L. (1997). Controlled and automatic forms of memory and attention: Process purity and the uniqueness of age-related influences. *Journal of Gerontology: Psychological Sciences, 52B*, P216–P228.

Saxton, J., Lopez, O.L., Ratcliff, G., Dulberg, C., Fried, L.P., Carlson, M.C., Newman, A.B., & Kuller, L. (2004). Preclinical Alzheimer disease: Neuropsychological test performance 1.5 to 8 years prior to onset. *Neurology, 63*, 2341–2347.

Scahill, R.I., Frost, C., Jenkins, R., Whitwell, J.L., Rossor, M.N., & Fox, N.C. (2003). A longitudinal study of brain volume changes in normal aging using serial registered magnetic resonance imaging. *Archives of Neurology, 60*, 989–994.

Scarmeas, N., & Stern, Y. (2003). Cognitive reserve and lifestyle. *Journal of Clinical and Experimental Neuropsychology, 25*, 625–633.

Schaie, K.W. (1988). Internal validity threats in studies of adult cognitive development. In M.L. Howe & C.J. Brainerd (Eds.), *Cognitive development in adulthood* (pp. 241–272). New York: Springer-Verlag.

Schaie, K.W. (2005). *Developmental influences on adult intelligence: The Seattle Longitudinal Study.* New York: Oxford University Press.

Schaie, K.W., Labouvie, G.V., & Barrett, T.J. (1973). Selective attrition effects in a fourteen-year study of adult intelligence. *Journal of Gerontology, 28*, 328–334.

Schmidt, R., Ropele, S., Enzinger, C., Petrovic, K., Smith, S., Schmidt, H., Matthews, P.M., & Fazekas, F. (2005). White matter lesion progression, brain atrophy, and cognitive decline: The Austrian Stroke Prevention Study. *Annals of Neurology, 58*, 610–616.

Schooler, C. (2007). Use it—and keep it, longer, probably: A reply to Salthouse (2006). *Perspectives on Psychological Science, 2*, 24–29.

Schooler, C., & Mulatu, M.S. (2001). The reciprocal effects of leisure time activities and intellectual functioning in older people: A longitudinal analysis. *Psychology and Aging, 16,* 466–482.

Schretlen, D., Pearlson, G.D., Anthony, J.C., Aylward, E.H., Augustine, A.M., Davis, A., & Barta, P. (2000). Elucidating the contributions of processing speed, executive ability, and frontal lobe volume to normal age-related differences in fluid intelligence. *Journal of International Neuropsychological Society, 6,* 52–61.

Schretlen, D., Pearlson, G.D., Anthony, J.C., & Yates, K.O. (2001). Determinants of Benton Facial Recognition Test performance in normal adults. *Neuropsychology, 15,* 405–410.

Schroeder, D.H., & Salthouse, T.A. (2004). Age-related effects on cognition between 20 and 50 years of age. *Personality and Individual Differences, 36,* 393–404.

Schuitt, A.J., Feskens, E.J.M., Launer, L.J., & Kromhout, D. (2001). Physical activity and cognitive decline, the role of the apolipoprotein e4 allele. *Medicine & Science in Sports & Exercise, 33,* 772–777.

Schwartzman, A.E., Gold, D., Andres, D., Arbuckle, T.Y., & Chaikelson, J. (1987). Stability of intelligence: A 40-year follow-up. *Canadian Journal of Psychology, 41,* 244–256.

Searcy, J.H., Bartlett, J.C., Memon, A., & Swanson, K. (2001). Aging and lineup performance at long retention intervals: Effects of metamemory and context reinstatement. *Journal of Applied Psychology, 86,* 207–214.

Sehl, M.E., & Yates, F.E. (2001). Kinetics of human aging: I. Rates of senescence between ages 30 and 70 years in healthy people. *Journal of Gerontology: Biological Sciences, 56A,* B198–B208.

Selnes, O.A., Royall, R.M., Grega, M.A., Borowicz, L.M., Quaskey, S., & McKhann, G.M. (2001). Cognitive changes 5 years after coronary artery bypass grafting: Is there evidence of late decline? *Archives of Neurology, 58,* 598–604.

Shenkin, S.D., Starr, J.M., Pattie, A., Rush, M.A., Whalley, L.J., & Deary, I.J. (2001). Birth weight and cognitive function at age 11 years: The Scottish Mental Survey 1932. *Archives of Diseases of Childhood, 85,* 189–197.

Sherwin, B.B. (2005). Estrogen and memory in women: How can we reconcile the findings? *Hormones and Behavior, 47,* 371–375.

Shukitt-Hale, B., McEwen, J.J., Szprengiel, A., & Joseph, J.A. (2004). Effect of age on the radial arm water maze—a test of spatial learning and memory. *Neurobiology of Aging, 25,* 223–229.

Shukitt-Hale, B., Mouzakis, G., & Joseph, J.A. (1998). Psychomotor and spatial memory performance in aging male Fischer 344 rats. *Experimental Gerontology, 33,* 615–624.

Siedlecki, K.L. (2007). Investigating the structure and age invariance of episodic memory across the adult lifespan. *Psychology and Aging, 22,* 251–268.

Siedlecki, K.L., Salthouse, T.A., & Berish, D.E. (2005). Is there anything special about the aging of source memory? *Psychology and Aging, 20,* 19–32.

Simons, L.A., Simons, J., McCallum, J., & Friedlander, Y. (2006). Lifestyle factors and risk of dementia: Dubbo study of the elderly. *Medical Journal of Australia, 184,* 68–70.

Singer, T., Verhaegen, P., Ghisletta, P., Lindenberger, U., & Baltes, P.B. (2003). The fate of cognition in very old age: Six-year longitudinal findings in the Berlin Aging Study (BASE). *Psychology and Aging, 18,* 318–331.

Singh-Manoux, A., Hillson, M., Burnner, E., & Marmot, M. (2005). Effects of physical activity on cognitive functioning in middle age: Evidence from the Whitehall II Prospective Cohort Study. *American Journal of Public Health, 95,* 2252–2258.

Singh-Manoux, A., Richards, M., & Marmot, M. (2003). Leisure activities and cognitive function in middle age: Evidence from the Whitehall II study. *Journal of Epidemiology and Community Health, 57,* 907–913.

Skinner, B.F., & Vaughan, M.E. (1983). *Enjoy old age: Living fully in your later years.* New York: Warner Books.

Sliwinski, M., & Buschke, H. (1999). Cross-sectional and longitudinal relationships among age, cognition, and processing speed. *Psychology and Aging, 14,* 18–33.

Sliwinski, M., & Buschke, H. (2004). Modeling intraindividual cognitive change in aging adults: Results from the Einstein Aging Studies. *Aging, Neuropsychology and Cognition, 11,* 196–211.

Sliwinski, M., Lipton, R.B., Buschke, H., & Stewart, W. (1996). The effects of preclinical dementia on estimates of normal cognitive functioning in aging. *Journal of Gerontology: B: Psychological Sciences, 51,* 217–225.

Small, B.J., & Backman, L. (2007). Longitudinal trajectories of cognitive change in preclinical Alzheimer's disease: A growth mixture modeling analysis. *Cortex, 43,* 826–834.

Small, B.J., Fratiglioni, L., Viitanen, M., Winblad, B., & Backman, L. (2000). The course of cognitive impairment in preclinical Alzheimer disease. *Archives of Neurology, 57,* 839–844.

Small, B.J., Hertzog, C., Hultsch, D.F., & Dixon, R.A. (2003). Stability and change in adult personality over 6 years: Findings from the Victoria Longitudinal Study. *Journal of Gerontology: Psychological Sciences, 58B,* P166–P176.

Small, B.J., Rosnick, C.B., Fratiglioni, L., & Backman, L. (2004). Apolipoprotein E and cognitive performance: A meta-analysis. *Psychology and Aging, 19,* 592–600.

Smits, C.H.M., Smit, J.H., van den Heuvel, N., & Jonker, C. (1997). Norms for an abbreviated Raven's Coloured Progressive Matrices in an older sample. *Journal of Clinical Psychology, 53,* 687–697.

Snowdon, D.A., Kemper, S.J., Mortimer, J.A., Greiner, L.H., Wekstein, D.R., & Marksbery, W.R. (1996). Linguistic ability in early life and cognitive function and Alzheimer's disease in late life: Findings from the Nun Study. *Journal of American Medical Association, 275,* 528–532.

Solomon, P.R., & Groccia-Ellison, M. (1996). Classic conditioning in aged rabbits: Delay, trace, and long-delay conditioning. *Behavioral Neuroscience, 110,* 427–435.

Solomon, P.R., Pomerleau, D., Bennett, L., James, J., & Morse, D.L. (1989). Acquisition of the classically conditioned eyeblink response in humans over the life span. *Psychology and Aging, 4,* 34–41.

Sorensen, H.T., Sabroe, S., Olsen, J., Rothman, K.J., Gillman, M.W., & Fischer, P. (1997). Birth weight and cognitive function in young adult life: Historical cohort study. *British Medical Journal, 315,* 401–403.

Sorenson, H. (1933). Mental ability over a wide range of adult ages. *Journal of Applied Psychology, 17,* 729–741.

Sorenson, H. (1938). *Adult abilities.* Minneapolis, MN: University of Minnesota Press.

Spencer, W.D., & Raz, N. (1995). Differential effects of aging on memory for content and context: A meta-analysis. *Psychology and Aging, 10,* 527–539.

Spielberger, C.D., Gorsuch, R.L., Lushene, R., Vagg, P.R., & Jacobs, G.A. (1983). *Manual for the State-Trait Anxiety Inventory (Form Y)*. Palo Alto, CA: Consulting Psychologists Press.

Squire, L. (1974). Remote memory as affected by aging. *Neuropsychologia, 12*, 429–435.

Srivastava, S., John, O.P., Gosling, S.D., & Potter, J. (2003). Development of personality in early and middle adulthood: Set like plaster or persistent change? *Journal of Personality and Social Psychology, 84*, 1041–1053.

Starr, J.M., Deary, I.J., Lemmon, H., & Whalley, L.J. (2000). Mental ability age 11 years and health status age 77 years. *Age and Ageing, 29*, 523–528.

Stein, R., Blanchard-Fields, F., & Hertzog, C. (2002). The effects of age-stereotype priming on the memory performance of older adults. *Experimental Aging Research, 28*, 169–181.

Stephan, B.C.M., Matthews, F.E., McKeith, I.G., Bond, J., & Brayne, C. (2007). Early cognitive change in the general population: How do different definitions work? *Journal of American Geriatrics Society, 55*, 1534–1540.

Stern, R.A., & White, T. (2001). *Neuropsychological Assessment Battery: U.S. Census-Matched Norms Manual*. Lutz, FL: Psychological Assessment Resources, Inc.

Stern, Y. (2006). Cognitive reserve and Alzheimer disease. *Alzheimer Disease and Associated Disorders, 20*, 112–117.

Stigsdotter Neely, A.S., & Backman, L. (1995). Effects of multifactorial memory training in old age: Generalizability across tasks and individuals. *Journal of Gerontology: Psychological Sciences, 50B*, P134–P140.

Stine, E.L., Wingfield, A., & Myers, S.D. (1990). Age differences in processing information from television news: The effects of bisensory augmentation. *Journal of Gerontology: Psychological Sciences, 45*, P9–P16.

Stine-Morrow, E.A.L., Parisi, J.M., Morrow, D.G., Greene, J., & Park, D.C. (2007). An engagement model of cognitive optimization through adulthood. *Journal of Gerontology: Series B, 62B (Special Issue)*, 62–69.

Stine-Morrow, E.A.L., Parisi, J.M., Morrow, D.G., & Park, D.C. (2008). The effects of an engaged lifestyle on cognitive vitality: A field experiment. *Psychology and Aging, 23*, 778–786.

Storandt, M., Grant, E.A., Miller, J.P., & Morris, J.C. (2006). Longitudinal course and neuropathologic outcomes in original vs. revised MCI and in pre-MCI. *Neurology, 67*, 467–473.

Sundet, J.M., Barlaug, D.G., & Torjussen, T.M. (2004). The end of the Flynn effect? A study of secular trends in mean intelligence test scores of Norwegian conscripts during half a century. *Intelligence, 32*, 349–362.

Swan, G.E., & Carmelli, D. (2002). Impaired olfaction predicts cognitive decline in nondemented older adults. *Neuroepidemiology, 21*, 58–67.

Sward, K. (1945). Age and mental ability in superior men. *American Journal of Psychology, 58*, 443–479.

Tabert, M.H., Liu, X., Doty, R.L., Serby, M., Zamora, D., Pelton, G.H., Marder, K., Albers, M.W., Stern, & Devanand, D.P. (2005). A 10-item smell identification scale related to risk of Alzheimer's disease. *Annals of Neurology, 58*, 155–160.

Tamura, T., Chiang, A-S., Ito, N., Liu, H-P., Horiuchi, J., Tully, T., Saltoe, M. (2003). Aging specifically impairs amnesiac-dependent memory in Drosophila. *Neuron, 40*, 1003–1011.

Tapp, P.D., Siwak, C.T., Estrada, J., Head, E., Muggenburg, B.A., Cotman, C.W., & Milgram, N.W. (2003). Size and reversal learning in the Beagle dog as a measure of executive function and inhibitory control in aging. *Learning and Memory, 10,* 64–73.

Taub, H.A. (1975). Mode of presentation, age, and short-term memory. *Journal of Gerontology, 30,* 56–59.

Teachman, B.A. (2006). Aging and negative affect: The rise and fall of anxiety and depression symptoms. *Psychology and Aging, 21,* 201–207.

Teasdale, T.W., & Owen, D.R. (2008). Secular declines in cognitive tests scores: A reversal of the Flynn effect. *Intelligence, 36,* 121–126.

Terracciano, A., McCrae, R.R., Brant, L.J., & Costa, P.T. (2005). Hierarchical linear modeling analyses of the NEO-PI-R scales in the Baltimore Longitudinal Study of Aging. *Psychology and Aging, 20,* 493–506.

Thompson, D.E. (1954). Is age kinder to the initially more able? *Proceedings of the Iowa Academy of Science, 61,* 439–441.

Thorndike, E. L., Bregman, E.O., Tilton, J. W., & Woodyard, E. (1928). *Adult learning.* New York: MacMillan.

Thorvaldsson, V., Hofer, S.M., Berg, S., & Johansson, B. (2006). Effects of repeated testing in a longitudinal age-homogeneous study of cognitive aging. *Journal of Gerontology: Psychological Sciences, 61B,* P348–P354.

Tisserand, D.J., Visser, P.J., van Boxtel, M.P.J., & Jolles, J. (2000). The relation between global and limbic brain volumes on MRI and cognitive performance in healthy individuals across the age range. *Neurobiology of Aging, 21,* 569–576.

Topic, B., Dere, E., Schulz, D., de Souza Silva, M.A., Jocham, G., Kart, E., & Huston, J.P. (2005). Aged and adult rats compared in acquisition and extinction of escape from the water maze: Focus on individual differences. *Behavioral Neuroscience, 119,* 127–144.

Tucker-Drob, E.M. (2009). *Global and domain-specific longitudinal changes in cognition throughout adulthood.* Unpublished dissertation, University of Virginia.

Tucker-Drob, E.M., Johnson, K.E., & Jones, R.N. (2009). The cognitive reserve hypothesis: A longitudinal examination of age-associated declines in reasoning and processing speed. *Developmental Psychology, 45,* 431–446.

Tucker-Drob, E.M., & Salthouse, T.A. (2008). Adult age trends in the relations among cognitive abilities. *Psychology and Aging, 23,* 453–460.

Tuddenham, R.D. (1948). Soldier intelligence in World Wars I and II. *American Psychologist, 3,* 54–56.

Turic, D., Fisher, P.J., Plomin, R., & Owen, M.J. (2001). No association between apolipoprotein E polymorphisms and general cognitive ability in children. *Neuroscience Letters, 299,* 97–100.

Tyas, S.L., Salazar, J.C., Snowdon, D.A., Desrosiers, M.F., Riley, K.P., Mendiondo, M.S., & Kryscio, R.J. (2007). Transitions to mild cognitive impairments, dementia, and death: Findings from the Nun Study. *American Journal of Epidemiology, 165,* 1231–1238.

Uttl, B., & Graf, P. (1993). Episodic spatial memory in adulthood. *Psychology and Aging, 8,* 257–273.

Valentijn, S.A.M., van Boxtel, M.P.J., van Hooren, S.A.H., Bosma, H., Beckers, H.J.M., Ponds, R.W.H.M., & Jolles, J. (2005). Change in sensory function predicts change in cognitive functioning: Results from a 6-year follow-up in the Maastricht Aging Study. *Journal of American Geriatrics Society, 53,* 374–380.

Valenzuela, M.J., & Sachdev, P. (2006a). Brain reserve and dementia; A systematic review. *Psychological Medicine, 36,* 441–454.

Valenzuela, M.J., & Sachdev, P. (2006b). Brain reserve and dementia: A non-parametric systematic review. *Psychological Medicine, 36,* 1065–1073.

Van den Heuvel, D.M.J., ten Dam, V.H., de Craen, A.J.M., Admiraal-Behloul, F., Olofsen, H., Bollen, E.K.E.M., Jolles, J., Murray, H.M., Blauw, G.J., Westendorp, R.G.J., & van Buchem, M.A. (2006). Increase in periventricular white matter hyperintensities parallels decline in mental processing speed in a non-demented elderly population. *Journal of Neurology, Neurosurgery, and Psychiatry, 77,* 149–153.

Van Dijk, K.R.A., van Gerben, P.W.M., van Boxtel, M.P.J., van der Elst, W., & Jolles, J. (2008). No protective effects of education during normal cognitive aging: Results from the 6-year follow-up of the Maastricht Aging Study. *Psychology and Aging, 23,* 119–130.

Van Gelder, B.M., Tijhuis, M.A.R., Kalmijn, S., Giampaoli, S., Nissinen, A., & Kromhout, D. (2004). Physical activity in relation to cognitive decline in elderly men: The FINE study. *Neurology, 63,* 2316–2321.

Veng, L.M., Granholm, A.C., & Rose, G.M. (2003). Age-related sex differences in spatial learning and basal forebrain cholinergic neurons in F344 rats. *Physiology & Behavior, 80,* 27–36.

Verghese, J., Lipton, R.B., & Hall, C.B. (2003). Low blood pressure and the risk of dementia in very old individuals. *Neurology, 61,* 1667–1672.

Verhaeghen, P. (2003). Aging and vocabulary scores: A meta-analysis. *Psychology and Aging, 18,* 332–339.

Verhaeghen, P., Marcoen, A., & Goossens, L. (1993). Facts and fiction about memory aging: A quantitative integration of research findings. *Journal of Gerontology: Psychological Sciences, 48,* P157–P171.

Verhaeghen, P., & Salthouse, T.A. (1997). Meta-analyses of age-cognition relations in adulthood: Estimates of linear and non-linear age effects and structural models. *Psychological Bulletin, 122,* 231–249.

Villarreal, J.S., Dykes, J.R., & Barea-Rodriguez, E.J. (2004). Fischer 344 rats display age-related memory deficits in trace fear conditioning. *Behavioral Neuroscience, 118,* 1166–1175.

Volkow, N.D., Gur, R.C., Wang, G.-J., Fowler, J.S., Moberg, P.J., Ding, Y.-S., Hitzermann, R., Smith, G., & Logan, J. (1998). Association between decline in brain dopamine activity with age and cognitive and motor impairment in healthy individuals. *American Journal of Psychiatry, 155,* 344–349.

Wahlin, A., MacDonald, S.W.S., De Frias, C.M., Nilsson, L-G., & Dixon, R.A. (2006). How do health and biological age influence chronological age and sex differences in cognitive aging: Moderating, mediating, or both? *Psychology and Aging, 21,* 318–332.

Walhovd, K.B., Fjell, A.M., Reinvang, I., Lundervold, A., Fischl, B., Salat, D., Quinn, B.T., Makris, N., & Dale, A.M. (2005). Cortical volume and speed-of-processing are complementary in prediction of performance intelligence. *Neuropsychologia, 43,* 704–713.

Wang, J.Y.J., Zhou, D.H.D., Li, J., Zhang, M., Deng, J., Tang, M., Gao, C., Li, J., Lian, Y., & Chen, M. (2006). Leisure activity and risk of cognitive impairment: The Chongqing aging study. *Neurology, 66,* 911–913.

Watson, J.D. (2007). *Avoid boring (other) people.* New York: A. Knopf.

Watson, D., Clark, L.A., & Tellegen, A. (1988). Development and validation of brief measures of positive and negative affect: The PANAS scales. *Journal of Personality and Social Psychology, 54*, 1063–1070.

Wechsler, D. (1997a). *WAIS III: Administration and scoring manual*. San Antonio: TX: The Psychological Corporation.

Wechsler, D. (1997b). *WMS III: Administration and scoring manual*. San Antonio, TX: The Psychological Corporation.

Wechsler, D. (1999). *Wechsler Abbreviated Scale of Intelligence (WASI)*. San Antonio, TX: The Psychological Corporation.

Weisenburg, T., Roe, A., & McBride, K.E. (1936). *Adult intelligence*. New York: The Commonwealth Fund.

Welford, A.T. (1958). *Ageing and human skill*. London: Oxford University Press.

Westervelt, H.J., Ruffolo, J.S., & Tremont, G. (2005). Assessing olfaction in the neuropsychological exam: The relationship between odor identification and cognition in older adults. *Archives of Clinical Neuropsychology, 20*, 761–769.

Weuve, J., Kang, J.H., Manson, J.E., Breteler, M.M.B., Ware, H.H., & Grodstein, F. (2004). Physical activity, including walking, and cognitive function in older women. *Journal of American Medical Association, 292*, 1454–1461.

Whalley, L.J., Starr, J.M., Athawes, R., Hunter, D., Pattie, A., & Deary, I.J. (2000). Childhood mental ability and dementia. *Neurology, 55*, 1455–1459.

Williams, K.T. (2007). *Expressive Vocabulary Test*. Bloomington, MN: Pearson Assessments.

Willis, S.L., & Schaie, K.W. (1994). Cognitive training in the normal elderly. In F. Forette, Y. Christen, & F. Boller (Eds.), *Plasticite Cerebrale et Stimuation Congitive* (pp. 91–113). Paris: Fondation Nationale de Gerontologie.

Willis, S.L., Tennstedt, S.L., Marsiske, M., Ball, K., Elias, J., Koepke, K.M., Morris, J.N., Rebok, G.W., Unverzagt, F.W., Stoddard, A.M., & Wright, E. (2006). Long-term effects of cognitive training on everyday functional outcomes in older adults. *Journal of American Medical Association, 296*, 2805–2814.

Willoughby, R.R. (1927). Family similarities in mental test abilities (with a note on the growth and decline of these abilities). *Genetic Psychological Monograph, 2*, 235–277.

Wilson, R.S., Beckett, L.A., Barnes, L.L., Schneider, J.A., Bach, J., Evans, D.A., & Bennett, D.A. (2002a). Individual differences in rates of change in cognitive abilities of older persons. *Psychology and Aging, 17*, 179–193.

Wilson, R.S., Bennett, D.A., Bienias, J.L., Aggarwal, N.T., Mendes de Leon, C.F., Morris, M.C., Schneider, J.A., & Evans, D.A. (2002b). Cognitive activity and incident AD in a population-based sample of older persons. *Neurology, 59*, 1910–1914.

Wilson, R.S., Li, Y., Bienias, J.L., & Bennett, D.A. (2006). Cognitive decline in old age: Separating retest effects from the effects of growing older. *Psychology and Aging, 21*, 774–789.

Wilson, R.S., Scherr, P.A., Schneider, J.A., Tang, Y., & Bennett, D.A. (2007). Relation of cognitive activity to risk of developing Alzheimer disease. *Neurology, 69*, 1911–1920.

Winblad, B., Palmer, K., Kivipelto, M., Jelic, V., Fratiglioni, L., Wahlund, L.O., Nordberg, A., Backman, L., Albert, L., Albert, M., Almkvist, O., Arai, H., Basun, H., Blennow, K., De Leon, M., DeCarli, C., Erkinjuntti, T., Giacobini, E., Graff, C., Hardy, J., Jack, C., Jorm, A., Ritchie, K., Van Duijn, C., Visser, P., & Petersen, R.C. (2004). Mild cognitive impairment—beyond controversies, towards a consensus: Report of the International working group on mild cognitive impairment. *Journal of Internal Medicine, 256*, 240–246.

Withaar, F.K., Brouwer, W.H., & van Zomeren, A.H. (2000). Fitness to drive in older drivers with cognitive impairment. *Journal of the International Neuropsychological Society, 6,* 480–490.

Wood, L. E., & Pratt, J. D. (1987). Pegword mnemonic as an aid to memory in the elderly: A comparison of four age groups. *Educational Gerontology, 13,* 325–339.

Woodruff-Pak, D. S., & Thompson, R.F. (1988). Classical conditioning of the eyeblink response in the delay paradigm in adults aged 18–83 years. *Psychology and Aging, 3,* 219–229.

Wu, B., Plassman, B.L., Crout, R.J., & Liang, J. (2008). Cognitive function and oral health among community-dwelling older adults. *Journal of Gerontology: Medical Sciences, 63A,* 495–500.

Wyss, J.M., Chambless, B.D., Kadish, I., & van Groen, T. (2000). Age-related decline in water maze learning and memory in rats: Strain differences. *Neurobiology of Aging, 21,* 671–681.

Yaffe, K., Barnes, D., Nevitt, M., Lui, L.-Y., & Covinsky, K. (2001). A prospective study of physical activity and cognitive decline in elderly women. *Archives of Internal Medicine, 161,* 1703–1708.

Yerkes, R.M. (1921). Psychological examining in the United States Army. *Memoirs of the National Academy of Sciences, 15,* 1–877.

Yoder, C.Y., & Elias, J.W. (1987). Age, affect, and memory for pictorial story sequences. *British Journal of Psychology, 78,* 545–549.

Yoon, C., Hasher, L., Feinberg, F., Rahhal, T.A., & Winocur, G. (2000). Cross-cultural differences in memory: The role of culture-based stereotypes about aging. *Psychology and Aging, 15,* 694–704.

Zelinski, E.M., & Burnight, K.P. (1997). Sixteen-year longitudinal and time lag changes in memory and cognition in older adults. *Psychology and Aging, 12,* 503–513.

Zelinski, E.M., Burnight, K.P., & Lane, C.J. (2001). The relationship between subjective and objective memory in the oldest old: Comparisons of findings from a representative and a convenience sample. *Journal of Aging and Health, 13,* 248–266.

Zelinski, E.M., Gilewski, M.J., & Anthony-Bergstone, C.R. (1990). Memory functioning questionnaire: Concurrent validity with memory performance and self-reported memory failures. *Psychology and Aging. 5,* 388–399.

Zelinski, E.M., & Kennison, R.F. (2007). Not your parents' test scores: Cohort reduces psychometric aging effects. *Psychology and Aging, 22,* 546–557.

Zelinski, E.M., & Stewart, S.T. (1998). Individual differences in 16-year memory changes. *Psychology and Aging, 13,* 622–630.

Zhang, Z., Davis, H.P., Salthouse, T.A., & Tucker-Drob, E.A. (2007). Correlates of individual, and age-related, differences in short-term learning. *Learning and Individual Differences, 17,* 231–240.

Zimprich, D., & Martin, M. (2002). Can longitudinal changes in processing speed explain longitudinal age changes in fluid intelligence? *Psychology and Aging, 17,* 690–695.

Author Index

Subject Index

Note: Page Numbers followed by *f* denotes figures and *t* denotes tables.